Gender and the Abjection of Blackness

SUNY series in Gender Theory
─────────
Tina Chanter, editor

Gender and the Abjection of Blackness

Sabine Broeck

SUNY PRESS

Cover art: Migdalia Valdes, "Every Year in Black and White," 2007

Published by State University of New York Press, Albany

© 2018 State University of New York

All rights reserved

For information, contact State University of New York Press, Albany, NY
www.sunypress.edu

Library of Congress Cataloging-in-Publication Data

Names: Bröck-Sallah, Sabine, 1954– author.
Title: Gender and the abjection of Blackness / Sabine Broeck.
Description: Albany, NY : State University of New York, 2018. | Series: SUNY
  series in gender theory | Includes bibliographical references and index. Identifiers:
LCCN 2017037080 | ISBN 9781438470399 (hardcover) |
  ISBN 9781438470405 (pbk.) | ISBN 9781438470412 (ebook) Subjects: LCSH:
  Women, Black. | Blacks—Race identity. | Racism. | Womanism. |
  Feminism. | Intersectionality (Sociology) | Slavery.
Classification: LCC HQ1201 .B83 2018 | DDC 305.896082—dc23
LC record available at https://lccn.loc.gov/2017037080

Contents

Acknowledgments

This book has been a long time in the making, dating back to first presentations around 2010. Parts of some chapters have appeared in previous publications. The entire text, however, has been written and revised for the purposes of this book. Some passages of the chapter "Abolish Property" were published in "The Challenge of Black Feminist Desire: Abolish Property," *Black Intersectionalities: A Critique for the 21st Century*, edited by Monica Michlin and Jean-Paul Rocchi, Liverpool University Press, 2013. Parts of chapter 4, "Abjective Returns," appeared in "Re-reading de Beauvoir 'after Race': Woman-as-Slave Revisited," *International Journal of Francophone Studies*, vol. 14, nos. 1–2, 2011. I thank State University of New York Press, and particularly Andrew Kenyon and Tina Chanter, for their patience and support. Heartfelt gratitude goes to Dana Foote and to Gordon Marce for kindness and swiftly provided expertise to help make text into book. To the numerous friends, acquaintances, colleagues, and students in Bremen, Berlin, Bielefeld, Hannover, Potsdam, Oldenburg, Erlangen, Munich, Hamburg, Bonn, Leipzig, Frankfurt, Rostock, Giessen, Dusseldorf, and Munster, as well as in Italy, Poland, Austria, France, Spain, Britain, Ireland, the Netherlands, the United States, Canada, Senegal, Mexico, Sweden, South Africa, and Russia, who I had the privilege to meet or work with for Erasmus visits, conferences, workshops, lectures, and seminars, and to learn from, I am deeply and sincerely grateful for your critical input, your always freely given listening and kind advice, your prodding and contradicting, questioning and thinking along with me, your pushing and pulling me to the finish line. You know who you are: thank you. Jana Geisler: nothing doing without your help. Christina Sharpe and Rinaldo Walcott: thank you for collegial "tough love"—interest in my work. Jane Desmond and Virginia Dominguez: your eager curiosity for the project gave me a beginning. Maria Diedrich: you trusted me to write another book. Sara

Lennox: thank you, again, for unerring guidance through the versions. Renate Hof: without you, this project would not have become a book. To Malick and Youssoupha Sarr: *jerejef,* but words don't really do it.

One

Against Gender

Enslavism and the Subjects of Feminism

How can one—in my case a senior white feminist German scholar who has struggled with and through decades of transnational, (post-)multicultural, intersectional, queered, intergenerational feminism—be against gender? Why—and how can one, or even need one—read the category of gender as constitutively anti-Black, not just in cases of racist practice but as a theoretical formation? This book is about a (self-)critical recuperation of white feminist interventions, which have paradigmatically shaped my generation's trajectory of gender studies. It could not have been written without Black feminism. Writing it has been about coming to terms with where I come from: the white habitus of gender and my own being implicated in the longue durée of enslavism. It responds to Elisabeth Spelman's pioneering attempt, as a white feminist philosopher, to question the essentialization and universalization of white women's feminist approaches to gender, and takes up her questions, still unanswered. For me, this reckoning with the history of my own formation as a white feminist recapitulates an epistemic challenge: white gender studies' evasion of the authority of Black theoretical interventions.

The book is neither a historiography of white feminism and gender studies, nor a painstaking discussion of lively and massive intramural debates in gender studies, including those over trans-difference, postcolonial and decolonial intersectionality, and queerness, which have shaped gender studies over the last half-century. It is a theoretical intervention focused on a, for me, paradigmatic set of intellectuals—Simone de Beauvoir, Jessica Benjamin, Judith Butler, and Rosi Braidotti—with an American and transnationally

1

effective white feminist trajectory, engaging it with my readings of what have been key Black texts of my generational formation, by Hortense Spillers, Sylvia Wynter, and Saidiya Hartman. It does look past the (de)constructionist, poststructuralist approaches of difference, performativity, and the nonidentity of gender, and at the ongoing racist agnotology of gender studies and the fungible status of Blackness within gender as a paradigm. Gender, as white feminism has known it, will be discussed here as an anti-Black concept in its inception and in a series of generative reiterations.

Accordingly, my interest lies in a critique of late twentieth- and early twenty-first-century white knowledge formations, and not in transmitting, ventriloquizing, or explaining contemporary Black feminist activism and scholarship. This activism and scholarship has created a resurgence that has been lighting up the pressure on white institutions, formations, and agents outside and inside academia—as anybody connected to social media will or might have realized over the last years. The following is not at all an inclusive list of activists, scholars, cultural producers, but names only a few: Christina Sharpe, Kimberly Brown, Tiffany Lethabo King, Patrice Douglass, Lisa C. Moore, Nadia Alahmed, Samiya Bashir, Korina Jocson, Mecca Jamilah Sullivan, Aneeka Henderson, Aishah Shahidah Simmons, Kai M. Green, Evie Shockley, Alexis Pauline Gumbs, Keisha Blain, and Jessica Marie Johnson. As this is a collective movement, it has also become manifest in the brilliant work of the e-journal *Feminist Wire*, in the special issues of *The Black Scholar* published on Black feminisms (*On the Future*), and a series of recent Black feminist symposia: for example, The Flesh of the Matter: A Hortense Spillers Symposium, on March 18, 2016, at Cornell University; Feminist Poetics: Legacies of June Jordan Symposium, on March 25, 2016, at University of Massachusetts, Amherst; and the Black Feminist Futures Symposium, in April 2016, at Northwestern University.

While much attention has been given to white supremacy, and white privilege, this attention has been largely directed at the social, political, or cultural racist white positionalities, agents, and practices, from which anti-racist white feminists have learned to distance ourselves. By contrast, I do not read for a dissection of white privilege or for instances of obvious racism in gender studies' theoretical pronunciations by way of finding imperfection and a "not enough" of feminist anti-racism, but for the anti-Blackness I see settled in the premises of gender theory's genealogy, in its rearticulation of post-Enlightenment discourses of white freedom, that is, in the very fiber of its programmatic intent. Black feminism has been pushing for this epistemic break in most explicit, but insistently unnoticed, terms—a white feminist theoretical reckoning with a Black feminist genealogy remains an urgency.

"Feminist leaders rooted in the second wave such as Gloria Anzaldúa, bell hooks, Kerry Ann Kane, Cherríe Moraga, Audre Lorde, Maxine Hong Kingston, Reena Walker and other feminists of color, sought to negotiate a space within feminist thought for consideration of race." This is from the *Wikipedia* article "Third-Wave Feminism." If *Wikipedia* may be seen as the reservoir of collective e-memory for the current and coming producers of knowledge in its most immediately accessible form, its acts of naming, framing, and formatting become crucial, signifying not just a particular information but a certain politics of knowledge and interpellation of knowers. The sentence quoted here situates Black and women-of-color feminist work squarely in the paradigm of "racial difference," which still pertains to much international gender scholarship. In this view, "women of color" are responsible for race. By implication—and this is so engrained in collective white majority habitus that the writers of this entry apparently write this fluently, without hesitation, as a standard phrase—any subjects related to race are of course Black or people-of-color. White gender studies moving into the third wave, the entry tells us, accept the difference "among women," and have responded to critical Black interventions by granting "space" to Black voices. This space, however, has but materialized in white feminism's ethnographic gains, in an attention to Black knowledge produced about Blackness. In the very same move, the very phrasing of this passage tellingly abjects Black being because apparently Black knowledge cannot be about gender or feminist issues in any generalized way, it is rendered unable to enter into a relation with gendered knowledge for and of women. That move leaves the space of race to Black knowledge and knowledge "of color" and keeps authority over "universal" gender issues as a white default. Thus, the white gender theoretical production of what Orlando Patterson has called a "genealogical" isolation (5) from Black knowledge amounts to a practice of anti-Black abjection, which has generated academic generations of agnotology.

In a first move, thus, my critique requires sharing a reading of those Black feminist theorists who have taught me to think about what Hartman calls the "afterlife" of enslavement, the "future slavery has made," in which white and Black people in the Euro-American West live, but about which white and Black people have told antagonistic stories. Black feminist theorists—and I will look at Wynter, Spillers, and Hartman paradigmatically—enabled me to think of a term, *enslavism*, for this continuity reaching into the future, in which anti-Blackness as violence, commodification, and repression is contained as a kind of ongoing legacy of New World enslavement. Chapter 2, "Abolish Property: Black Feminist Struggles against

Anti-Blackness," thus reads the theoretical advances of Black feminism's history in the United States as epistemic rupture of contemporary white gender theory. It is decidedly not an exhaustive and inclusive report of recent Black feminist activism and scholarship, particularly of the younger, post-Obama, Internet-based textual and activist production in its manifold academic and nonacademic articulations. This restriction is owed to the particular nature of my enterprise here: to produce a reckoning within white gender studies scholarship of my generation and its evasion of foundational Black feminist theory, and not to repeat gestures of white-on-Black ethnography. At the moment of writing this, in the wake of an escalation of state and fascist killings of Black people in recent years, the movement Black Lives Matter, organized by Black feminists, with a strong queer and transgender constituency, has garnered nationwide and international Black support and coactivism, based on its instant and constant dissemination on social media like Black Twitter. The work of these activists is more than amply visible, if one is interested; in its presence to the historical moment, it does not at all need or bear, and even interdicts, white mediation or translation.

In chapter 3, "Gender and the Grammar of Enslavism," I will elaborate on the term, its justification, and the mutually constitutive relation I see between gender, as a modern and postmodern conceptual advance, and enslavism. Chapter 4, "Abjective Returns: The Slave's Fungibility in White Gender Studies," performs exemplary readings of crucial moments in the post-Enlightenment career and ever growing sophistication of gender as a concept, which hinge on the concept's anti-Blackness in and by the very move that the selected texts work as anti-patriarchal critique. This chapter focuses on Simone de Beauvoir, Jessica Benjamin, and Judith Butler. In a coda, I look at the contemporary moment of theorizing the posthuman moment in the work of Rosi Braidotti, who, as a theorist of gender, suggests vitalism as a solution to the impasses of humanism's legacies, including gender theory's—a turn that, however, repeats anti-Blackness in its very disavowal of post-Enlightenment narratives.

I am not claiming that these texts are per se canonical, or that they are the universally most important representative texts of all Western/transnational gender studies. The selection is due (a) to a personal generational trajectory of feminist education spanning almost five decades, for which all the selected texts have been constitutive, and (b) to my theoretical premise that those particular texts—if from rather different angles, given their historical context and specific respectively different ideological, theoretical, and philosophical loyalties—share certain white premises of (post)humanist worldviews for which Black being, as well as Black knowledge (in many intellectual circles an oxymoron to this day), does not exist but as fungible flesh, spectacle, or otherwise commodified entity. So, my interest was not to create or reinstate a canon but to make visible certain structures, terms, articulations of anti-Blackness that have permeated existing theoretical repertoires, which until now have exacted considerable influence in gender and cultural studies departments, social sciences, and philosophy. The overall gist of the book is to put gender as a heuristic concept in more intimate but quite agonistic relation to enslavism, as the historical and ongoing practice of structural anti-Blackness, with the result of seeing the persistent intergenerational blockage on the part of white gender studies against Black epistemological interventions not just as an individual white supremacist practice but as a structural problem of theory. The concept of gender, as we know it, has been a means of intrahuman differentiation, serving to analyze and make claims on white post-Enlightenment patriarchal societies. As a term then, gender has cast Blackness as the signification of human absence, captured in Black flesh, which has served largely symbolic purposes for representations of oppression, violence, and discrimination. This very signification, of the slave or the "n----," provided the metaphorical horizon of what woman, if she was to achieve fully human status, was not to be. The maintenance of this metaphorical fungibility has been serving generations of white feminist articulations of gender.

My discussion demonstrates a diachronic continuity between the selected texts beyond otherwise crucial distinctions of humanism and posthumanism. It also, putting the selected texts in synchronous connection, shows how the various strands of thinking taken from the post–World War II feminist metaphoric apparatus of *woman as* slave are contiguous with early twenty-first-century metaphorical employments that capitalize on Black critical notions of social death, that evade an engagement with Black critiques of humanism, or that rejoice in a kind of revindication of certain white philosophies' satisfaction about the collapse of humanism without even addressing the problem that the visions of the posthuman responding to that collapse share in very old practices of anti-Blackness: textual dismembering, silencing, overwriting, and desubjectification of Black being. The point to me is that there is no break between humanism and posthumanism, when it comes to intellectual enslavism as a shared ground of thought. Current deliberations of posthumanism, as I will argue in the chapter on Braidotti, cannot be seen as epistemic and ethical ruptures. They, too depend on referential absence paired with rhetorical fungibility of Black abjection in order to draw their allegedly raceless, not-species-bound human lines of flight from what they see as the oppressive shackles of humanism.

I propose enslavism as a term necessary to situate current anti-Black practices in the future that slavery has made (see Hartman, *Lose*), and thus to critique them as the ongoing afterlife of enslavement, instead of addressing slavery as an event in bygone history. To produce those critical protocols means to reread the longue durée of humanism in a way that abolishes the human's reign of being and knowledge, based as it has been on Black nonexistence for the human. Rather than taking recourse, thus, to the established paradigm of multiple and trans/differentiation—which, again, has been enabled by Black corporeality marking the "difference"—I suggest reading the epistemology of gender as a function of enslavism, as a function of a changing same: the continuity between the regimes of Euro-American and Caribbean enslavement and its anti-Black afterlife. The term points to a present tense of anti-Blackness engrained in modern and postmodern epistemic trajectories which have, for the most part, not acknowledged their rootedness in the wake (Sharpe, *In the Wake*) of transatlantic enslavement. The employment of the term abjection for white enslavist practices of anti-Blackness provides the overarching frame for the selection of texts discussed here. Arguably, while the selected texts have operated in different theoretical fields and periods, and were bound into different feminist loyalties and epistemic allegiances, they share a claim to posit and mobilize the concept of the binary human gender antagonism over and against Black being. The political effects of this binary division, ultimately bolstering the claims of Western white cisgender women at the expense of all Black being and some people-of-color, as well as of Black and some white LGBTQ communities' struggles, have been critiqued severely from within those communities. My contribution to this debate seeks to provide a genealogical foray into the theoretical premises of those politics, which have remained untouched by white critical self-inspection.

As the reader might have guessed from the employment of the personal pronoun and other markers, my selection of the texts under discussion and my rather involved criticism of those texts is a specific individual response to Black critique, based in my years of scholarship at the crossroads of gender studies, African American studies, and Black feminist theory, and, as such, it might be regarded as a project of intellectual autobiography. Thus, the book shares an agonistic return to my own scholarly and intellectual trajectory, and, indeed, it partakes in the genre of the polemic essay, rather than in the genre of an academic research piece with its appeal of uninvested oversight, neutrality of tone, and multiperspectivity. It does not develop its train of argument in linear, chronological fashion through a series of points evolving in progressive sequence. Rather, it consists of a series of essays that encircle the intimacy between enslavism and white feminist gender studies, and that tries to find a—certainly nonexhaustive—mode to address this intimacy.

A note on this book's citation politics: readers will be asked for their patience with digesting a number of extensive quotations from primary sources. Crucially, it is in formal terms of textual address, that is, in the overwhelming amounts of ornate repetition, in excessive but vacuous employment of rhetorics that anti-Black abjection becomes visible beyond the mere content of respective pronouncements. Finally, I ask readers to employ necessary caution with respect to my highly problematic employment of the terms "slave" and "slave/Black." Theorizing enslavism results in a methodological as well as ethical conundrum. While one must inevitably use those words in order to critique the ongoing violence of enslavism, they need to be read with an alert awareness of the very term slave's racist naturalization as a signifier for Black enslaved being, as an anti-Black signification of Black life forced to figure as a nonhuman species in those ongoing white discourses and practices of abjection in urgent need of being destructed.

Two

Abolish Property

Black Feminist Struggles against Anti-Blackness

Remembering

This chapter reads the theoretical advances of Black feminism's history in the United States as epistemic rupture of contemporary white gender theory. For a small number of white scholars and activists of today's middling generation, the ones who came of age with the civil rights movement and early second-wave feminism, Black feminism has figured prominently in the controversial debates between Black female post–civil rights movement activist intellectuals and their male opponents both in the Black leftist and the Black nationalist organizations. Alice Walker's anti-patriarchal advances in her short stories and in novels like *Meridian*, Michelle Wallace's book *Black Macho and the Myth of the Superwoman*, Ntozake Shange's play *For Colored Girls Who Have Considered Suicide When the Rainbow Is Enuf*, for example, met with enthusiastic feminist acclaim, but also scandalized conservative audiences. Those publicly drawn out instances of Black women's struggle attacked both reactionary white racist and sexist stereotypes and the Black male misogyny complicit with the post–Moynihan Report (*Moynihan Report [1965]*) mold of unveiled contempt of Black women.

As it appeared to the general, mostly white public, it was all of a sudden that Black women thinkers and writers, anthologized in collections like *This Bridge Called My Back: Writings by Radical Women of Color* (Moraga et al.), claimed a powerful public voice, which also made visible the ignorance, indifference, and downright racism of the white feminist movement at the

9

time. Epitomized in the landmark contribution *All the Women Are White, All the Blacks Are Men, but Some of Us Are Brave* (Hull et al.), those controversies and the ensuing Black women's studies have created productive and lasting responses within and beyond the academy. Any even cursory glance at department faculty listings, class syllabi, or web publications, or at Sherri Barnes's stunning multidisciplinary web bibliography *Black American Feminisms* will show that Black women scholars have entered the US academy to stay—even if against all odds, if need be, and in many cases in very precarious positions. This was by no means predictable when Alice Walker, June Jordan, Toni Cade Bambara, Mary Helen Washington, and many others took up arguing—for a wider audience—Black women's social, cultural, and political claims in the early 1970s, and when a text like Toni Cade Bambara's *The Black Woman* in 1970, in one fell swoop, put the Black woman as the subject of her own life on the public agenda in ways immensely clairvoyant, and lasting until this day (see also Broeck, "Enslavement"; for a bibliography of Black feminist work in response to Bambara, see Traylor).

Those post-1970s Black female intellectuals traced Black feminist articulation way back to the first Black poet, Phyllis Wheatley; way back to female Black preaching against the sins of slavery, movingly recaptured by Alice Walker; way back to the first women freedom narratives of the enslaved, which created wide transatlantic echo space for the abolition of human propertization; way back to the late nineteenth century, when Anna Julia Cooper published *A Voice from the South*. Way back to the Black women moderns of the Harlem Renaissance; way back to marginalized 1940s and 1950s Black Caribbean women intellectuals like Sylvia Wynter, Beryl Gilroy, and Elsa Goveia; way back to communist post–World War II militancy of a Claudia Jones and to the radical grassroots resistance Dayo Gore's book *Radicalism at the Crossroads: African American Women Activists in the Cold War* chronicles so painstakingly. Way back to Black women testimonials in the Works Progress Administration collection of narratives of the 1930s, to the 1950s insister poet Gwendolyn Brooks, to the 1960s prophet poetess and novelist Margaret Walker. For some readers it might be a reminder that the post-1970s explosion of literary talent, political acumen, and academic sharpness of the intellectual generation of (on the American scene) bell hooks, Deborah McDowell, Hortense Spillers, Patricia Williams, Nell Painter, and Patricia Hill Collins, among many others, owes its strength to a stubborn ancestry. Today's endeavors of Black feminism in disciplines no one would have dared dream of—like law, anthropology, prison studies, history, sociology, political sciences, and more—are connected all the way back to seventeenth-, eighteenth-, and nineteenth-century knowledge formations created by Black women.

It has also been a Black feminist prerogative, and *not* a white theoretical virgin birth, to intervene into the debates of gender from the point of view of interlocking oppression (to use the Combahee River Collective's term from 1977) by race, gender, class, and sexuality; a point of view which made it impossible to look at gender as the only, or even as the privileged, signifier of any woman's life. Dating back to Frances Beal's 1969 exhortation in "Black Women's Manifesto; Double Jeopardy," intersectionality has been on the agenda—even if it has taken white feminism more than two decades (in Europe, even longer than that!) to catch on. Texts like Alice Walker's pioneering *In Search of Our Mothers' Gardens*, Angela Davis's *Women, Race and Class*, and Audre Lorde's *Uses of the Erotic: The Erotic as Power* have set radical standards to refocus the US and transnational feminist debates around the exclusiveness of gender as an epistemic and analytical category. The fact that this work has not internationally acquired the same theoretical currency as its white counterparts and, as epistemic contribution, has been disacknowledged persistently—being relegated to cursory footnoting and empty appraisals in the bylines of much transnational gender theory—is due to white feminism's and gender studies' entrenched anti-Blackness, and cannot in the least diminish the importance of Black feminist epistemology.

Hesitation

Talking about the challenge of Black feminism entails, of course, a problematic for a white gender studies descendant like myself, and a German at that, who needs to steer clear of ventriloquism or unbidden translation. Instead I speak here as a white scholar who considers herself an *addressee*, a spoken-to, of the epistemic challenge which Black feminism has posed to any critical theory of transatlantic modernity—in my case, white gender studies. To read Black feminist contributions epistemically is to acknowledge an intervention, which goes straight to the core of transatlantic modernity: the issue of property and its consequences. It is to Black feminism, I argue, that critical attention needs to be directed to overcome the lasting theoretical agnotology, in Robert N. Proctor and Londa Schiebinger's term, or studied epistemic ignorance, in Charles Mills's term ("White"), that has marked Western critical theory, including gender theory, for generations. What would it entail for a radical critique of modern subjectivity, including modern and postmodern gender relations, to hear a position that has consistently spoken from the location, the materiality, and the inherited memory of having been literal property?

That is to say, I have been challenged by Black feminism to hear a female slave singing to a passing traveler about having been raped on order of her master, and being in grief—because of the impossibility of legal redress, since a thing would not be treated like a vulnerable and violated human being before the law. I tried to hear the curses of the Black freedwoman during reconstruction, whom the Freedmen's Bureau tried to reeducate as Mrs. John Freeman. Her radical stance against propertization would not tolerate the replacement of a white master with subjection by a free Black husband, so that she would end up as second order property. The liberal promises of post-slavery contract law must have looked too much like just another form of inacceptable commodification of body and soul to hold a promise of freedom. I have tried to hear the courage of a middle-aged, very well educated female African American teacher submitting her dissertation to the Sorbonne (of all places), in 1925—no mean feat, just given the plain basics of this event, whatever the topic. The topic, however, was the Haitian revolution against enslavement, and Cooper's strident critique of French refusal to acknowledge the meaning of enslavement for French metropolitan society. Cooper's dissertation—a daring knowledge project if there ever was one—struggles to conceptualize transatlantic enslavement as the most suppressed subtext of European modern societies (see May, *Anna Julia Cooper*). And one last example: I have been challenged to hear Ida B. Wells's enraged campaign against lynching, in which she fearlessly attacked the most appalling legacy of Black abjection, and of white hot hysteria against what racist white communities perceived as the loss of their entitlement to Black property. In all those articulations I hear a will to be done with abjection, a rage for change, and a wild longing for *unownedness*, altogether a stunning recombination of social sentiment, which gives subjectivity and desire an entirely new name.

My interest has been to trace a lineage of Black feminism that needs to be acknowledged for its profound critique of white Western post-Enlightenment capitalist societies, including their narratives of freedom struggles, as in gender studies. It needs to be appreciated for making available to critical knowledge projects a location at once historically particular and generative of the most radical social, cultural, and political consequences. Historically marked by the enforced location of being treated as *propertized Black* female flesh, Black women have articulated practices, discourses, cultural repertoires, and memories, which by logical necessity criticized Western modernity in the most incorruptible ways. Theorizing from the position of enslavement has made it necessary to address a system of abjection of Blackness by white abjectorship. Departing from Kristeva's psychoanalytical employment of the term, and also from white feminist theorizing of the abject, as in Tina Chanter's work (*Picture*), I am taking up the term abjection here in the post-Fanonian vein in which it appears in Saidiya Hartman's and Hortense Spiller's work. *Abject* thus has changed from a category descriptive of individual subjectivity and its contours into a theoretical concept to discuss the underside of white Western modernity's terms of human sociability and subjectivity. One needs the term to be able to talk about the positioning of human beings as female flesh, as that abject which has been most radically beyond the pale of the subject in an Enlightenment vision, as that abject which has been structurally, not contingently, cut off from the human, from the self-possessed possessor of the world and its things. The abject unlocation of the prototypical thing, the movable laboring property, was the only position from which to reckon with Western modernity and its self-conceptions without any of the narcissistic screens of post-Enlightenment philosophies and subject theories.

Ever since Angela Davis's 1971 "Reflections on the Black Woman's Role in the Community of Slaves" put slavery on the agenda of Black feminist theorizing, the debate has become more and more sophisticated. Groundbreaking theoretical texts by Sylvia Wynter, Hortense Spillers, Patricia Williams, Adrienne Davis, Kathryn Gines, Saidiya Hartman, Cathy Davis, Alexis Gumbs, and Christina Sharpe—to name but very few scholars—have created a sustained epistemic intervention of sorts. This concerted theorizing resulted in a crucial knowledge project of the connection between property of the self and abjection of the Black, and accordingly in a demolition project: a project which situates itself in our present as the future slavery has made, to paraphrase Hartman ("Venus"). Therefore, I want to proceed by reading a selection of Black feminist interventions spanning three decades of intellectual continuity, the possible epistemic impact of which has been largely ignored by transnational postmodern gender studies. Even though a handful of quotations by Hortense Spillers have traveled through recent white scholarship, they have mostly been used in iconic ways to illustrate Black feminism, and to precisely ward off white feminist autocritique.

In this chapter, I address the following texts as paradigmatic epistemic interventions: Sylvia Wynter's "Beyond Miranda's Meanings: Un/silencing the 'Demonic Ground' of Caliban's 'Woman,' " Hortense Spillers's "Mama's Baby, Papa's Maybe" and "Interstices: A Small Drama of Words," and Saidiya Hartman's "Seduction and the Ruses of Power," the germinal study for her monograph *Scenes of Subjection: Terror, Slavery, and Self-Making in Nineteenth-Century America*. I am looking back at these older texts in a double gesture of mnemonic recuperation and unanswered claimancy to gender studies. With this decision, I do not at all intend to reduce Black feminist theorizing to a limited retrievable number of essays. As I hope will become clear, I am rather interested in their generative potential across generations ranging from the continuum of their respective moments to today's articulation of Black feminism—such as documented in the recent collection of Black feminist essays in *The Black Scholar* (*On the Future*)—as much as I am interested in pursuing a continuity of gender studies' agnotological nonresponse to those repeated interventions.

I am working from the following premises that are grounded in my study of Black feminism, Black historiography, and recent Black theory, which will then also be explored in the chapter "Gender and the Grammar of Enslavism": Western modernity has been constituted and motorized by, and deeply embedded in, enslavism, which most importantly must be read as a continuous regime of propertization of Black being. The discourse and practice of gender as we know it today is a contingent historical formation that owes its existence to modern white Enlightenment struggles around human subjectivity. As a prototypical modern emancipatory discourse, gender carries a baggage of propertization and abjection of Blackness, which needs to be addressed from within white gender studies. If enslavement is the vantage point from which to read modernity, it follows that property needs to be that reading's counterpoint. But property with a double difference: first, in a sense that goes beyond a post-Marxist critique. That is, property needs to be seen not just as means of production and as ownership of natural and man-made resources, but as property of Black life in its actuality, as property of Black reproductive capacity, of Black capacity to generate a future. Thus, property becomes a term that signifies not the metaphorical slavery of white post-Enlightenment theories of subjection, but the literal accumulation and fungibility, as Saidiya Hartman has called it in *Scenes of Subjection*, of Black being.

The implications of this critique point away from the notion of women's internal "difference" and non-homogeneity, which have dominated gender studies for the last decades, towards a realization of the anti-Blackness inherent in the very category of gender, for which women and men as humans have been the default reference, and which thus cannot see, as it were, Black life. Thus, we should, to paraphrase Frank Wilderson, not speak about differentiation among women, but about an antagonism between "woman" and Black being (*Red* 57). That is to say, difference is a category of lateral comparison, which avoids acknowledgment of a fundamental structural opposition, borne by white enslavist power, and thus cannot address white power—male and female—over, and use of, Black being (see chapter 3). I also take critical issue with the recently established paradigm of intersectionality. Adding the feature of race to gender analysis has caused almost as many problems as it has suggested to solve in its acknowledgment of so-called gender diversity. Given that race generally appears as a descriptor in analyses of Blackness (people, practices, discourses) without examining racialization as grounded in Euro-American white consciousness and subject positions, it has a problematic function to begin with: it ethnographically demarcates an object of observation, critique, and reflection characterized by its inherent given particularity.

In and by way of this particularity, the Black female, the one marked by "race," the so-called other, carries the weight of "difference" in theoretical terms, and it serves to provide embodiment to historical, sociological, and literary-cultural analyses of multiple "oppressions." Intersectional work—as reflected, for example, in the recent series The Politics of Intersectionality by Ange-Marie Hancock and Nira Yuval-Davis—has mostly compounded that problem, because it has not asked the question of white abjectorship and its multiple power sources, in any thoroughgoing historical perspective. Most white feminist work on intersectionality used the insights first formulated by Black feminists as early as the 1970s, like Fran Beal, Toni Cade Bambara, and Pat Robinson, to perform analyses of the "other woman" with more sophistication (see Bambara). At the point when Black interventions could not be ignored any longer, white texts conceded that the other woman was not only oppressed within gender relations but also racially and or ethnically discriminated against, and a subfield of intersectional oppression studies in ethnography, literature, cultural studies, and social sciences has emerged. This perspectival shift in the observation of the so-called Other has spread from US academic discourse, which itself has oftentimes disavowed the Black genealogy of intersectionality, to transnational scholarship. It has resulted in an influential body of texts in which race and gender figure as structural axes of oppression, in interconnectedness and interdependence.

However, the intersectionality of white empowerment and white abjectorship, of which gender has been an indispensable momentum for white women, ever since early eighteenth-century feminist remonstrations of humanity, has not figured much in those recent debates, outside the scholarly segment in the humanities clustered as whiteness studies. The radical question has been posed by Black and, in her case, Caribbean intellectuals like Sylvia Wynter, who, throughout her massive and ongoing, if widely unreceived text production, has raised the bar to the epistemic level, which keeps one from avoiding repetitions of the additive argument that in order to produce state-of-the-art gender studies we have to incorporate racial oppression into the analysis "as well."

Rereading the Human: Repercussions of Sylvia Wynter's Epistemic Project

It is not that I am against feminism: I'm appalled at what it became. Originally, there was nothing wrong with my seeing myself as a feminist; I thought it was adding to how we were going to understand this world. If you think about the origins of the modern world, because gender was always there, how did we institute ourselves as humans; why was gender a function of that? I'd just like to make a point here that is very important. . . . Our issue is the issue of the genre of "Man." . . . Now when I speak at a feminist gathering and I come up with "genre" and say "gender" is a function of "genre," they don't want to hear that.

—Sylvia Wynter, "Proud Flesh Inter/Views: Sylvia Wynter"

I focus on an address of Wynter's issue with gender, gender studies, and gender theory, which means I will not look at the wide range of challenges her work has raised and questions her writing has left unanswered for us to ponder. Wynter's work has moved the discussion away from descriptions of "difference," which remains a category to describe variations of differently endowed and empowered incarnations of the human, to a radical critique of the Enlightenment and post-Enlightenment (re)production of the human. In a rather post-Fanonian and post-Césairean vein, Wynter has turned her gaze to examining the human's existence as based on the Black nothingness against which it has been measured. I conceptualize this white practice as abjectorship (see also chapter 3). My reason to invoke the abject here is based on a rejection of the (post-)Hegelian and (post)psychoanalytic framework of subject and object, or self and other, as a pertinent conceptualization of white modernity's thingification of the slave/Black. To theorize Black thingification as othering to me does not respond to the state of Blackness as social death. It does not do justice to the sentient thingness of the Black/slave who is not alive as a human but instead is a fungible (see Hartman; subsequent passages in this chapter), accumulable, and dispensable—if laboring, thus its closeness to animal—all-round commodity to its owner. Thus, there is a need for a term that reaches beyond the binary structure underlying feminist and postcolonial discourses of otherness and difference, because these terms logically assume the sine qua non intrahuman negotiability of those positions, however messy, fragile, endangered, and aborted those negotiations might appear to human agents. It is important to stress, though, that, while I am borrowing from Kristeva's notion of the abject as that which threatens the subject's secure anchoring in the symbolic from an elsewhere, I am in contradiction to Kristeva. I am not interested in her question of what the abject does to an individual or collective subject—plunge it into states of disorientation—but in the way in which the white modern subject (male or female) might be considered an abjector, that is, a motorizing force which needed Black thingification to "know," socially, culturally, politically, and epistemically, its subjectivity and its social being.

To speak of self and other, or its Hegelian foil, of subject and object, also contains a white ethical presumptuousness that borders on the grotesque. Because the potentially reversible dialectics of agency of the "subject versus other" binary, in which the subject *is* because of and in the object's recognition, or in its resistance, seems patently absurd in the face of the Middle Passage. To sustain a post(-Hegelian)-paradigm would require sustained advocacy for mass suicides of the millions of shipped beings. The enslavist history of Black life turned into shippable and tractable commodities explodes the Hegelian model of a struggle for recognition between *Herr und Knecht* and renders any notion of sublation, as well as the postmodern play of otherness as difference defunct (see chapter 3).

Abjection of Blackness was the constitutive figuration of Euro-American modernity, in that it was Black enslavement in the Caribbean and the New World that has enabled free, bourgeois white capitalist societies to flourish into world hegemony; it was colonial Black enslavement that made Western democracy, freedom, and the conception of rights a desirable and pursuable project, since it provided both the wealth and the philosophical horizon for the human to thrive, as opposed to the abhorred figure of slavery. White feminist movements have—from Wollstonecraft through Beauvoir to Butler—always known that in order to be recognized in their gendered but human existence, and in order to make claims for their gendered interests against discrimination, violence, and abuse, they had to aggressively draw a philosophical, political, and sociomaterial line between "woman" and "slave," between "human" and "thing."

One needs to recall Wynter's particular scholarly trajectory before addressing her early 1984 intervention to shift epistemic practice to the question of the future human, after what she calls, with capital letter, "Man." As for her biography, I refer you to the introduction of the 2005 *Caribbean Reasonings: After Man, towards the Human,* written by its editor, Anthony

Bogues, in which he, as one of her former students, traces her extensive trajectory as a writer, scholar, critic, and activist. Beyond that, it would be detective work to trace Wynter's reception, or, better, its strange history of disappearance in the Western academy into a cult among a rather limited number of younger scholars who have had the privilege and satisfaction to work with her and who have been referring their own work back to her (see McKittrick, *Sylvia Wynter*; Bogues).

After all, she was indeed a crucial but forgotten agent in the founding of *Social Text*, together with Frederic Jameson; she published a wealth of extended, almost book-length essays in influential Caribbean and US journals. There was a conference in her honor organized at Brown by a group of former students and colleagues. She worked closely with Black philosopher Lewis Gordon, with Walter Mignolo, and with other prominent representatives of Caribbean and decolonial studies. She has lectured widely and internationally at conferences, and there are a number of individual US and Canadian scholars—like Eudell, Ambroise, Thomas, McKittrick, Walcott, and Gumbs—who acknowledge her palpable influence on their own work. An array of her articles have appeared in scattered quotations in studies about Caribbean slavery, New World colonialism, or Jamaican history. Recently a collection of essays about Wynter's trajectories has been published as *Sylvia Wynter: On Being Human as Praxis* by Katherine McKittrick.

But the epistemic breakthrough, which she engineered as early as 1984—which, if recognized, might have shifted the debates in gender studies, critical race studies, and Black studies in considerably radical ways—has not been duly recognized in white gender studies. Just for one example, European feminist scholar Rosi Braidotti (see chapter 5), who also has profoundly engaged with the question of the human, seems not to be cognizant of her work. In *Transpositions*, Braidotti sketches out a vision of conviviality beyond difference, borrowing from Deleuze and Guattari, on one hand, and from Paul Gilroy, on the other, beyond the techno-capitalist world of the human, and explores the human-animal divide as one of the destructive features of (post-)Enlightenment, but her historical framework is devoid of colonial modern enslavement in any profound sense. Wynter, as one of the most radical questioners of the idea of the human, and its "genres," has obviously not crossed her orbit.

This seems all the more strange if one considers the transdisciplinary, irreverently nonaligned, and *multiconnectable* nature of Wynter's intellectual contributions. Ranging from literature through theology to natural sciences, queering philosophy and history, and always keeping an alert political perspective—if one wanted to search for an organic intellectual, it would be her. One can only speculate as to how much anti-Black, misogynist, and hegemonic power of quotation cartels and publishing venues have silenced her possible impact. Her work has, as it were, fallen through the cracks of the last twenty-five years of competitive discursive communities, as well as through the mutual indifference of various postcolonial scholarly communities mired in monolingualism and late-colonial national and regional pieties (see Winks).

In 1984, grounded in Fanon, Césaire, and C. L. R. James, as well as in an unorthodox post-Stalinist Marxism, in dialogue with Said's *Orientalism* of 1978, but before Spivak's *A Critique of Postcolonial Reason: Toward a History of the Vanishing Present* of 1999, before Gilroy's *The Black Atlantic* of 1993, before Bhabha's *Nation and Narration* of 1990, she published "The Ceremony Must Be Found" in *boundary 2*, a high postmodern journal which did not lack sophisticated and powerful audiences. That article was but one move in her ongoing negotiation of Western modernity's racist, anti-Black coloniality—a structure, a system, a regime, and a praxis that she located very early on not in the "colonies," on the periphery, exclusively, but marked as the very *movens* of "degodded" European humanism in the creation of the white subject, of what she calls the genre of Man 2. (Man 1 was the pre-Renaissance version of the subject in the feudal grip of king, church, and theocentric belief.) In Wynter's project, coloniality and enslavement have always already extended to epistemology, cognition, the psychic apparatus of the human, the economy of reproduction and sexuality, and to all social, cultural, and political practices on micro- and macro-levels, that is, to the very maintenance of what has been regarded as human life.

My project now begs the question of whether there can be a language in support of struggles for freedom "after Man" in material, political, and epistemic terms, beyond "gender," or, to pick up Wynter's phrasing, beyond Miranda? A language that could facilitate alliances, which trace their trajectories back to the "demonic grounds" (see McKittrick, *Demonic*) of enslavement and Black abjection, and not to the distributions of "gender," "race," and "sexuality"—inflected ascriptions of Man in the liberal play of differences.

Obviously, those Black feminist critics who have worked with Wynter's work, like Carole Boyce Davies and McKittrick, have read her as enabler. Their work (Davies and Fido; McKittrick, *Demonic*) has employed her texts as ample support to articulate questions of Black female agency, of Wynter's admonition to make the displaced but nevertheless articulate interventions into the enslavist coloniality of being, hearable and visible. My approach here, as a white reader embedded in a framework of gender discourses that I, of course, also cannot voluntarily transcend, is to read her work as a farsighted incipient critique of the very concept of gender, which has been inextricably tied to the white Western self-universalizing paradigm of what she calls Man 2. Wynter's 1990 essay "Beyond Miranda's Meanings: Un/silencing the 'Demonic Ground' of Caliban's 'Woman,' " the afterword to the pioneering and by now classic, and still in print, collection of scholarship on Caribbean's women's writing *Out of the Kumbla*, edited by Carole Boyce Davies and Elaine Savory Fido, is a groundbreaking achievement on a number of counts. Taking on—as squarely and elaborately as the genre of an afterword permitted, but in keeping with the entire collection's purpose to make visible Black Caribbean women's literary and cultural accomplishments—white feminist "high theory's" unacknowledged universalist posturing, Wynter's afterword intervened into a discourse that theoretically preempted and practically ignored any need to recognize, name, and circulate individual and collective authorship of Black women artists, writers, and scholars.

Pars pro toto, and in keeping with the discourses of its moment, the afterword takes issue with Luce Irigaray's "purely Western assumption of a universal category 'woman,' whose 'silenced ground' is the condition of what she defines as an equally universally applicable, patriarchal discourse" (Wynter, "Beyond" 355). Against this white myopia, Wynter's text pits a purposefully Black move: borrowing the term "womanist" from Alice Walker, she inserts a double-forked contradiction into the debate. She maintains, "The term 'womanist/feminist,' with the qualifying attribute 'womanist' borrowed from Afro-American feminist Alice Walker, reveals the presence of a contradiction, which, while central to the situational frame of reference of both, Afro-American and Caribbean women writers/critics, is necessarily absent from the situational frame of reference of both Western-European and Euromerican women writers" (355). The term womanist was first coined by Alice Walker. It appeared in various places, as in *MS Magazine* in 1974, for instance, its most enduring location being on the title of her 1983 collection *In Search of Our Mothers' Gardens: Womanist Prose*, in which she defines the term as follows: womanist stands for "[a] Black feminist or feminist of color. From the Black folk expression of mother to female children . . . [and] [a]lso: A woman who loves other women, sexually and/or non-sexually. Appreciates and prefers women's culture. . . . Committed to survival and wholeness of entire people, male and female" (Walker, *In Search* xi).

As you will realize, at this point in the late 1980s, way before white feminism began to theorize the challenge posed by the nonidentity of women, Wynter was able to project a transnational, politically informed Black diasporic perspective into the emerging controversies. That this transnational connection is crucial and amply available to her argument seems obvious enough to Wynter as not to warrant any elaborate explanation; the fact, even, that she can mention Alice Walker without footnoting her, and thus without giving the term a genealogy, bespeaks the self-evident familiarity on the part of *Out of the Kumbla*'s diasporic readers with Walker's work, which Wynter could take for granted. It seems also vital to stress, in hindsight, that Wynter's term is "a contradiction." With this term, the afterword takes a clear and prophetic distance to ensuing theorizations of the differentiation of woman along the additive lineup of race, class, and gender, a mantra which would successively saturate multicultural gender studies of the 1990s. Stressing the potential contrariness of the concept of womanism, Wynter does not only speak of a "paradoxical relation" between Caribbean, and by extension Black diasporic women as a collective, and their Euro-American peers, in which femaleness is always already qualified by the power imbalance caused by white supremacy. She describes Black women writers/critics' position vis-à-vis feminism as one of "contradictory dualism by which the writers [of *Out of the Kumbla*, in her example] both work within the 'regime of truth' of the discourse of feminism, at the same time as they . . . point towards the epochal threshold of a new postmodern and post-Western mode of cognitive inquiry; one which goes beyond the limits of our present 'human sciences,' to constitute itself as a new science of human forms of life" ("Beyond" 356). The last words here echo Walker's definition, which made it clear in 1983 that the intellectual challenge of Black womanist knowledge aimed against and beyond the parameters of gendered difference. To push the point, Wynter's argument conjures up "the emergent 'downfall' of our present 'school like mode of thought' and its system of 'positive knowledge' inherited from the nineteenth century and from the Industrial epoch of which it was the enabling mode of rationality and participatory epistemology; and that it does this in the same way as feminist theory itself had earlier inserted the contradiction of the variable *gender* into the ostensibly 'universal' theories of Liberal Humanism and Marxism-Leninism" (357). For Wynter, with enslavement and coloniality, the "primary code of difference . . . became that between 'men' and 'natives' with the traditional 'male' and 'female' distinctions now coming to play a secondary—if none the less powerful—reinforcing role within the system of symbolic representations" (358). Accordingly, from that "secondary position," white Western women—for whom she reads Shakespeare's Miranda in *The Tempest* as an allegorical figure—had an entry into the social formation of the human, based on their share in the symbolic and material system of racist coloniality. So, the alignment is as follows: "Caliban, as an incarnation of a new category . . . that of the subordinated 'irrational' and 'savage' *native* is now constituted as the lack of the 'rational' vis-a-vis the Master Mind Prospero, and the 'now capable-of-rationality Miranda' " (358). While Miranda, the white heiress, becomes the bearer and "genitrix of a superior mode of human 'life' " (360), the Black woman glares as an absence from the triangle. She remains off scene, as only a potential mate for Caliban, which points to the masterfully orchestrated genealogical rupture that colonialism wrought for enslaved populations. The Black woman's absence stands for the intended or collateral enslavist and colonial "obliteration" of populations. In Wynter's analysis, moreover, it dramatizes the profound contradiction within gender analysis created by the disavowal of Black female cognitive and reproductive agency. The white logic of gender can only "see" Miranda in this play, because she possesses gender. Miranda, that is, has become a visible actor in the script of Man 2, if in a severely subordinated role. "In consequence," as Wynter says, if

> before the sixteenth century what Irigaray terms as "patriarchal discourse" had erected itself on the "silenced ground" of women, from then on, the new primary silenced ground (which at the same time now enables the partial liberation of Miranda's hitherto stifled speech), would be that of the majority population-groups of the globe—all signified now as the "natives" (Caliban's) to the "men" of Prospero and Fernando, with Miranda becoming both a co-participant, if to a lesser *derived* extent, in the power and privileges generated by the empirical supremacy of her own population; and, as well, the beneficiary of a mode of privilege unique to her, that of being the metaphysically invested and idealized object of desire for all classes (Stephano and Trinculo) and all population-groups (Caliban). (363)

Consequently, Wynter proposes to "diacritically draw attention to the insufficiency of all existing theoretical interpretative models, both to 'voice' the hitherto silenced ground of the experience of 'native' Caribbean women and Black American women as the grounds of Caliban's woman . . ." (364) and to interrogate the function of their silencing, "both as women, and more totally, as 'native' women." Her question is: "Of what mode of speech is that absence of speech both as women (in masculinist discourse) and as 'native' women (in feminist discourse) an imperative function?" (365).

For Wynter, the concept of gender has been a particular *function* of the genre of Man 2, that is, of the ethnocentric, white, capitalist, secularized formation of post-Renaissance humanism, which has universalized itself politically, socially, culturally, and epistemically. The very discourse and practice of nationhood, by way of cognitive extension, is also obviously a discourse of Man 2. As such, it does not offer desirable parameters of conviviality for the "wretched and dispossessed," who have been at the center of Wynter's pronounced interest, but it has become subjected to Wynter's critical deconstruction. I don't see her arguing against gender in order to ignore masculinist hatred of women, let alone to tolerate the masculine unwillingness to respond to women's demands and struggles in nationalist Black politics. Instead, she reconsiders the universalized term gender and the politics it has motorized ever since it became a focal point of reference in the Enlightenment interventions of white European women, because of its colonialist, anti-Black baggage. To me, it is crucial to acknowledge and own that baggage as white critical feminist intellectuals, because it haunts contemporary formations of gender, both in gender mainstreaming, and in the absolute absence of white anti-Black abjection in contemporary gender theorizing. So, Wynter's polemics against gender indeed refers us to a far-reaching objection against the political, cultural, social, and epistemic implications of gender theory which does not want to, or has not been able to, acknowledge the active white feminist involvement in claim to rights and civilization based on the polar binarity of gender as ownable by white European women only. The exclusive possessability of gender by white women made gender itself into a modus of rendering Black being abject. Therefore, for my project, it has been crucial to read Wynter's work into an intertextual dialogue with Spillers and Hartman. Coming from a Caribbean context, her terms of address are the Black colonial and postcolonial abject of Western domination. She does acknowledge the slave as a phenomenon, and she does speak, in passing, of the "obliteration" of the Black/slave but her emphasis is not on scrutinizing the mass shipping of Black being, its "accumulation and fungibility," to use Saidiya Hartman's terms. The Black/slave, as opposed to Caliban, was not happened upon on his or her own island as a native and made a stranger and a lesser human on his or her own grounds, however demonic they were made to be, but instead became a sentient thingbeing characterized by genealogical rupture, a species without analogy, as Wilderson would say, an unsubjectified mass item without claim to even be an object of human relation. Answering back to Wynter, Spillers and Hartman argue that the slave is not an other, it is conceptualized and treated as a thing, fungible, and dispensable, workable and killable, and thus cannot be seen in the paradigm of self and other, which, after all, logically is an intrahuman binary. This insight, of course, has decisive bearings on talking about "Caliban's mate," on a theoretical level: the slave has flesh; neither the "biologically" male nor "biologically" female enslaved "have gender," because the thing/flesh transported through the Middle Passage has been abjected from the system of Western (post)-Enlightenment genderization. Black feminist work about the Caribbean and about the United States has consistently struggled with this conundrum ever since Sojourner Truth's appeal to the white Women's Rights Convention in the late nineteenth century: "Ain't I a Woman?" From Truth there runs an unbroken line to Black feminist theorizing today, trying to install a *vocabulary* and a *syntax*, that is, a grammar (in Spillers's phrase) to grapple with a paradigmatic contradiction: the paradigm of gender and the location it afforded for white women constitutively worked to enable white women's access to full human entitlement; at the same time, the very possibility of this advance necessarily separated woman as human from the slave as thing.

Spillers: Gender and Black Flesh

The captive body, then, brings into focus a gathering of social realities as well as a metaphor for *value* so thoroughly interwoven in their literal and figurative emphases that distinctions between them are virtually useless. Even though the captive flesh/body has been "liberated," and no one need pretend that even the quotation marks do not *matter*, dominant symbolic activity, the ruling episteme that releases the dynamics of naming and valuation, remains grounded in the originating metaphors of captivity and mutilation so that it is as if neither time nor history, nor historiography and its topics, shows movement. . . .

[W]e would regard dispossession as the *loss* of gender, or one of the chief elements in an altered reading of gender.

—Hortense Spillers, "Mama's Baby, Papa's Maybe:
An American Grammar Book"

At the moments of their first publication, Spillers's essays appeared as a kind of theoretical densification and condensation of the post–civil rights struggle's decades of Black feminist activism and scholarship. They take up the politics of white supremacist as well as Black male nationalist stereotyping of Black women. In intertextual, if indirect, conversation with many other Black feminist and Black womanist interventions at the time Spillers addressed the disastrous social, cultural, and political effects of the notorious Moynihan Report (Gewertz) of the late 1960s, a state intervention aiming at undermining Black communities' coherence and anti-racist politics by aggressively and successfully promoting the racist relegation of Black women to the status of culprit for the hysterically perceived disintegration of Black communities and for the assumed deviance from patriarchal symbolic law because of their alleged matriarchal power over males and children; thus making the victims of racist and sexist violence responsible for their and their families' economic and social suffering. Her work engaged a host of disciplines and intellectual fields, like psychoanalysis, feminist theory, and historiography of slavery, in the process of resituating Black women, who white supremacy rendered as "an example of signifying property *plus*" (Spillers, "Mama's Baby," 65), at the center of an inquiry into the possible relation Black women could or could not entertain to feminist interventions of the decade. Because of Spillers's strategy of calling specific texts or authorial names of early gender studies theorists into the debate only indirectly (an exception is her direct citation of Suleiman's *The Female Body in Western Culture*), much subsequent white gender studies theory did allow itself to not see its raison d'être, a gender-based social and cultural critique, as implicated in her intervention—whereas, in my reading, these moves were made to precisely forward the principal and generalizable character of her conceptual deconstruction of gender.

I need, then, to go back to those moments in her rich writerly (in Barthes's sense) essays that, almost three decades ago, laid more groundwork, after Wynter, for a critique of gender as we know it. That means I will not pay closer attention to Spillers's scorching indictment of white supremacist violence against Black women and the Black community, nor to the ingenious ways that the article moved sexual violence to center stage of Black intramural debates, nor to the necessity she insisted upon for Black men *and* women to recover a maternal line of nurturance as resistance to white power—an argument which has stirred up eager Black response and controversy to this day (see "Introducing," and the conversation with other Black feminists in Spillers et al.). I try, that is, not to read Spillers's text by way of a white parasitical and ventriloquist ethnography of Black female being but want to recover those parts of her argument that I see as a direct launch of a critique of gender as another "white mythology" (see Maart, "Decolonizing"). That momentum of her article has not been taken up by white gender studies, it went missing even in the politics of eventually numerous iconographic citations of "Mama's Baby." Spillers's passages on Blackness as "flesh," at the time, could have been seen as a challenge to white gender theory to move away from facile talk about racial difference and from a politics that did suggest enfolding Black women in the purview of gender but left the premises of gender theory's embeddedness in enslavism intact. The reason for this kind of double gesture is that gender theory—in keeping with all other Euro-American post-Enlightenment discourses—has, as I will try to show in chapter 3, not seen a critique of enslavism as its imminent and pressing prerogative, but as a domain of Blackness. This conceptual splitting between seeing women's subjectivization as a prerogative of gender studies and (post-)enslavement as a prerogative of Black studies, not as the white subject's historical legacy and responsibility, maintained the intactness of gender theory as an epistemic discourse about the realization of free subjectivities for women as human agents, over and against the slave and its Black progeny. If enslavism established a wide range of unredressable anti-Black doability for white (post)modern subjects, gender theory has figured into that range with a consistent refusal to acknowledge its own historical and present embeddedness in the afterlife of slavery. One element of this enslavist commodification of Blackness has been the power to ignore epistemic rupture, the power to concede or not to concede the possibility of being addressed by Black feminist knowledge as critical authority vis-à-vis one's white intellectual trajectories and loyalties. But for white agnotology, this horizon of Spillers's essays might have opened for gender studies at an early junction, but this has been continuously deferred.

In "Interstices" (76), Spillers opens her debate with gender studies with a Fanonian predicative move, reminding the overwhelmingly white readership of the anthology that "[t]he Black person mirrored for the society around her and him what a human being was not." So, her critique starts from a structural division between "humanness" and "Blackness" that theory needs to take into account in foundational manner. She pushes her point by calling for new semantic and syntactical modes of address, because the white feminist language at disposal cannot grasp the synchronic and diachronic range of Black abjection, which to her is a "structure of unreality" (77). This structure "originates in the historical moment when language ceases to speak the historical moment at which hierarchies of power (even the ones to which some women belong) simply run out of terms because the empowered meets in the Black female the veritable nemesis of degree and difference." This is one of the crucial moments for gender studies at which Black feminism calls for a change in theorems. She insists that between white women ("the empowered") and Black women there exists no relation of differentiation but an antagonistic opposition ("nemesis") between being and "non-being." In contrast to white woman as marked by "historical apprenticeship as inferior being," Black woman is marked by "the paradox of non-being," which aligns Black male and female existence as Black "as absolutely equal" (77). "Interstices" takes the reader through the epistemologies of feminism's binary gender investments, teasing out a bizarre quality of theoretical evasion on the part of gender theory. The essay also lays out a series of key terms that Spillers will come back to in "Mama's Baby": among them, empowerment, sexuality, history, the power of the symbolic, the "disaster" of Black life under the reign of white power, and practices of "mythical signification" of woman. As the longue durée of anti-Black terror during and after the Middle Passage has "divided the empire of women against itself" (78), so female sexuality, as a paradigm for "symbolic domination" (80), needs to be seen as a one of the domains which have become a "frontier" for white women to fix their human existence against the threat of enslavement embodied in Black women, who "do not participate in the legacies of symbolic power . . . not even in the form of contestation," which was white feminism's terrain (86). This could only be achieved, Spillers argues as long as critique held on to the "store of mythical signifiers," like "woman," which did serve to turn away from the historical particularities of enslavist terror. "Mama's Baby" therefore takes pains to detail the ravages of enslavement trade and New World enslavement (based on historiography dating back to Donnan's four volume history from 1932), which leads to an analysis of enslavement that foreshadowed debates even in Black studies by decades and has never fully registered in gender studies. Before the Nobel Prize winning success of Morrison's *Beloved* that helped catapult national interest in slavery (as token as it might have been) and research in history, literature, and cultural studies contexts to a previously unknown reach in institutions of higher education, in museums, the art world, and in popular culture, Spillers outlines enslavement in a pathbreaking way. It becomes visible in her argument that New World enslavement was philosophically and ethically significant not because it was exploitative of labor (which it was, of course), not because it worked by means of legal, political, and social subjugation (which it did), and not because it created a system of white individual and collective profiteering from other people's dependency (which it did, too), but because it made Black being into a usable, shippable, transactable, disownable, atomizable, brandable, breedable, and inheritable item, a being severed from kinship, "consanguinity" (73), genealogy, and a proper name. Thus, "Mama's Baby" prefigured an insight which later Black theorists like Hartman and, most recently, Wilderson and Jared Sexton have taken up: that enslavement resulted in a system of racist capitalist modernity which has not known any *relation* between the human subject and Black being. Even after formal emancipation, inheritable thingness versus inheritable owner- and usership thus characterized that system, and not—as in the widespread understanding held in the realms of education, politics, social, and cultural life—a relation of "submission," "discrimination," power hierarchy, and maltreatment. She pits against that a phrasing of Black experience as a perpetual "fall, as a veritable descent into the loss of communicative force" (69). I read the latter phrase—to be without "communication"—to indicate that any human negotiation, claimantship, protest, between subject and slave was legally, politically, and socially nil. Similar to Patterson's magisterial argument, her discussion comes to the conclusion, without using the same term, that transatlantic slavery was the constitutive production of Black social death on a global scale: "Though the notorious 'Middle Passage' appears to the investigator as a vast background without boundaries in time and space, we see it related in [Elizabeth] Donnan's account to the opening up of the entire Western hemisphere for the specific purposes of enslavement and colonization" (69).

The debodying terror of enslavement was one of the crucial issues in her argument in "Interstices" that she then took up in "Mama's Baby," published in *Diacritics* in 1987. This terror is immediately connected to propertization (and therefore thingification) of Black being, showing up in the first paragraph of this essay: "In that regard, the names by which I am called in the public place render an example of signifying property *plus*" (65). Against compelling discourses of "gender undecidability" emerging at the time, Spillers maintains a necessary distance; in her view (post-)enslaved Black life would have to first "gain, in short, the *potential for gender differentiation* [italics mine] as it might express itself along a range of stress points, including human biology in its intersection with the project of culture" (66). That is to say, the Middle Passage, the plantation (political) economy and postemancipation afterlife of enslavement are being read on a continuum of violence under which the foundational "*theft of the body*—a willful and violent . . . severing of the captive body from its motive will, its active desire" has never been compensated, human ownership of and authorship over body never restored to Black being: "But I would make a distinction in this case between 'body' and 'flesh' and impose that distinction as the central one between captive and liberated subject-positions. In that sense, before the 'body' there is 'the flesh' that zero degree of social conceptualization. . . . If we think of the 'flesh' as a primary narrative, then we mean its seared, divided, ripped-apartness, riveted to the ship's hole, fallen or 'escaped' overboard" (67). This is the second time in a decade that she urges a realization, which might have changed the course not just of gender theory but also of white feminist politics. She presses for the exigency to understand the inadequacy of gender as an analytics, if a struggle against white patriarchal-capitalist supremacy were to be indeed the goal, and not just the professed mantra of "race, class, gender" alignments: "Under these conditions, we lose at least *gender* difference in the outcome, and the female body and the male body become a territory of cultural and political maneuver, not at all gender-related, gender-specific" (67). Anti-Black violence, she details in all gruesomeness, resulted in Black existence lived, in the eyes of state, civil society, and human agents, as usable flesh that adhered to no symbolic bodily integrity, that was not looked upon as a corpus which could and did house an ego, flesh undynamically sealed in what she called the "vestibularity" of culture.

The challenge of this vestibularity to culture resides in a perspective on the human (post-)Enlightenment world which potentially breaks its "customary lexis"; prevalent terms of Spillers's contemporary feminist "grammar books," like subject, gender, desire, sexuality, motherhood, fatherhood, reproduction, family, labor, pleasure, women's history, domesticity, to name but a few of the most current ones at the time, are thrown into "unrelieved crisis" (76). Thus she suggests that "the human cargo of a slave vessel—in the fundamental effacement and remission of African family and proper names" offers a *counter*-narrative to "notions of the domestic," which I take to signify both in a feminist and in a US national register (72). She also introduces a, however indirect, critique of psychoanalysis into the debate, calling the enslaved's suspension in the Middle Passage "oceanic," with deliberate reference to Freud's notion of undifferentiated identity, and thus evoking the idea of quite a different ur-scene for psychoanalysis (72).

However, this potentially disruptive perspective was absented from influential investigations of "the female in Western culture," as in Susan Suleiman's monograph, or the "reproduction of mothering," as in Nancy Chodorow, both of which she alludes to specifically, but certainly metonymically. This white decision has resulted in discourses failing to realize that the "materialized scene of unprotected female flesh—of female flesh 'ungendered' [and by extension of her argument, Black male flesh as well]—offers a praxis and a theory, a text for living and for dying, and a method for reading both through their diverse mediations" (68).

White Culpability, Enjoyment, and Gender in Hartman's Work

In 19th-century common law, rape was defined as the forcible carnal knowledge of a female against her will and without her consent. Yet the actual or attempted rape of an enslaved woman was an offense neither recognized nor legislated by law. Rape was not simply unimaginable because of purported Black lasciviousness, but its repression was essential to the displacement of white culpability that characterized both the recognition of black humanity in slave law and the designation of the black subject as the originary locus of transgression and offense. . . . If subjectivity is calculated in accordance with degrees of injury, and sexual violation is not within the scope of offenses affecting slave existence, what are the consequences of this repression and disavowal in regard to gender and sexuality?

—Saidiya Hartman, "Seduction and the Ruses of Power"

One of Saidiya Hartman's most compelling points in her first book, *Scenes of Subjection*, has been the exposure of white American society's libidinal, emotional, cultural, and legal investments and pleasure in, and the "enjoyment," of the enslavement and racist abjection of Black people (see also Farley, "Black Body," which speaks of the "race pleasure" of white power). My work is hugely indebted to the clarity of this pronunciation, even though the term she used at the time, abjection, did only register in my thinking at a later point, when I thought about a term that could signify anti-Blackness as a practice and came up with *abjectorship* as a word that addresses the continuous *doing* of anti-Black agency (more in chapter 3):

Although assertions of free will, singularity, autonomy and consent necessarily obscure relations of power and domination, the genealogy of freedom, to the contrary, discloses the intimacy of liberty, domination, and subjection. This intimacy is discerned in the inequality enshrined in property rights, the conquest and captivity that established "we the people," and the identity of race as property, whether evidenced in the corporeal inscriptions of slavery and its badges or *in the bounded bodily integrity of whiteness secured by the abjection of others.* (Hartman, *Scenes* 123; italics mine)

Indirectly, Hartman has extended this argument in her last book, *Lose Your Mother*, with her focus on the modern machine of triangularized trading in enslaved Black being, which saturated the entire transatlantic world with its regime. Hartman's symptomatic reading of the "dead book," as she calls the vast archive of enslavement, follows a textual strategy by which every elusive archival trace of slavery becomes charged with referential value clearly in excess of the term's metaphorical workings. Enslavement becomes visible as proactive white history, not as a bygone deplorable but disowned state of affairs. This strategy of re-referentializing, of calling thingification to consciousness, has become the crucial political lever for Hartman's work to turn the tables on critical theory, including gender theory. Her two books' very amassment of detail makes readable the catalogued but previously neutralized transgressions of the enslavist trading machine and as such forces a white reader to reconsider one's own white investment in, as well as the short- and long-term benefits of the discourses and practices of, enslavism for modern white European societies:

> Impossible to fathom was that all this death had been incidental to the acquisition of profit and to the rise of capitalism. . . . Death wasn't a goal of its own but just a by-product of commerce, which has had the lasting effect of making negligible all the millions of lives lost. Incidental death occurs when life has no normative value, when no humans are involved, when the population is, in effect, seen as already dead. . . . To my eyes this lack of intention didn't diminish the crime of slavery but from the vantage of judges, juries, and insurers exonerated the culpable agents. In effect, it made it easier for a trader to countenance yet another dead black body or for a captain to dump a shipload of captives into the sea in order to collect the insurance, since it wasn't possible to kill cargo or to murder a thing already denied life. (Hartman, *Lose* 31)

Past the contemporary international debates for monetary reparation, Hartman's work goes straight for a Euro-American white public, which has programmatically deluded itself about the pertinence of enslavism to white Europe and America. As she has repeatedly argued, the slave barracoon must be looked at not just as a holding cell, but more importantly as a modern episteme which controlled the practices of history and of collective white memory; it created a "second order of violence" by way of disappearing, abjecting Black life in the figurative and most material sense (*Lose* 5). I am interested here in discussing the implications of her analysis for gender theory. Therefore I will look at her early article, "Seduction and the Ruses of Power," from 1996, which became a chapter in her extensive study *Scenes of Subjection*, published a year later. In contemporary Black feminism, and for much of contemporary Black Studies, this intervention has been canonized next to Hortense Spillers's work as foundational for a young generation of scholars and activists who employed Hartman's and Spillers's work as a theory of unrecuperable negativity (see Ricks's discussion of Spillers) within and against both the ongoing anti-Black violence against Black life and the pervasive white liberal desire for so-called postracial ignorance and wishful innocence.

"Seduction and the Ruses of Power" first appeared in a 1996 *Callaloo* special issue on emerging Black women writers; the 1997 publication of *Scenes of Subjection* has been reactivated by Black critique and remembered as a game changer for years. Even though, like Spillers's essays, "Seduction and the Ruses of Power" was anthologized early on in *Between Woman and Nation: Nationalisms, Transnational Feminisms, and the State* (Kaplan et al.), white gender studies, if cognizant at all, have largely refused its theoretical impact.

In "Seduction and the Ruses of Power," Hartman walks her reader through a grim catalogue of the white quotidian *tractation* of the enslaved within the plantation orbit. I am using this specific word because, as Hartman also ponders, the words humans have at their disposal to name physical and mental or spiritual violence enacted on another being—rape, violation, transgression, abuse—do not adequately signify in the context of enslavement: "What does sexuality designate when rape is a normative mode of its deployment? . . . How can we discern the crime when it is a legitimate use of property?" (Hartman, *Scenes* 85). Questions like these may point the reader towards a conundrum of critical thinking and its language, because the implication of her statement is that if sexual violence against Black enslaved women was not coded and readable as that, let alone as rape, then, for all practical purposes of white law and ownership, Black women could not be raped. In turn, this implies that the language gender studies has used, fails Black women's existence, because in trying to claim a category, which can only be defined because a transgression against a victim is applied by its inherent value system, the history of their captive existence becomes again invisible: there is—another impossibility—no transgression against the enslaved, because there is no subject, no will, in the first place. Gender's very language, that is to say, assumes a human subject who can be violated. Gender's very language excludes the enslaved. Obviously, something's got to give.

Hartman's immediate object of concern is disarticulation and disfiguration of Black life in the codes, legal decisions, and the records of what passed for jurisprudence in the annals of American slave law. The enslaved's body, particularly the female body, becomes an exposed site of use value, without any possible redress on the part of the enslaved in the law's "dismissal of sexual violence as an 'offense not affecting the existence of the slave' " ("Seduction" 553). In stark difference to the legal stipulation of rape as a violation for white women (even though actual legal redress was, of course, impossible in many cases), this legal impossibility of raping a Black enslaved "made the body prey to sexual violence. . . . The ravished body, unlike a broken arm or another site of injury, did not bestow any increment of subjectivity because it did not decrease productivity or diminish value—on the contrary, it might actually increase the female captive's magnitude of value—nor did it apparently offend the principles of Christian enlightenment" (553).

By way of examining court records and legal documents, Hartman exposes the cultural, political, and legal encoding of Black enslaved women's violation (and, by implication, of Black male's violation) as a white slave-holder's fiction that relied on the white invention of a complicated web of masterful benevolence and responsibility for the slave's life, on the one hand, and submission-cum-lasciviousness on the side of the enslaved, crucially, the female enslaved, on the other. The intricate combination of Black women's purported submissiveness with insatiable sexual desire was then used, in the context of slave law, to cast the nonrelation between master and slave as a relation based on Black women's powers of seduction.

Seduction by weakness (in exchange for a never actualized promise of protection), in the narrative of stakeholders of white patriarchal power, as in observers, judges, masters themselves, and also as in a great number of white women who were enraged at their husbands' sexual dealings with their enslaved property, was considered the weapon of the meek to in fact dominate the desires and the lives of masters and owners. Thus, Hartman says, "we are to believe that the exercise of control by the weak softens universal despotism, subdues the power of the father by commanding his care, and guarantees the harmony of slave relations" (547). This notion of "control by the weak" was met with disdain and fascination, potently bolstering white power, and kept being negotiated, debated, and rejuvenated in a highly charged sexualized register of discourse way into the historical afterlife of slavery. This practice in fact made the enslaved, entirely vulnerable and permanently available, by force, to her master's every whim, into the "master of her [own] subjection" (547), as Hartman phrases it. As such, the enslaved was—in blatant negation of her actual situation as sentient property without any claim to a treatment as human—culpable before the law as a person. That means, she could be sentenced and legally punished, in case she should resist participation in her own destruction. Hartman uses the legal case of "Celia" who was indicted for having murdered her master, because she did not want to bear more years of rape and violation. Her violation would have only registered before the law as such in the case of some other man's abuse of her, as a theft, as it were, of her master's possessive power of sexual entitlement (see McLaurin; and the recent "Celia Project"). That is to say, in the eyes of white law, the Black enslaved being did not participate in human life but was instead a sentient piece of property—except that, as soon as she managed to threaten the system with acts of resistance, she became liable. In that moment of violatedness and response, she became a "person," that is, an object of interest for the law's regulatory containment procedures. If patriarchal protection was forthcoming at all—which was hardly ever the case, because violence against the enslaved did not have a recognized limit, as long as it served the master's will and interest, as Hartman explains—it became "an exemplary dissimulation, for it savagely truncated the dimensions of existence, inasmuch as the effort to safeguard slave life recognized the slave as subject only as she violated the law, or was violated (wounded flesh or pained body)" (552). And she goes on:

> The designation of person was inescapably bound to violence and the effort to protect embodied a degree of violence no less severe than the excesses being regulated . . . , *for the recognition of the slave as person depended upon the calculation of interest and injury.* The law constituted the subject as a muted, pained body or as a body to be punished; this agonized embodiment of subjectivity certainly intensified the dreadful objectification of chattel status. Paradoxically, this designation of subjectivity utterly negated the possibility of a non-punitive, inviolate or pleasurable embodiment, and instead the black captive vanished in the chasm between object, criminal, pained body, and mortified flesh. The law's exposition of sentiment culminated in a violent shuttling of the subject between varied conditions of harm, juggled between the plantation and the state, and dispersed across categories of property, injury and punishment. (552)

Inasmuch as it was only the decisive factor of this "shuttling" of what was framed as a will-less entity that made the Black person visible to white society in terms of gender, Hartman concludes that "[i]t was not simply fortuitous that gender emerges in relation to violence; that is, gender is constituted in terms of negligible and unredressed injury and the propensity for violence" (554).

I turn now from her exposition of the law's politics, literally enacted upon the body of the enslaved, to the questions her article raises, as a consequence, for gender theory. There are a number of intensifying instances in the article, where Hartman asks questions addressed to gender studies directly as to what constitutes engendering. I need to quote at length, because, in my view, they have not adequately been answered. She takes issue both with the neglect of Black women's histories and articulations in self-universalizing gender theory and with a widely accepted framing of the Black woman as somehow existing "outside the gendered universe because she was not privy to the entitlements of bourgeois women within the white patriarchal family" (556). Quoting Elisabeth Fox-Genovese, who maintains quite euphemistically that "[v]iolation of the norm painfully reminded slaves that they *did not enjoy the full status of their gender* . . ." (Fox-Genovese 193; italics mine), her point is, precisely, that abjective violence was what engendered Black women. Seen in that light, Fox-Genovese's phrasing, which assumes a possibility to claim or "enjoy" gender status by degree—from little to full, as it were—obscures the antagonism between white person and Black property. Coming through a reading of Spillers's argument that concepts like gender, motherhood, and other feminist key tropes could not adhere to any "symbolic integrity" because of the way enslavement condemned Black being, in the eyes, minds, and hands of white society, to the zero degree of fleshness, I read Hartman's insistence on gender as an objection against a white feminist relegation of Black women to a zone of nonbeing in the realm of gender studies. As my reading of prominent gender theoretical texts argues, this relegation and condemnation, as much as it has been reason to argue for a recasting of gender in order to acknowledge Black women's trajectories, might also be a reason to speak out against gender as an analytics in the first place. This is the vantage point from which I have been reading the terms of Hartman's address:

> As a consequence, gender becomes a descriptive for the social and sexual arrangements of the dominant order rather than an analytic category. As well, it enchants the discourse of protection and mystifies its instrumental role in the control and disciplining of the body, and, more importantly, maintains the white normativity of the category "woman." What I am attempting to explore here is the divergent production of the category woman, rather than a comparison of black and white women, which implicitly or inadvertently assumes that gender is relevant only to the degree that generalizable and universal criteria define a common identity. "Can we . . . name as 'woman' that disenfranchised woman whom we strictly, historically, geopolitically *cannot imagine* as a

literal referent." . . . By interrogating gender within the purview of "offenses to existence" and examining female subject-formation at the site of sexual violence, I am not positing that forced sex constitutes *the* meaning of gender. . . . (Hartman, "Seduction" 556; Brown qtd.; italics in original)

Instead, Hartman poses the following questions, which all point towards the inadequacy of gender theory's language to frame and name the (sexual) politics of enslavement on Black flesh. First, "the extremity of power and the absolute submission required of the slave, not only renders suspect, or meaningless, concepts of consent and will, but the sheer lack of limitations regarding the violence 'necessary' to the maintenance of slave relations, that is black submission, unmoors the notion of 'force' " (539). Second, "[t]he abjection of the captive body exceeds that which can be conveyed by the designation or *difference* between 'slave' women and 'free' women. In this case, what is at issue is the difference between the deployment of sexuality in the contexts of white kinship—the proprietorial relation of the patriarch to his wife and children, the making of legitimate heirs, and the transmission of property—and black captivity—the reproduction of property, the relations of mastery and subjection. . . . Kinship and captivity designate *radically* different conditions of embodiment . . ." (541; italics mine). With this seminal argument, the mantra of *multicultural differences among women* could have been abandoned a long time ago, because, precisely, kinship and captivity are antagonistic terms that do not lend themselves to differential comparison on and within an unruptured scale of "woman" as a name or gender as a category. I am interested in the hegemony the category of gender (even in its more recent articulations as dispersed, non-homogeneous, and performative) acquired over feminist discourses to the extent that I see that hegemony as a continuation of foundational moments in gender's history to make gender work on the site, and side, of kinship—over and against the thingified slave's prerogatives of existence.

Scenes of Subjection then proceeds to introduce the two terms central not just to Hartman's argument but also to the recent Black critical formation of Afro-pessimism, as well as to the critique of gender as an analytics, which Black feminism has advanced. The concepts behind these terms have been implicit in Black critical thinking ever since the earliest articulations of Black consciousness in so-called slave narratives and texts by free Black thinkers. The terms themselves, though, were new and generative of a paradigm shift to counter the vogue of postracial quietism in the first decade of the twenty-first century (see Weier; Wilderson, *Red*): accumulation and fungibility.

With respect to the first term, accumulation is not only at work, Hartman claims, in the literal propertization (the white capacity to buy and sell Blackness as laboring capital) of the enslaved Black sentient being, but has survived legal emancipation into the afterlife of slavery as a white mechanism of symbolic and material power. This power enacts the ignorability, serviceability, rentability, and enjoyability, even the pitiability, of Black being at its digression. For the scene of theory, including gender theory, this pertains—apart from downright suppression of Black knowledge—to practices in the cracks of white argumentation, as it were. The most important of those practices are, first, the seclusion of Black knowledge as ethnography of Blackness; second, the wholesale reference to Blackness as opposed to a responsive interaction with Black knowledge and authorship; and, third, a facile discourse about "race" as an identitarian category, as opposed to an examination of the production of racialization, which would entail an acknowledgment of white abjectorship (see next chapter for discussion). Any distance to the practice of slave ledgers, which Spillers so graphically discussed, becomes one of degree: the "destruction of the African name, of kin, of linguistic, and ritual connections is so obvious in the vital stats that we tend to overlook it" (Spillers, "Mama's Baby," 73).

These practices served to accrue sophistication, cultural capital, in Bourdieu's term, in a turn-of-the-century neoliberal economy of human differentiation, the attention of which focused on the plurality of difference as a value-generating paradigm. This paradigm enabled a sidelining of the history of enslavement and its violent anti-Black effects as a negligible entity for gender theory, while it rejuvenated gender studies with largely presentist ethnographic particularity. Such instances of accumulation on epistemic and analytic levels have been contingent and dependent on ongoing Black fungibility. It affords the possibility and white capacity of nonrecognition, for which Blackness remains a cipher without human reference.

For the conceptual archive of Western modernity, no Black human, and consequently, no Black woman existed. This insight urges gender studies to move away from benevolently adding the talk of race to its postmodern thinking about human subjectivation. Instead, we need to discuss the modern white gendered subject as situated in a nexus of white female successful fight for access to the category *human* over and against Blackness as abjection. The white violence, to call on Frank Wilderson here, of enslavement forced Blackness outside the defining categories of modern subjectivity. At the same time, it was the fine white line drawn between women and slaves—even by way of prolonged conflicted negotiations of oppression and discrimination—that necessarily and consequentially contained gender relations within human society. That is to say, the founding difference of early modern transatlantic societies was the splitting of white propertied and sovereign humanity from thingified Black flesh; gender as modern category, comes to figure within that split social economy, that epistemology. It became a category to negotiate, for white European and US women, towards a status of sovereignty, subjectivity, and property rights, due to them as human members of post-Enlightenment societies, however marginalized and discriminated against.

The point being made here, of course, is not that African societies did not organize themselves around particular and various cultural, social, and economic interpellations of humans, nor that in New World enslavement and in colonial societies African-origin female beings were not subjected to particular politics and practices—most importantly, enforced genital availability and the theft of motherhood. Nor is it to deny intramural (in Spillers's term) male violence. However, as the texts discussed here have illuminated, enslaved beings of African ancestry, because of their status of nonhumanness, were not interpellated to partake in the ongoing social construction of gender, and its contestation of patriarchal oppression.

In transatlantic Western societies, the very category of binary gender emerged in political and philosophical rhetoric precisely in the context of creating a space for white women, who refused to be treated like slaves, like things, to lay claim to subjectivity. Modern gender, with early modern feminism, constituted itself discursively precisely in the shift from eighteenth-century white female Christian empathy with the enslaved to the paradigmatic feminist rhetorical and material distancing of self-possessed women from slaves, a process that repeated itself in the late nineteenth-century American negotiations of suffrage and anti-racism (see my discussion of Wollstonecraft in chapter 3). The fact that many Black women have consistently fought for an access to the category gender to occupy a space of articulation, however performative a gesture of human freedom that might be (see Wilderson, *Red*), does not alter the structural consanguinity of gender with the formation of the sovereign modern white subject. Black feminist thought and activism struggling against the abjection of an ungendered condition necessarily involved "the potentially liberating prospect of (re)coding the slave's body as a decidedly gendered one," because being situated "as internal to bourgeois rational modes of human difference is not the same thing as being installed at the limits of rational order where bourgeois (sexual) difference dissolves into the categorically nonhuman site of racialized embodiment" (Carr 135, 141). White feminism has not answered to that pressure in ways that might have justified a discourse of women across the difference of "race," because that would have required a persistent disinvestment from the enslavist nature of their own structural position. That is to say, to have or to be of female gender, which could demand and deserve certain kinds of rights and civil treatment, exclusively staked the claim of white eighteenth-century women to full human subjectivity, based on, and in contrast to, the condemnation of Black life to thingness. Thus, the infamous and persistent use of the analogy of "women" with and as "slaves" provided a springboard for white women to begin theorizing a catalogue of their own demands for an acknowledgment of modern, free subjectivity as antagonistic to enslavement. As a discursive construct, then, modern gender served the differentiation of white human from Black property. White gender theory, therefore, needs its own critique of anti-Black abjection as its constitutive grounds, instead of a fixation on additive discourses about the other woman, on the racialized ethnography of Black women's supposed difference.

White feminism, to which gender theory is still and again indebted, has been a discourse of negative analogy—We are not slaves, we are not property!—ranging from Wollstonecraft through Simone de Beauvoir to second- and third-wave feminism, and not stopping there. These white feminist remonstrations have left, however, the modern and postmodern grammar of propertization as an inevitable part of the anti-Black capitalist machine untouched. Disturbing traces of this linger, when Judith Butler—for example, in a text about queer kinship—all of a sudden mechanizes Orlando Patterson's key term for slavery, social death, into her argument. She still and again mobilizes an epistemic reservoir for which "slavery" marks the limit of unwanted terror; she does not, however, engage with Black positions on her specific issue of queer kinship, nor does she show any interest in the question of how a reckoning with Black enslavement might impact on her argument. One could say she transposes the negative analogy from the language of political claims to the language of theory, but its function remains the same (Butler, *Antigone's*; see chapter 4). In order to accept the work of Black female intellectuals like the ones discussed here as a source of epistemic authority over one's own thinking, however, instead of practicing negative analogy, gender studies needs an affective and cognitive response to the burden of our theories' genealogies.

Because Black epistemology has compounded the challenge for an activist study of enslavism not to recycle abolitionist titillation, a demolitionist project will be necessary to enable a turn away from the solipsistic presentism of much contemporary theory and make it answerable to its own indebtedness to the history of early modern Europe, the United States, and the New World. Wynter's, Spillers's, and Hartman's texts, taken as examples, force white readers into a challenging closeness to that conceptual archive's gaze. At the same time, they disrupt a renewed take on enslavism by way of quasi-abolitionist empathy with Black suffering. For a white constituency of gender studies communities to adapt itself to what Hartman calls "the redress project" (Hartman, "Venus") means a relocation into the time of enslavism, into a genealogical continuum that reaches from the early modern period into postmodernity. This relocation entails far-reaching implications for the conglomerate of post-Enlightenment Western critical thinking, be it for post-Hegelians, critical theory, post-Marxists, Black nationalists and other radical factions, and white gender theories. All liberation philosophy steeped in a post-Hegelian dialectics of oppression has evaded a theorization of abjection, which lies outside the potentially reversible subject-object struggle; so also white gender studies have foregone the issue of propertization of Blackness. To follow this analysis requires white critical communities to read Black feminist work, such as Wynter's, Hartman's, or Spillers's, not as native informants, but as epistemic lessons in redress.

Black feminist theory has clearly spoken the desire for a sociability not based on any propertization of being. It seems to me Black feminism as a political, cultural, and social project necessarily and consequently figures a demolitionist desire, a longing for something, which has not been realizable within capitalist enslavist modernity. That "something" of desire still remains on the horizon of an enslavist and megacapitalist present. It posits the utopia of a sociability formed by unowned and unowning selves, for which the issue is not *belonging* but *convivial association*. That something of desire refuses to articulate humanness articulated in enslavist possession but instead desires a sociability of mutual beholding. Even to see this collectively as a possibility, will need the end of the world as we know it, to refer once again to Césaire through Fanon and Wilderson.

This project, at this point in history, can only be a fugitive one, as Hartman suggests in her article "Venus in Two Acts." By necessity, it bears the marks of mourning anti-Black violence and not of transcendent exuberance. Hartman's "I, too, live in the time of slavery" (Best and Hartman 15)—is a statement not echoed by white gender theory. At a time of rampant takeover by globalized forces of neoliberalism, for (white) gender studies theory the challenge is to achieve agony instead of complicity with the corporate projects and, particularly in Europe and the United States, with recent rampant eulogies of European Enlightenment as the mythical ground of universal freedom. White gender theory, as much as it has been a modern critical agent in the white-on-white negotiation of patriarchal power, has also mechanized the violence of discursive formations that produced the disposable lives of Black flesh. White gender theory's transcultural and transdisciplinary expansion, recently marked by terms like the posthuman, the queered ungendered, the postracial, and the postcolonial cosmopolitan, needs to check fantasies of untethered, mobile subjectivities with the subject's white history deeply implicated in propertization and abjection of Blackness. White gender studies, that is, needs to theorize enslavism, and it needs to come to its own grief. This *grief* needs to be thought of as a self-deconstructive practice, it is, by necessity, a white conundrum.

Three

Gender and the Grammar of Enslavism

The Anti-enslavist Challenge of Blackness

In *Demonic Grounds*, I suggest that the markers of captivity so tightly
adhere to the black body that seeing blackness involves our collective
willingness to collapse it into a signifier of dispossession. . . . While
I certainly suggest there, as I do here, that black dispossession reveals
the limits of our present geographic order and opens up a way to
imagine new modes of black geographic thought, it is challenging to
think outside the interlocking data of black erasure, unfreedom, and
anti-black violence. Putting pressure on archive numbers that, particularly in the case of the middle passage and plantation life, are the
only documents that tell us about the ways in which the practice of
slavery set the stage for our present struggles with racism, is difficult.
So, what do we do with the archival documentation that displays this
unfree and violated body as both naturally dispossessed and as the
origin of new world black lives? How do we come to terms with the
inventory of numbers and the certain economic brutalities that introduce blackness—the mathematics of the unliving, the certification of
unfreedom—and give shape to how we now live our lives? And what
does it mean that, when confronting these numbers and economic
descriptors and stories of murder and commonsense instances of anti-
black violence, some of us are pulled into that Fanonian moment, where
our neurological synapses and our motor-sensory replies do not result
in relieved gasps of nostalgia or knowing gasps of present emancipation
(look how far we have come/slavery is over/get over slavery/post-race/
look how far) but instead dwell in the awfulness of seeing ourselves

43

and our communities in those numbers now? . . . This is the future the archives have given me.

—Katherine McKittrick, "Mathematics Black Life"

I begin with this long quotation from Katherine McKittrick because I want to give myself an epistemic signpost. The "I" and "us" she addresses do not include me. It is this Black articulation that I want to respond to.

This chapter will walk the reader through a series of terms that have become crucial for my argument: enslavement, abjection, ongoing abjectorship, and anti-Blackness, all of which serve to critique enslavism as a specific white Western post-Enlightenment grammar. It will need to do this because I maintain that white gender studies cannot and should not claim aloofness or agnotological innocence vis-à-vis transatlantic enslavement and its afterlife, as the constitutive enabling formations for the female modern and postmodern subject, the analytic discussion of which has been, after all, the raison d'être of its terms of address.

Gender as an analytic for women's liberation, or, better, for generating knowledge necessary to work towards overcoming patriarchal power structures and social, political, cultural and economic formations, is at the same time a reiteration of enslavism. I argue that gender as a term, and the propagation of worldly knowledge based on the insight of modern human genderedness as a specific contingent construction of human distribution of power and access to any subject position, and its very sophisticated permutations through the modern and postmodern moment, have created a changing same of anti-Blackness as abjection. That is, gender and its theory have supported and mobilized the installation of a space of resonance for a split at the base of Western societies between "the human," and the Black (post-)slave thing that has no claim to human relationality. Gender, as a discourse of free women, thus mobilized a struggle—by now widely successful for a substantial number of white Western women—for social, cultural, political, and economic participation in the project of the human and of the human's freedom. White feminism and gender theory have thus played active roles in the constitution of modern societies as we know them, in shaping and negotiating the expectations and frameworks of how to do gender properly, even in its critical modes—creating gender formations devoid of an acknowledgment of Black people's humanness and agency. To me, the epistemic corruption inherent in this history demands a disruption of the category gender, a reconnection of gender theory to enslavism, to lose its assumed innocence. Making this kind of connection will also challenge gender studies to go beyond the epistemologically restrictive gender-race analogy which fired the politics of generations of white feminism in various historical movements and articulations—an ideological position untenable for gender theory that wants to respond to anti-enslavist "clamor" (Morrison, *Beloved* 275).

Gender studies, too, live "in the time of slavery," in the "future created by it" (Hartman, *Lose* 133). It is the economic, cultural, and epistemic regime of human commodification, that transgressive nexus of white violence, desire, and property which first formed the horizon of the Euro-American modernity that Euro-American philosophers and intellectuals, including in gender studies, have known and claimed. The Enlightenment's realization of human subjectivity and rights created a vertical structure of access claims to self-representation and social participation from which, however, Black people, as hereditary commodities, were a priori abjected. It is on the basis of that abjection that the category of woman, and consequently of the gender binary, was constituted as a framework to negotiate the social, cultural, and economic position of white Euro-American women. To accept that the very constitution of gender as a term in European early modernity was tied to a social, cultural, and political system that paradigmatically prefigured Black death throws contemporary notions of gendered subjectivity into stark relief.

My interventions take an epistemic turn away from the solipsistic presentism of contemporary gender theory and make it answerable to its own indebtedness to the history of early modern Europe and the New World. Wynter's, Hartman's, and Spillers's interventions have thus become my deconstructive guides to read a series of programmatic gender studies texts, because white gender theory, as much as it has been a modern critical agent in the negotiation of patriarchal power, has also partaken in and promoted the violence of discursive formations that produced the disposable lives of Black being. In opposition to that, I will address the humiliatability, the ownability, the availability, the usability, the workability, and the shipability of Black being in the discourses and practices that shape Euro-American collective memory, as well as in the contemporary white repertoires of thinking Blackness. These discourses and practices add up to a longue durée of white abjectorship and unhumanization of Black being from the early modern period, through Enlightenment modernity, and into the postmodern moment. The slave's assumed slavishness, that persistent topos in which Blackness has been contained in white philosophy from Hegel to de Beauvoir, has blatantly disregarded the histories of Haiti and other local and globally important acts, practices, and Black discourses of Black rebellion, and of Black freedom narratives, and has kept negating all forms of Black life. It has been fixed most enduringly in white intellectual and popular thought in Germany, by Nietzsche's pertinent musings on what he called "slave morality" in his *Beyond Good and Evil* and *On the Genealogy of Morality*. The topos's ubiquity and its lasting racist value has ensured the same structural positionality for post-enslaved diasporic Black life forms, as Rinaldo Walcott in "The Problem of the Human" has phrased it, until today. I argue thus for a recognition of the continuity of enslavist white Euro-American abjectorship, lasting from the sixteenth century, through the late nineteenth and the twentieth centuries, into contemporary practices of anti-Black abjection. Even though legally sanctioned ownership of and access to Black flesh was abolished as a result of long and hard radical anti-slavery struggles, violent practices of anti-Black abjection have morphed and thus continued into the lasting afterlife of enslavement.

This book comes as the result of a sustained effort to let myself be addressed by Black epistemology, to become a spoken-to, as it were. It is possible because of the work of contemporary thinkers, most important among them for my work being Orlando Patterson, Toni Morrison, Paul Gilroy, Hortense Spillers, Saidiya Hartman, Lewis Gordon, Charles Mills, Fred Moten, Frank Wilderson, Sylvia Wynter, Kwame Nimako, Egbert Martina, Grada Kilomba, Françoise Vergès, Stephanie Smallwood, Nell Painter, Jared Sexton, Katherine McKittrick, Rinaldo Walcott, and Christina Sharpe, and, as earlier presences, Fanon and Césaire. As with Ian Baucom's magisterial study, *Specters of the Atlantic*, on the constitutive role enslavement and the system of trading with enslaved Africans played for the foundation and development of modern transatlantic societies, my work could not be articulated without interaction with decades of Black intellectual and epistemic labor antecedent to it, and generative of it.

The legacy of the white European early modern production of Black social death, to use Orlando Patterson's by now notorious phrasing, and the philosophical disappearance of the white European role in modern transatlantic enslavism have created a kind of perverted frame for the discourses of Black being. Human life has not been perceived as a social, cultural, physical, and virtual space for which enslavism and colonialism have been constitutive and that thus needs be considered as always already saturated with its proper anti-Blackness (Sexton, "Ante-Anti-Blackness"; Wilderson, *Red*).

Reading Enslavism: A Hermeneutics of Absence

Black studies have produced a wealth of historiography of Euro-American modernity with respect to the productive function that the transatlantic enslavement trade and New World slavery took on in their constitution, development, and constant economic, social, cultural, and philosophical (re)articulation. This discourse has only of late slowly trickled into adjacent humanities disciplines and, to a surprisingly hesitant degree, into philosophy and critical theory. Thus, even though New World enslavement as an object of historiography has become one of among the best-researched phenomena of the Western academic machine, other disciplines have been largely resistant to engage the connection between enslavement, modernity's Enlightenment, and transatlantic history. By way of carefully maintained disciplinary boundaries, an examination of this connection has hardly reached beyond scattered admissions of modernity's so-called paradox.

As I have shown in my previous chapter, the study of Black feminism calls for the thoroughgoing reexamination of modernity's white mythologies (see Maart, "Decolonizing"), of which I take gender to be one. In order, however, to critique the durable nexus between Euro-American transatlantic enslavement practices and (post)modern discourses, and not keep slavery safely entombed in the humanities' archives of deplorable events in the past, we need a term. A term that puts theoretical-critical thinking about modernity as a regime of slavery (to turn Saidiya Hartman upside down, who amply discusses slavery as a regime of modernity in *Lose Your Mother*) on an "equal footing" with established generalizing critical terms—like Anti-semitism, racism, colonialism/coloniality, patriarchy—that allow us to see structures, patterns, and power systems instead of singular and isolated events. That kind of term, and I have suggested the neologism *enslavism* (Broeck, "Legacies"), will make it possible to criticize a white practice the legacies of which are ongoing. It is a telling fact that humanist education, including recent so-called avant-garde theory, has so utterly abjected modern transatlantic enslavement from its purview to not even have a generalizable term for it. Slavery, as a term descriptive of a limited temporal and spatial sequence, at best, relegates the practice of enslavement to the realm of a phenomenological particular, which may or may not be included in versions of history. If retrievable at all, then it functions again only as event, as come and gone, not as a structure-generative systematic practice, including its theorizable genealogical function; as object of historiography, that is, which is by definition a string of particulars, not able to generate metacritical, epistemic potential.

We have the concept of militarism, so we can theorize wars. Without that frame which then points research to generalizable insight into patterns of imperial designs, capital investments, technological destruction, psychology of war, and other components of war-making, particular instances of war—say, Vietnam, Iraq, Afghanistan—would not be theorizable. We have been able to theorize colonialism as a practice of subjection, exploitation, and dominance in the modern arsenal of European power, beyond its various particular instantiations in and by respective countries, because we have a term, even though it had to be reappropriated from imperial historiography critically and agonistically. Slavery, by contrast, exists in the Western intellectual critical imaginary only as an isolated event, since our very language has axed it from our inner and outer worlds of critical thought. The "event" can be described, and historiography, at this point, fills libraries, but it does not translate into a cause for and lever of theorization, and that is not coincidence, but has method and purpose. The humanist white subject, including the subject of gender, has been supposed to remember, address, articulate, empathize with, rejoice in, question the brutality of, and elicit other particularly emotional responses to the specific situation, to the imagined event of being a slave in slavery. The image of slavery as traumatic occurrence, situated often beyond the frame of human rational understanding, that limit event—in an act of perverse theft—has given metaphorical heft to modern and postmodern protest against white human suffering and bondage. The idea of slavery as event, and of the slave as a generic, naturalized term for the being held in slavery, however, has never put the white subject's practice of forcing Black being into enslavement and of parasitically profiting on any conceivable level from Black abjection, sustained for centuries, on the agenda. On the contrary, the enlightened outrage at the event of slavery has served to screen perpetual white practices of enslavement off from view. Accordingly, in the German language, we have the term *Sklaverei*, which is the state of slaves; it is the history, the event, the phenomenon without an agent, but not *Versklaverei*. In English it is very similar: we use slavery, but have not said enslavism, the term I am suggesting; in French the term is *esclavage*, but not *esclavagisme* (or whatever French theory could have come up with). There is a second severe problem with nongeneralizability: the event may elicit only affect vis-à-vis the victimized—as ad hoc white pity, terror, or revulsion—meaning white responses to slavery are all and still in the realm of Christian emotions, have never passed beyond the abolitionist empathy Marcus Wood has so adroitly deconstructed. Moreover, the event of slave*ry*, as such, always remains the isolated disembodied entity *apart* from, outside of, the white subject's abjectivizing agency on and against Black being, that which does not and cannot speak about the white subject's active role in the very production of abjection. In Western white modes of thinking, including gender studies, the making of slavery into an event has thus successfully preempted theoretical cognition, as well as epistemic leverage.

Enslavism as a term, as a horizon of common reference from disciplines as varied as history, philosophy, modern literatures, cultural anthropology, law, and social and political sciences, could also facilitate the necessary transdisciplinary research and pedagogy we urgently have to put in place. This is particularly urgent for the Euro-American academy, still a bastion of white subjectivity, where the humanities have been drained towards remaining atoms of individual decolonial, anti-enslavist scholars working away in isolation at their institutes, never commanding enough critical mass to garner attention and possible support of the national and supranational research funding apparatuses, and not willing to dilute their own research to the point of nonrecognizability in research networks with positivist, presentist, philological, or other idealist multi-, inter-, and even transcultural agendas.

Such anti-enslavist labor requires a *hermeneutics of absence* (see Broeck, "Lessons" 356). This hermeneutics of absence has brought me up against the confines of established methodologies, research, and dissemination; thus this book suggests practices of reading and argumentation, which necessarily run counter to the canonical positivism of the disciplinary frames and archives, including that of gender studies.

White Machinations

> In fact, human society is only possible because some human beings accept being slaves instead of fighting to the death; a community of *masters* would be impossible.
>
> —*No Subject: An Encyclopedia of Lacanian Psychoanalysis*

European modernity as an empowering fiction and the free European subject as humanist telos rose to prominence in early modernity as a tool of political and epistemic self-empowerment of European white men and eventually also white women. The breakthrough of poststructuralist skepticism in academia and the ensuing academic discourse about the subject as constituted in social practices, as an effect of interpellation and as "always out of step with itself" notwithstanding, the white subject's universalist reign keeps resurfacing, for instance, in much of the recent feuilleton and academic discourse about the legacy of Enlightenment as a haven of freedom, entitled subjectivity, and human rights. This proactive discourse has endured not only in the face of hundreds of years of enslavism and colonialism, but also in our presence of white neoliberal capitalist expansion.

Critical theory's affective and epistemic liaison with post-Enlightenment theory resulted in an avoidance of a radical historiography of Europe's and the Enlightenment's splitting of the world into humans and Black/slaves and of its own historical position on the side of white abjectorship, of enslavism, within this split. The assumption of freedom provided the philosophical foundations for white ethico-political intellectual authorities such as Hegelian philosophy, Nietzschean anti-modernity, Marxism, critical theory, postmodern ethics, and white feminism. Yet this assumption required a massive break within cultural memory. It required a self-inscription of European modern subjects as not enslaved and, by automatic and unexamined extension, as opponents to enslavement at a historical juncture at which white modernity was in most profitable ways articulated with enslavism in intimate and effective ways.

Paradigmatically, therefore, I read three textual (post-)Enlightenment scenes to illustrate the horizon before which, and in ongoing response to which, gender studies' theoretical interventions have unfolded (see chapter 4 on de Beauvoir, Benjamin, Braidotti, and Butler). Those scenes are Wollstonecraft's and American feminism's woman-as-slave analogy, Hegel's *Herr* and *Knecht* dialectic and Nietzsche's remonstrations against slave moralities. These scenarios have been chosen because their different rhetorical strategies achieve remarkably similar results. Wollstonecraft's effective move established a white discursive monopoly over the rhetorical employment of enslavement way into the twentieth century, beyond its immediate usefulness; the Hegelian allegory, spinning out through Kojève to Lacan, evades and thus erases the historical abjection of the enslaved as a necessary third term to insist on a binary structure of recognition; Nietzsche's trope of slavishness aggressively mobilizes the anti-Black, abjectivizing jouissance already embedded in the Hegelian prerogative of a free subjectivity profiled against servility and submission. This ancestral reservoir of anti-Blackness needs to be purposefully ruptured. So far, it still shines through, or becomes reactivated in gender theory's allegiances to it, be it by way of postmodern embodiments in Deleuze and Guattari, in Lacanian analysis, or in post-Hegelian theories of recognition as aptly universal articulations of subject formation.

Woman as Slave Mobilized

Another white mythology (and racist and sexist to boot) is the romantic idea of mourning the imbalanced opposition between nature and culture, and—as synonym to that—the lack of balance between "creator" and "matter." If one looks at the history of work on matter, in the Western history of production by a masterly will, one has to take into view the ones who actually did the labor. In case of the enslaved, a particularly convenient construction because not only did they perform—by force—the master/creator's will, but they were made into self-reproducing matter property as well—something that white women managed to distance themselves from over centuries of feminism, aspiring successfully to come down on the side of creation/culture/will. To me it seems as if the much decried dis-harmony between culture (will) and nature (matter) is anchored in the fact, precisely, of the philosophical negation of labor. Not to sound Hegelian, though, by any means and fall into another white mythology: as if the "slave" ever was in more direct contact, somehow, with matter, and from that experience could develop a subjectivity in the "Auseinandersetzung," could see his own indispensability in the direct negotiation, by sweat and tears, with matter so that he could force the master/creator/will into a confrontation. The "slave" being disposible, fungible, had no such relation to the objects she sweated on: being matter among matter, no recognition springs from there. And white women knew that.

—Sabine Broeck, "White Mythologies"

What Miss Stone demands is, simply, that in marriage, woman shall be legally the equal of man so that her personal rights shall not be invaded and she shall have the control of her own property.

—William Lloyd Garrison, *Liberator*

The nexus of slavery, abolition, and articulations of women's rights in the long eighteenth and nineteenth centuries, has been amply studied and documented, so that at this point the question becomes unavoidable: How does one explain the ongoing theoretical isolation of white women's feminist claims and gender analyses from Black studies and Black feminism? If the roots of early modern feminism and, consequently, gender studies have so clearly been traceable to early modern anti-slavery campaigns, and if second-wave feminism had, as has been thoroughly documented by historiography (Breines), an intricate connection to Black decolonization struggles and the Black civil rights movements—a fact which might suggest the sharpest critical self-reflection of white female empowerment—then why has that history not widely entered the genealogy of modern and postmodern gender theory's epistemic premises?

As Garrison's remark amplifies, the mid-nineteenth-century early feminist clamor he alludes to pertained only to free white women, since Black enslaved women were not considered women before the law, were property themselves as legally certified laboring commodity. The threat of not having control over their own property did not pertain to Black enslaved being (male or female), whereas, the threat to be divested of command over her property could, until legal Black emancipation at least, entail very well the loss of control over their own slaves for some white women, as recent historiography has documented (see Jones-Rogers). That means that any common interest in the destruction of slavery, as a system could not at all be taken as a given joint interest for all white women and Black slaves. Even for women who did not come from wealth, their situation as legally free human, entitled-to-protection-and-rights beings differed starkly from that of Black slaves, even though their dependence on and legal, cultural, social, and political subordination to white men as husbands and fathers was, of course, extensive. One cannot assume a given congruence of interests between "all women," as much as early feminist literature and women's abolitionist propaganda tried to create that picture. To what extent an (always already potent) *conflict* of interest between a legacy of human freedom and a legacy of enslavement played itself out in the feminist afterlife of legally sanctioned enslavement becomes visible in the gradual, if controversial, abandonment of Black women's interests on the part of the white woman's movement after abolition, as Helen Quanquin (basing her work on both DuBois and Sánchez-Eppler) has recently observed again. To say it in even more pronounced fashion, white women's movements—which recurringly sprang to theoretical and political life in the wake of Black anti-slavery and civil rights struggles—have maintained a parasitical connection to anti-Black abjection, as Black feminists have repeatedly maintained from Hull et al.'s *But Some of Us Are Brave* to *On the Future of Black Feminism*, the 2015 special edition of *The Black Scholar*.

Therefore it is crucial to discuss the contemporary theoretical response to this trajectory, which is in the position to reflect on decades of Black feminist historiography and epistemic work. The article "There Are Two Great Oceans: The Slavery Metaphor in the Antebellum Women's Rights Discourse as Redescription of Race and Gender," by Quanquin, thus stands here prototypically for contemporary white gender studies that ostentatiously respond to the challenge of Black feminist work by offering an intersectional position but actually replay a white feminist dream of analogy, recast here as mutuality of interest. The author addresses the successful dissemination of the woman-as-slave analogy in the nineteenth-century US white women's suffrage and rights movement pre– and post–American Civil War. Quanquin's piece builds on the pioneering work on the subject, published as early as 1988, Elisabeth Spelman's *Inessential Woman*. Spelman traced the roots of the woman-as-slave metaphor to white women's antithetical reading of Aristotelian pro-slavery philosophy, for which both woman and slave were disentitled from rights, expected to surrender themselves to submission, and entirely dependent on patriarchal masters for existence and protection. In indirect response to Spelman, Quanquin's article critically observes the agnotological indifference and active racism within the US white women's movement vis-à-vis Black people, and specifically vis-à-vis Black women's political agency; it makes a move to question the validity of comparison between nineteenth-century white women under the laws of coverture, disenfranchised but legally free individuals endowed with violable rights and Black women as enslaved things, for whom "both the terms of the metaphor had been . . . everyday realities: on the one hand, the slave auction and the Ku Klux Klan, the symbols of racist oppression; on the other hand, unjust marriage laws, and more generally speaking, sexism" (76). For one, the article remains mired, though, in the metaphorics it purports to critique: calling the slave auction and the Klan "symbols of racist oppression" might make sense for the white political imagination, but does not address the violent material realities of Black flesh. Moreover, "unjust marriage laws" certainly were not a problem of enslaved Black women, and neither was "sexism" for free Black women "generally" in the sense that Quanquin's white feminist appeal would under-stand it, because free Black male misogyny cannot be equated with white patriarchy's sexist reign. Even though the free Black middle-class activists Quanquin discusses in her engagement with Black male misogyny did have to attack free Black men for their lack of support for or aggression against Black female independence and subjectivity, the term "sexism, generally speaking" does, precisely, not apply to the situation either of enslaved Black being or of only nominally free Black women. The very term assumes a human being discriminated against by another human being for reasons of her gender, but none of these terms serves to represent the (post-)enslaved Black female, as I have discussed with recourse to Spillers's work. Ultimately, Quanquin's terms of address aim to understand the position of, speak from within, and refer her readers back to the interests of white feminism. In her however skeptical return to the woman-as-slave analogy, the two poles of the analogy's effectiveness—"slave" and "woman"—become recoded as "race" and "gender," and the rhetorical goal is to establish their intersectionality. This, in itself, is as flawed a move as its early modern original, reassigning race to Black being and gender to (free, white) women. Only, as Quanquin argues in keeping with gender studies debates of the last two decades, if the connection of these poles comes into clear view, will women's existence across race and gender be adequately addressed:

The slavery metaphor also revealed the ambivalence inherent in the universalism of the *antebellum antislavery* and the *women's rights movement* [italics mine; she refers by default to the white movements]. While the analogy contributed to the idea that race and gender might be considered comparatively, it did not ensure the effective integration of both causes, often obscuring their specificities, as in the displacement of the experiences of African American women in favor of those of white women. At the same time, the slavery metaphor resonated deeply with white feminist-abolitionists, allowing them to work out intimate issues related to identity and autonomy. These conflicted uses of the slavery metaphor expose the failure of white female activists to bridge the tension between their personal and collective claims to equality. They also show the impossibility of thinking about the intersections of race and gender without acknowledging the existence of simultaneous situations of oppression and privilege. (97)

This paradigmatic statement makes assumptions that need to be unpacked. First of all, its language is driven by an ahistorical post-multicultural feminist white imaginary of difference, which has allowed key terms like "effective integration" of both "causes"—race and gender—to emerge. While it bespeaks best intentions of inclusivity, that very language reinstates a possibility of the separation of potentially competitive causes. "Race" and "gender" function again as distinct formations—a constellation in which obviously Black women and Black feminism cannot fully occupy either position or both, in a kind of contentious hypervisibility, given their specific experience; while white women stand for gender, inhabiting and owning—as the semantics imply here—the general experience, from which Black experience has been "displaceable." It is Black women's "race" whose particularity has to be squared with gender. Second, to employ the repertory of race and gender neutralizes anti-Black violence; both of these terms are descriptive of specific variations of humanness, which cannot represent the structural position of the Black post-enslaved; the adjectival quality of these ascriptions obscures the issue of "whiteness as property" (Harris), the history of enslavism resulting in the antagonism between white human freedom and Black social death. Its vocabulary of "privilege" moreover absents attention to the trajectory of white women's interest in human rights over and against the "slave," and the Black post-enslaved. That trajectory has been characterized not by privilege, which again, by its very semantics, implies a differential system, but instead by structurally exclusive histories of white power, kinship, of white feminist struggles to fully occupy the structural position of a progenitor of freedom. These histories speak not of displacement of "experiences," but of the abjection of Black life forms. Also, what sense does it make to speak of "conflicted uses" with respect to the woman-as-slave analogy in face of its complete political, social, and cultural uselessness for Black women? I also suggest resisting the implied discourse of "failure" and "missed bridging." Those terms imply the idealistic notion that anti-Black violence could be overcome by more honesty about the tension between personal and collective desires. The term "failure" refers to good intentions gone awry because of weakness or incapability; it depoliticizes its own employment of Black feminist historiography to the effect of recentering white feminist ethical will.

In order to articulate this as a challenge to gender theory's longue durée recapitulations, I now go back to Wollstonecraft's foundational Enlightenment text, which anchors the white Western women's movement within the emerging discourse on humanity and rights by way of separating "woman" from "slave" in the very move of analogizing their situation. This reading will show that (a) there is no such thing as "effective integration" between a discourse of rights, and a state of thingification and abjection; (b) race and gender as terms are a screen to hide that fact from view; and (c) the problem is that the analogy never served, in fact, to bring white women closer to effective solidarity with Black women, but instead fostered white agency at the expense of Black life.

Taking my readership's general familiarity with the crucial concepts of early modern transatlantic articulations of women's rights for granted, as they were formulated in texts like the *Vindication of the Rights of Woman* and in a whole slew of pamphlets, poems, plays, diaries, books of manners, propagandistic needlework, and other genres, I refer you to the rich textual body thoroughly assessed by historians and literary and cultural studies scholars from both sides of the Atlantic (see, e.g., Knott and Taylor; Yeo; Carruth). On the basis of this extensive historiographical research, I argue the following: early feminist arguments pushed the rights of free women to female gender as part and parcel of human life in order to exempt white women in the emerging capitalist societies they inhabited from the onslaught of patriarchal epistemic, cultural, social, and economic violence in the globalizing colonialist and enslavist world. They established the "fair sex" of white women as a human agent within early modern intramural Euro-American power negotiations of emerging post-Enlightenment societies; their expedient trope of choice was slavery. Himani Bannerji has already commented on this textual centrality of the trope for *The Vindication of the Rights of Woman*. She writes:

> From this point of view, the *Rights of Woman* is marked by the iconic centrality of "slavery" used in various metaphoric and analogical ways. It is not an exaggeration to say that it serves as an interpretive and organizational device of the text. . . . Thus, metaphors, similes and analogies of bondage, ranging from sadism to sadomasochism, deriving from the complex of slavery, provide the point of departure for her reform and utopian proposals. Without the figurative layer underwriting its philosophical and moral arguments, the *Rights of Woman*, which is otherwise a rather repetitive and formless text, would not have its internal coherence or sense of urgency. (Bannerji 229)

What Bannerji's insight points to is the textual construction, the foundational writing of gender as a discourse that needs slavery as an analogy. By force of enslavism's regime, the "slave," as the horizon of modern gendered (as all other) social, cultural, and political negotiations, then, could emerge as abjected metaphorical foil of the human's struggles. When white women, as in Wollstonecraft's text, began using the term "slave" as critical boundary of their own inscripted, textualized subjectivity, they fixed a practice of distinction—the founding gesture of gender struggle requires woman not to be slave—in Western post-Enlightenment cultures and societies. Enslavement was the practice that white women had to understand and consequently reject in order to become gendered humans with rights, as Spillers has observed:

> [T]he captive female body locates precisely a moment of converging political and social vectors that mark the flesh as a prime commodity of exchange. While this proposition is open to further exploration, suffice it to say that this open exchange of female bodies in the raw offers a kind of Ur-text to the dynamics of signification and representation that the gendered female would unravel. (Spillers, "Mama's Baby," *Diacritics* 76)

In contrast to those competitive and successful white female negotiations of the human, which centralized the recognition of gender difference as a motor of humanism, "slave" was a term that enabled a different series of significations, allowing, as the necessary negative foil, feminism to think "freedom" (and "gender"), because "unfreedom" and "thingness" was perpetually fixed on the site of abjected Black being. Wollstonecraft's textual genius, then, looked back on (post-)Aristotelean philosophy of the slave, it participated in the raging anti-slavery discourses of her contemporary moment, and, most crucially, it laid a groundwork for later redeployments of the slave's—note the very ungenderedness of the very term—fungibility.

To illustrate the *Vindication*'s textual and political saturation, even infatuation, with the slave as a troping device, I have contracted three paradigmatic passages, which illustrate the paramount value of slavery for Wollstonecraft's argument. These passages also amplify the process by which a progressive and liberatory textual concept of women's genderedness—a concept to write woman into Enlightenment as a subject, that is, a mode to create intelligibility for the female complaint and her demand—emerges by way of writing woman as *not* a slave.

Wollstonecraft's project is white women's liberation from the constraints of early modern patriarchal society that renders them childlike, immature, bereft of property, education, and rights, subject to sexual exploitation and abuse, and submitted to legal, political, and social dependency on husbands or families. In order to realize this project, she needed to construct woman as a promising antagonist to man. Woman needed to be cast as a subject who could and would be able to struggle for and negotiate, via a call for the acceptance of her gender's humanity, the rights of women to participation in civil society and for equality with men in political, cultural, and social life. In order to create gender as a potentially successful site of struggle for the reform of modern views of humanity, that is, in order to gender the human, Wollstonecraft needs to position white woman as human in the first place. The rhetorical device most immediately available, given Wollstonecraft's historical context, is the dramatic and proactive separation of white woman from the slave. Only if woman can be clearly separated from the slave, can she enter the discourses and practices of civil society as a human member, however discriminated against. This maneuver entails that, on one hand, the *Vindication* makes use of the slave as a richly productive metaphor in absurd profusion, but, on the other hand, that metaphor must be safely kept severed from its potential to signify actual enslavement of Black being. That means the metaphor must be kept within a referential horizon of the white female complaint. At the time of the *Vindication*'s publication, however, this was by no means a settled issue; the material presence of the Black abject slave thing, and the latency of white women's closeness to slave, or slave-like status, always already threatened to destabilize the workings of gender as a manageable binary intrahuman contradiction. Shrewdly, Wollstonecraft positions white women as willing cooperands in what she considers their slavery and exhorts them to abandon the state of slavishness which keeps them fastened to patriarchy's reign. Only if women will abandon this slavishness—so their dramatic appeal—will civil society recognize white women as human agents, because they are not slaves, which they demonstrate by the very propagandistic refusal of their own slavishness.

One needs to acknowledge the very political ingenuity and textual creativity to have lit upon anti-slavery to preemptively counteract the latent threat, in Wollstonecraft's moment, of women being left behind by the humanist, bourgeois revolutionary ferment emerging in Western societies, and abandoned to poverty, childbearing, and drudgery, or wealth and boredom. At our point in time, to see the woman-as-slave metaphor in operation might not strike one as particularly innovative, but for the late 1700s, with actual Black enslavement being a controversial fact of public life in enslavist nations like Britain, it must be considered a breathtaking textual breakthrough: to have found a rhetorical device which would speak to Wollstonecraft's potential female audience by appealing to their social, cultural, and political emergence as civic actors, thus giving them the horizon of futurity and a possible genealogy of freedom that the slave precisely could not have. It also launched a sense of white feminist avant-gardeness based on the textual installation of a necessary female abhorrence vis-à-vis the slave's assumed slavishness, that even at her historical moment could have—and did with Black protest—registered as an interested white fiction. And, last but not least, this device shrewdly enabled more progressive, enlightened masculine potential support by way of illustrating to interested parties the social, political, and cultural *waste* dynamic that rapidly modernizing and capitalizing societies would risk by keeping woman in the state of frivolous, under-challenged and dependent ridiculousness of the slave's purported flippancy, incapacity, ignorance, and mental weakness. The gross anti-Black violence here lies in the supreme irony with which Wollstonecraft's astute observations of wealthy women's actual behavioral frilliness and inconsequential existence—kept as they were as ornamental appendages to their husbands and families—is being scripted back on the slave, making a specifically aristocratic version of white femininity the sign of the slave's inherent character. This rhetorical move of purposefully endowing the slave and his or her Black progeny with ascriptions of useless femininity attached to the adynamic commodity has lasted way into our contemporary moment. Here are the *Vindication*'s passages (Macdonald and Scherf), which I quote at length and give together, for rhetorical effect:

Is not the following portrait—the portrait of a house slave? "I am astonished at the folly of many women, who are still reproaching their husbands for leaving them alone, for preferring this or that company to theirs, for treating them with this and the other mark of disregard or indifference; when, to speak the truth, they have themselves in a great measure to blame. Not that I would justify the men in anything wrong on their part. But had you behaved to them with more *respectful observance*, and a more *equal tenderness; studying their humours, overlooking their mistakes, submitting to their opinions* in matters indifferent, passing by little instances of unevenness, caprice, or passion, giving *soft* answers to hasty words, complaining as seldom as possible, and making it your daily care to relieve their anxieties and prevent their wishes, to enliven the hour of dullness, and call up the ideas of felicity: had you pursued this conduct, I doubt not but you would have maintained and even increased their esteem, so far as to have secured every degree of influence that could conduce to their virtue, or your mutual satisfaction; and your house might at this day have been the abode of domestic bliss." Such a woman ought to be an angel—or she is an ass— for I discern not a trace of the human character, neither reason nor passion in this domestic drudge, whose being is absorbed in that of a tyrant's. (97–98)

A slavish bondage to parents cramps every faculty of the mind; and Mr. Locke very judiciously observes, that "if the mind be curbed and humbled too much in children; if their spirits be abased and broken much by too strict an hand over them; they lose all their vigor and industry." This strict hand may in some degree account for the weakness of women; for girls, from various causes, are more kept down by their parents, in every sense of the word, than boys. The duty expected from them is, like all the duties arbitrarily imposed on women, more from a sense of propriety, more out of respect for decorum, than reason; and thus taught slavishly to submit to their parents, they are prepared for the slavery of marriage. I may be told that a number of women are not slaves in the marriage state. True, but they then become tyrants; for it is not rational freedom, but a lawless kind of power resembling the authority exercised by the favourites of absolute monarchs, which they obtain by debasing means. I do not, likewise, dream of insinuating that either boys or girls are always slaves, I only insist that when they are obliged to submit to authority blindly, their faculties are weakened, and their tempers rendered imperious or abject. I also lament that parents, indolently availing themselves of a supposed privilege, damp the first faint glimmering of reason, rendering at the same time the duty, which they are so anxious to enforce, an empty name; because they will not let it rest on the only basis on which a duty can rest securely: for unless it be founded on knowledge, it cannot gain sufficient strength to resist the squalls of passion, or the silent sapping of self-love. But it is not the parents who have given the surest proof of their affection for their children, or, to speak more properly, who by fulfilling their duty, have allowed a natural parental affection to take root in their hearts, the child of exercised sympathy and reason, and not the over-weening offspring of selfish pride, who most vehemently insist on their children submitting to their will merely because it is their will. On the contrary, the parent, who sets a good example, patiently lets that example work; and it seldom fails to produce its natural effect—filial reverence. (160–61)

I agree with Rousseau that the physical part of the art of pleasing consists in ornaments, and for that very reason I should guard girls against the contagious fondness for dress so common to weak women, that they may not rest in the physical part. Yet, weak are the women who imagine that they can long please without the aid of the mind, or, in other words, without the moral art of pleasing. But the moral art, if it be not a profanation to use the word art, when alluding to the grace which is an effect of virtue, and not the motive of action, is never to be found with ignorance; the sportiveness of innocence, so pleasing to refined libertines of both sexes, is widely different in its essence from this superiour gracefulness.

A strong inclination for external ornaments ever appears in barbarous states, only the men not the women adorn themselves; for where women are allowed to be so far on a level with men, society has advanced, at least, one step in civilization.

The attention to dress, therefore, which has been thought a sexual propensity, I think natural to mankind. But I ought to express myself with more precision. When the mind is not sufficiently opened to take pleasure in reflection, the body will be adorned with sedulous care, and ambition will appear in tattooing or painting it.

So far is this first inclination carried, that even the hellish yoke of slavery cannot stifle the savage desire of admiration which the black heroes inherit from both their parents, for all the hardly earned savings of a slave are commonly expended in a little tawdry finery. And I have seldom known a good male or female servant that was not particularly fond of dress. Their clothes were their riches; and, I argue from analogy, that the fondness for dress, so extravagant in females, arises from the same cause—want of cultivation of mind. When men meet they converse about business, politics, or literature; but, says Swift, "how naturally do women apply their hands to each other's lappets and ruffles." And very natural is it—for they have not any business to interest them, have not a taste for literature, and they find politics dry, because they have not acquired a love for mankind by turning their thoughts to the grand pursuits that exalt the human race, and promote general happiness.

Besides, various are the paths to power and fame which by accident or choice men pursue, and though they jostle against each other, for men of the same profession are seldom friends, yet there is a much greater number of their fellow-creatures with whom they never clash. But women are very differently situated with respect to each other—for they are all rivals.

Before marriage it is their business to please men, and after, with a few exceptions, they follow the same scent with all the persevering pertinacity of instinct. Even virtuous women never forget their sex in company, for they are forever trying to make themselves *agreeable*. A female beauty, and a male wit, appear to be equally anxious to draw the attention of the company to themselves; and the animosity of contemporary wits is proverbial.

Is it then surprising that when the sole ambition of woman centres in beauty, and interest gives vanity additional force, perpetual rivalships should ensue? They are all running the same race, and would rise above the virtue of mortals, if they did not view each other with a suspicious and even envious eye.

An immoderate fondness for dress, for pleasure, and for sway, are the passions of savages; the passions that occupy those uncivilized beings who have not yet extended the dominion of the mind, or even learned to think with the energy necessary to concatenate that abstract train of thought which produces principles. And that women, from their education and the present state of civilized life, are in the same condition, cannot, I think, be controverted. To laugh at them then, or satirize the follies of a being who is never to be allowed to act freely from the light of her own reason, is as absurd as cruel; for, that they who are taught blindly to obey authority, will endeavor cunningly to elude it, is most natural and certain. (193–94)

Early feminism's motto, "We are not slaves," then, inaugurated and kept rearticulating the disarticulation of subjectivity from Black being, since Blackness of skin as the inheritable and ineluctable sign of enslavement by necessity resulted in the denial of modernity's human kinship to Black being. Free women's rights could only be secured on the basis of shared kinship, and, as Wollstonecraft urged, of male and female companionship as human beings; consequently, even post-enslaved Black being inherited, as it were, not a state of entitled freedoms and rights, but the disbanded state of unfreedom accruing from a legacy of thingification that made human kinship impossible across generations.

I have been interested here in the slippage at the core of the late eighteenth- and early nineteenth-century doubled subject of abolition and early feminism that Wollstonecraft pars pro toto serves to represent. Progressively, that very doubleness was resolved by gradually slipping into a politics of the first person white female, in which slavery and the slave but functioned as a metaphorical prop, a signifier which was to lose its referent in actual enslavement entirely. Instead of seeing themselves as the guardians of civilization who were meant to save the "slave woman" from her fate at the hands of patriarchal abuse (as was the argument of earlier white female Christian abolition), Wollstonecraft and her followers propagandistically threatened the position of free white women with a likeness to the slave's existence as superfluous except for the use of enforced drudgery, would they not struggle for the right to own property and to live lives independently of their husbands and families.

Emerging gender theory as Wollstonecraft's capitalized proactively on the presumption of the slave's slavish foolishness. The very logic of that argument puts enslaved Black beings and their progeny in the structural position of perennial foolship and irrational sentience. The slave then, that woman was not, became the bulwark against white women's potential renaturalization into noncivic state, as it were. White women, in this progressive logic, were not men, but they also were neither primitive nature nor things in possession of men. The slave as a trope became a primary site of signification to mark women's *human difference* from men; it enabled white women, precisely in the recognition of that very difference, to point to a shareable antagonism outside differentialized kinship. In the later course of white feminism, this constructive trope moved any actual solidarity of struggle with Black women off the feminist agenda. Troping the slave was a successful feminist practice of white civilization, one can argue, in that it widened the human community to include white women's eventual recognition, at the expense of both the struggle against enslavism and Black life. In fact, the early modern textualization of gender naturalized the slave's, and subsequently Black being's, dispensability from social dynamics and—in this abjection from history's progress into the timeless and static existence of always already frivolous flesh, of thingified matter—his or her release into exclusion from history's engendering progress until our contemporary moment.

In Wollstonecraft's argument, the thing's frivolousness becomes aligned with and articulated as "savagery," a state of being fixed in brute nature, incapable of sociability and refinement, of civilization. Women, of course, had figured as "nature" to the realm of the social and to culture in the Western symbolic for the longest time, but, given the colonial moment, this signification gained new urgency. In the maturing global enslavist societies, nature in relation to Europe and new world culture takes on a different gestalt. On the one hand, it becomes synonymous with the far away and unattainable, the monstrously foreign, the undomesticated alien, the dangerous *outside* of transatlantic white modern culture in the making; on the other hand, it becomes epistemically enthinged, demythologized, a target of aggressive measurement, classification, surveillance, and improvement, but also a locus of ravage and possession.

In the transatlantic economic, social, and cultural commerce, the "nature" of the colonial slave arrives as the absolute "beyond" of patriarchal white culture, an extraterritorial but ubiquitous signifier to haunt and threaten the symbolic stabilization of colonial enslavist regimes (see Nussbaum). A fair amount of epistemic hysteria thus arose around the issue of Black being in the transatlantic traffic, which figured as natural thing, as chattel, but not without rhetorical expense and excess, as the history of abolition and counter-abolition amply demonstrates. White women had to enter this rhetorical economy aggressively—which was Wollstonecraft's genius to realize—because otherwise they would not have transcended the conundrum of being, as white people, part of the human regimes of enslavism but, as females, too close to "usable" or expendable nature, and thus to potentially enthinged chattel themselves. However much struggling for full subjectivity, women had to be conceptualized urgently as the progenitors of human freedom, which means they had to be purposefully disarticulated from both slavishness and concomitant natural "savagery."

Underneath the religiously grounded sentiment and compassion that undoubtedly fired abolitionist and philanthropic campaigns, that always already threatening debasement in the embodiments of Black slavethings was the negative horizon for educated emerging middle-class white women's precarious existence—themselves, exceptions few and far between, being subjected to male legal power of coverture and always just so many steps away from destitution, with only a-well-to-do and faithful husband, or a reliable family, to stand in the way. The tension between the modern West's humanity and the slave always already split Western societies along an axis of abjection that threatened to leave white Western women conceptually behind, on the side of the "primitive," premodern, natural, dispensable, and enslavable existence. The problem generated by early modern globalized enslavist regimes was the specific threat of the mobile slavething as something of a socially, culturally, and politically new mediating link between white colonialist metropolitan power and colonized so-called nature which actually enabled enslavist power to become a ubiquitous force beyond any fixed locus of actual colonization. The ubiquitous slave could be ideologically useful in ways that the distant "savage" in the colonies was not. The artificially produced, entirely commercialized and marketable entity of the modern slave thus does not point back to a nostalgically charged contradiction between modern progress and "primitive tradition." That means, it is not an entity pointing back to natural being left behind by the development of colonialist Western modern science, exploration, and domination; it does, on the contrary, refer to a threateningly productive dimension of progress, to the global makeability of abjectedness. Enslavement produces a conceptual joint entity between man as human agent and nature as the material site for the production of organizable, movable, autoregenerative, workable, and economically productive property, which could be transposed according to global circuits of capital interests.

The particular threat of that anti-Black abjection in the perception of white women differed in quality from the prospect of losing ground and stakes in the intramural contest around citizenship and subjectivity of the burgeoning nation states on both sides of the Atlantic—chilling enough, of course, as that very prospect was already for large numbers of free women in the early modern West. Here the material that socialist feminist author Silvia Federici has assembled, is very helpful to understanding the pressure that emerging colonial, enslavist capitalism put on the mass of non-middle-class, emerging female working class. In *Caliban and the Witch: Women, the Body and Primitive Accumulation*, she amply details a process of gender-classing that submitted poor white formerly peasant women to regimes of waged labor, in many instances, as documented carefully in her book, by sheer terror, as the witch hunts at the point of transition from medieval feudalisms to early capitalism emblematically demonstrate. Federici establishes a continuum of witch hunt, early conquest, and enslavism, which generated a capital-generative onslaught on the masses of European women, on so-called indigenous populations in the New World, and on the enslaved. My interest here, however, lies not so much in the history of that emerging terrorized female future proletariat who, as Federici holds, was at least structurally an ally of the enslaved and colonized. My perspective focuses the protestations of white middle-class notions of gender, which were to serve them in their articulation of the rights of the *citoyenne* in the face of capital's global formation and their part in it in Western European and North Atlantic societies. For white women to compete with white men for civil rights and entitlements within emerging modern cultural, social, and economic fields, discursive operations were required that could home white women in patriarchal enslavist modernity, even though not immediately enable them to access full subjectivity, as we know. Wollstonecraft's solution was to create a productive antagonism between woman and slavething. It lay in pushing the fact of white women's human kinship with the white male patriarchal subject by way of claiming white sociability, and thus rationality, agency, civic and social freedom, and natural rights. That distinction was distilled in a long process of controversial social, political, and cultural negotiations—in the emergence of modern gender difference *within* a kinship of enlightened subjects as a means of white individuation.

The urgent representation of woman as rational subject of human kinship, which was Wollstonecraft's and her successors' crucial project, thus had a twofold function. Its goal was as much to push white women into the unviolatable center of public life as to erect a discursive boundary against the onslaught of male transgression and domination that white women might have been stuck with had they *not* managed to separate themselves successfully from matter in modernity's enslavist context. By attacking male self-indulgence, mercantile greed, a pornographic culture, egotistic tyranny, and other patriarchal vices, early modern feminists like Wollstonecraft were addressing vestiges of former feudal social formations, to be sure. More urgently, though, they responded to practices of their contemporaneous social, political, and cultural world in action, which was inextricably tied to enslavism, on the plantation as much as in metropolitan life.

The patriarchal ravages white women addressed were massively afforded, bolstered, and strengthened by the involvement of metropolitan elites and power structures (like the state apparatus, the press, the church, and the educational system) in the culture of enslavement. As both Marcus Wood and Saidiya Hartman (*Lose*) have shown, the ubiquitous corruption of transatlantic white societies in the seventeenth, eighteenth, and early nineteenth century was a function of the metropolitan involvement in enslavist investments, practices, and discourses (see also Baucom). Both have commented on the massively rapist and pornographic discourse undergirding the slave trade and slavery; but also on the voyeuristic machinery of abolition vis-à-vis Black people, and female Black people specifically. Hartman's point, then, becomes to bracket the difference (in interest and articulation) between slavery's agents, pro-slavery advocates, and abolition, and to refocus readerly attention on what Spillers has called the "pornotroping" of Black slavethings and, subsequently, Blackness itself. For white female audiences, the brutal treatment and public abuse of Black female flesh epitomized the threat of anti-social violence at its most visible extreme, signifying the symbolic horizon of utter commodification that they needed to reject and to transcend. The terror of commodification must have been a similar threat for educated white middle-class women in the young American republic, albeit for different reasons. Early modern Enlightenment philosophy and the revolutions of the late eighteenth century abrogated feudalism but Black enslavement and anti-Black abjection embodied vividly and persistently structures and practices of violent enslavist terror of life as usable thing to which nonhuman subjects were treated. Adrienne Davis has recently termed Black women and men "extralegal creatures" ("Don't" 114), which corresponds with Spiller's notion of Black flesh, and Wilderson's term of Black life's reduction to "sentience." Sharifa Ahjum's contribution to this debate, "The Law of the (White) Father," amplifies that one needs to see this "creatureliness" compounded by its "extrasymbolic" position. Her argument supports my point that genderization, in the demands for recognition of free humanity of woman, produced Black abjection because that abjection became the negative frame of reference before which embodied states of female civic status could be enacted and represented: ". . . the degendering, paradoxically, cannot operate without a gendered point of articulation," and she speaks about gender programmatics as a humanist ideology which "must strategically affirm gender in order to render its effacement for slaves so powerfully exclusionary" (Ahjum 91–92). In consequence,

> [t]he phallic rationale for self-representation therefore precludes
> any parallel psychical-social relation between white femininity and

slave women. In other words, an autonomous white masculinity, whose "possession" of the phallus corresponds with its positioning at the apex of colonial hierarchies of power and difference, is predicated on the "exchange" of white women among white men as mothers and wives, while slave women and men function, in different ways, solely as use value. That is, excluded from the humanizing imperative of desire, slaves exist in a different order of being: that of dehumanized property, as opposed to a gendered order of masculine mobility vis-à-vis passive femininity installed by the patronymic Proper name. (86)

Hegelian Fallacy and Its Lacanian Echoes

Thus the relation of the two self-conscious individuals is such that they prove themselves and each through a life-and-death struggle. They must engage in this struggle, for they must raise their certainty of being *for themselves* to truth, both in the case of other and in their own case. And it is only through staking one's life that freedom is won; only thus is it proved that for self-consciousness, its essential being is not [just] being, not the *immediate* form in which it appears, not its submergence in the expanse of life, but rather that there is nothing present in it which could not be regarded as a vanishing moment, that it is only pure *being-for-self*. The individual who has not risked his life may well be recognized as a *person*, but he has not attained to the truth of this recognition as an independent self-consciousness.

—Georg Wilhelm Friedrich Hegel, *Phenomenology of Spirit*

To come into being, the European subject needed its underside, as it were. The crucially integral but invisible part of the human subject has been his or her *abject*, created in the European mind by way of racialized thingification. The African enslaved, seen as an unhumanized species, were tied by property rights to the emerging modern human subject so tightly that they could, structurally speaking, never occupy the position of the dialectical Hegelian object as other. Thus, they remained outside the dynamics of the human. Hegel's rather localized response to the history of bourgeois rebellion against feudalist constraints, contained in his fable of a struggle between Herr and Knecht was displaced onto a philosophical speculation equating the Herr (the self) with master, and the Knecht (other) with the slave, which since then has traveled through the transatlantic realm. Arriving in philosophy in its post-Marxist Kojèvean reception, the narrative has allegorized slavery and its overcoming into a seductive model of a container for idealized dialectical opposition, by severing the signifier slave from any New World referent (Kojève). Agnotologally ignoring the history of the Middle Passage and contemporaneous Black protestations, this practice of metaphor has celebrated the modern European subject as "former Knecht as slave" who has overtaken his master (that is, feudalism), who has mastered mastery, as it were. Thus, in the transnational Hegel reception, two things beneficial to the white Western subject happened at once: it could celebrate its own genealogy as a history of freedom because of its own transcendence, its successful overcoming of Knechtschaft; it also displaced the responsibility for enslavement onto the actual slaves which the free white subject held in contempt, because the slaves had not tried to attain their freedom by struggle. This philosophical scaffolding of the white subject needs to be seen as the result of abjective labor, because it had to disappear knowledge of the Haitian revolution, as well as of countless local revolts of the enslaved and of practices of living Blackness that were acts of resistance against social death on a daily basis. Post-Hegelian metaphorics obscured the fact that the previous Knechte, the emergent anti-feudal bourgeois as modern humans, had enabled themselves to become masterful subjects not only by their successful struggle for *liberté*, *egalité*, and *fraternité* in Europe, but also by means of the exploitative colonialist regimes of enslavism and imperialism abroad. As the popular English hymn has it, "Brittania rule the waves, we Englishmen never shall be slaves"—the fact that in order to rule the waves, *owning* slaves became an instrumental, useful, and productive way of ordering their affairs (see, most recently and encompassingly, Lowe) has been overwritten in Western philosophy departments and collective memory by the enduring legacy of the Hegelian master allegory, until Black historiography has refocused attention on the Middle Passage. The free human citizen subject of Europe gained this very freedom, this mastery of his (and eventually her) destiny by the creation of a mental, physical, political, economic, legal, and social border around the free human, which was marked and maintained by the existence of the slave/Black, by the free human subject's "n----." In an entirely undialectical relation to the free subject, this sentient thingbeing was structurally severed from human subjectivity, forcefully submitted to white use and benefit as laboring commodity, and abjected into what Patterson famously called the state of social death (see Patterson; Vergès; Wynter, "Unsettling").

By way of its Kojèvean installation as master-slave relation, as a frame for political, psychoanalytical, and philosophical ruminations on recognition by the other as an indispensable motor of the subject's becoming, Hegel's allegory moved into Lacanian theory, and thus into wide dissemination in all kinds of postmodern fields and disciplines, including various strands of gender theory and its critique of the masculine "master" subject. Lacan famously translated the "master-slave dialectic" into psychoanalytical investigation of subject-object relations in his reading of libidinal economy: in his metaphorical labor, the master and slave binary became the opposition between (patriarchal) "self" and (feminized) "other," in which the other, structurally speaking, remains subordinated to the self. However, this subordination functions as a *relation*, if negative, which can be worked on so as to achieve deobjectification: the other owning desire, gaining voice, becoming subject, achieving recognition. Obviously, the allure of this frame for gender theory (as well as for postcolonial and cultural studies) lay in the possibility of its subversion and potential reversal. Speaking back, and thus proactively claiming the position and perspective of the binary's object in struggle, enabled individual and collective empowerment on political, cultural, social, and economic levels for the previously disregarded and suppressed other.

This conscious political entry of an object-to-become-subject into the binary dynamics of gender division has been the mobilizing drive of feminism and gender studies since their early modern inception in Wollstonecraft's and Olympe de Gouges's demands for women's civil and human rights. However, this drive has suppressed white abjection of Black being as the motor of its success. This pertains to both the abstract level of its articulation in the Lacanian template and to the gender politics critically derivative of it.

In its abstraction, the Lacanian reading of subject formation is riddled by suppression of its historical referent, as was Hegel's model. Letting the master-slave allegory purposefully echo in elaborations of master consciousness and its imposition on the other, by implication connected to the "slave," closed the door again on the necessary third term of the abjected and, more so, on the practices of abjection which produce subject formation without the reciprocity of mutual recognition. The cynicism in face of (post-)enslaved Black being carries over from Hegel to Lacan, and into the ongoing Lacan reception, in striking ways. If seen from a perspective of the allegory's potential referent, its almost caricature-like inadequacy becomes alarming. Both ascriptions to the "master" and "slave" positions respectively can only be sustained on condition of a hermetic enclosure of this framework against the history of the Middle Passage and New World slavery. One must maintain that neither could the enslaved gain authority over their destinies via mediation of work, because they were shippable laboring propertied commodities, nor did the owners of Black flesh end up in "existential impasse." The annals and philosophies of slaveholding—

as in the notorious Thistlewood memoir, for example—bespeak unbridled jouissance in the practice of using their "slave property." At most, if any human response to the slave's existence could be detected, slavers' diaries, pamphlets, and traits evince forms of masters' panic conjured up by fear of slave resistance. There is no evidence, however, that they ruminated about existential angst or philosophical regret because they did not actually live a life of labor, and thus were not able themselves to factually shape their empirical reality. This also shows the second cognitive flaw in the voluntaristic transferal of Hegel's Herr and Knecht pair to the so-called master-slave relationship: read against the backdrop of modernity's historiography, one needed to see, if any translation to a register of slavery should be sought out, the Hegelian Knecht, the emerging bourgeois, pitted against his master, the system of feudalism, in the position of the master in becoming. For the actual enslaved, there is no position available in the Hegelian binary. The post-Kojèvean reception only served to further displace the Black (post-)enslaved being from the horizon of twentieth-century emancipatory theory.

To wit, I cite at length from *No Subject*, a kind of academic Lacan wiki, because it is in these forms of condensed e-circulations that the metaphorical anti-Black abjection—zooming, in this case, in on the submissive "slave" as "obsessional neurotic"—now manifests itself to and for a wider intellectual public. One cannot help but hear echoes of Nietzsche's contempt, in a psychoanalysis of the human that relies so heavily on marking the slave for staging the horizon of pathology, despicableness, and (social) illness: "Furthermore, the slave who resignedly 'waits for the master's death' offers a good analogy of the obsessional neurotic, who is characterized by hesitation and procrastination." This site, as with all wiki entries, is anonymously written. However, given the sophisticated nature of the entire website, one may safely assume that its authors are well-meaning, serious students of Lacan's work, trying to break down Lacan's complexity, in a well-footnoted manner, for a somewhat wider scholarly audience of non-specialists, but without vulgarizing the Lacanian oeuvre:

> According to Kojève, the dialectic of the master and the slave is the inevitable result of the fact that human desire is the desire for recognition. In order to achieve recognition, the subject must impose the idea that he has of himself on another. However, since this other also desires recognition, he also must do the same, and hence the subject is forced to engage in combat with the other. . . . This fight for recognition, for "pure pres-

tige" must be a "fight to the death," since it is only by risking his life for the sake of recognition that one can prove that he is truly human. However, the combat must in fact stop short of the death of either combatant, since recognition can only be granted by a living being. Thus the struggle ends when one of the two gives up his desire for recognition and surrenders to the other; the vanquished one recognizes the victor as his "master" and becomes his "slave." In fact, human society is only possible because some human beings accept being slaves instead of fighting to the death; a community of masters would be impossible. . . . After achieving victory, the master sets the slave to work for him. The slave works by transforming nature in order that the master may consume it and enjoy it. However, the victory is not as absolute as it seems; the relation between the master and the slave is dialectical because it leads to the negation of their respective positions. On the one hand, the recognition achieved by the master is unsatisfactory because it is not another man who grants him this recognition but only a slave, who is for the master a mere animal or thing; thus "the man who behaves as a Master will never be satisfied." On the other hand, the slave is partly compensated for his defeat by the fact that, by working, he raises himself above nature by making it other than it was. . . . In the process of changing the world the slave changes himself and becomes the author of his own destiny, unlike the master who changes only through the mediation of the slave's work. Historical progress is now "the product of the working slave and not of the warlike Master." The outcome of the dialectic is therefore paradoxical: the master ends up in a dissatisfying "existential impasse," while the slave retains the possibility of achieving true satisfaction by means of "dialectically overcoming" his slavery. . . . Lacan draws on the dialectic of the master and the slave to illustrate a wide range of points. For example the struggle for pure prestige illustrates the intersubjective nature of desire, in which the important thing is for desire to be recognized by another. The fight to the death also illustrates the aggressivity inherent in the dual relationship between the ego and the counterpart. Furthermore, the slave who resignedly "waits for the master's death" offers a good analogy of the obsessional neurotic, who is characterized by hesitation and procrastination. . . . Lacan also takes up the dialectic of the master and the slave in his theorization of the discourse of the master. In the formulation of this discourse, the master is the master signifier (S1) who puts the slave (S2) to work to produce a surplus (*a*) which he can appropriate for himself. The master signifier is that which represents a subject for all other signifiers; the discourse of the master is thus an attempt at totalization (which is why Lacan links the discourse of the master with philosophy and ontology, playing on the homophony between *maître* and *m'être*). However, this attempt always fails because the master signifier can never represent the subject completely; there is always some surplus which escapes representation." (*No Subject*)

Since, in this formation, the master consciousness knows only one adversary—namely, its other—a position which feminists post de Beauvoir then resurrected as a radical antinomy to all kinds of patriarchal master discourses and practices, (post-)enslavist Black abjected life forms have been obscured from view. This becomes crucial, particularly if transplanted from theory into social life and politics. The work of Western feminism of exposing and ultimately transcending the gender binary between masculine/subject and feminine/object positions entrenched in modern post-Enlightenment societies has been carried out in inheritance, however postmodernized, of the post-Hegelian subject-object formation, even though in the last decades this model has come under much critical scrutiny for its dialectical optimism, and, post-Butler, gendered subject positions have become regarded not as immutably fixed to sexual existence but as performative iterations.

The willful misapprehension of reading Hegelian metaphorics as a comment on, or even (see Buck-Morss) a critique of transatlantic enslavement, has altogether ignored the fact that the modern Black enslaved thing was *not* the result of an individual struggle (as in Hegel's Herr and Knecht narrative) but the result of an economic transaction that produced the Black structural condition of "being owned and traded" (Wilderson, *Red* 14). The idealized master's self that the transatlantic Hegel reception speculates about, is an entirely voluntaristic white fiction which blatantly disregards the reality of the enslavement trade and New World enslavement.

The Euro-American "master and slave" version of Hegelian narrative orchestrates enslavement as an idealized one-to-one struggle between wills, for recognition. The slave who remains slavishly overdetermined by his desire for life, not willing to risk death, in this scenario, deserves enslavement. This seems patently inappropriate in light of enslavism as a practice of globally operatic white human agents who made themselves into propertied subjects by way of transacting Black thingified being which existed outside human relationality. Thus, one must reject the assumption of a dynamics of recognition between Black being and the white subject. Following Frank Wilderson's political ontology, the modern human subject needs to be seen as borne by unlimited power over fungible Black being as a structurally afforded possibility, for every white person. Wilderson writes:

> Humanist discourse, whose epistemological machinations provide our conceptual framework for thinking political ontology, is diverse and contrary. But for all its diversity and contrariness it is sutured by an implicit rhetorical consensus that violence accrues to the human body as a result of transgressions, whether real or imagined, within the symbolic order. That is to say, Humanist discourse can only think a subject's relation to violence as a contingency and not as a matrix that positions the subject. Put another way, Humanism has no theory of the Slave because it imagines a subject who has been either alienated in language, or alienated from his or her cartographic and temporal capacities. It cannot imagine an object who has been positioned by gratuitous violence and who has no cartographic and temporal capacities to lose—a sentient being for whom recognition and incorporation is impossible. In short, political ontology, as imagined through humanism, can only produce discourse that has at its foundation alienation and exploitation as a grammar of suffering, when what is needed (for the Black who is always already a Slave) is an ensemble of ontological questions that has at its foundation accumulation and fungibility as a grammar of suffering. The violence of the Middle Passage and the Slave estate, technologies of accumulation and fungibility, recompose and reenact their horrors on each succeeding generation of Blacks. This violence is both gratuitous (not contingent on transgressions against the hegemony of civil society) and structural (positioning Blacks ontologically outside of Humanity and civil society). Simultaneously, it renders the ontological status of Humanity (life itself) wholly dependent on civil society's repetition compulsion: the frenzied and fragmented machinations through which civil society reenacts gratuitous violence on the Black—that civil society might know itself as the domain of Humans—generation after generation." (*Red* 54–55)

The (post-)Hegelian notion of modern sociability as the product of struggle for recognition, however symbolically cast, in which freedom is gained only by transcending the fear of death in mutual struggle, articulates a rather particular and interested anti-Black violence if juxtaposed with the fact of ten million (the established rough number) enslaved thingbeings. Not even having the faintest choice of risking death for freedom, those enslaved "shippable items" were forced to stay alive as sentient cargo in order to fetch revenue for the traders. Or else they died as "collateral damage" of shipping and handling, as Hartman unflinchingly called it (*Lose* 31). The total number of African deaths directly attributable to the Middle Passage voyage is estimated at up to two million; a broader look at African deaths directly attributable to the institution of slavery from 1500 to 1900 suggests up to four million African deaths (Rosenbaum 98–99).

It appears more than cynical to entertain the logic of recognition in the context of early modern enslavism. Thus, Hegelian allegory becomes a philosophical speculation with Black mass suicide, to imply self-annihilation as the only option for the millions of enslaved beings to become recognized as a human subject. This does not go to say that individual Black enslaved beings did not resist thingification by way of starving themselves to death or finding a way to jump overboard. Of course one will never know their reasons, but it seems appropriate to judge that none of them will have annihilated their existence to enforce a dialectical logic of "risking death." There was no possible price for the act: killing oneself as an enslaved did not entail "risk" but the certainty of one's physical erasure as property, and thus might at best have had the lure of successful theft; it did not promise freedom, but only physical death as "deliverance" from social death. As a practice of abjection, the logic of subject-object recognition, in its application to the enslaved, and their descendants, has evacuated any possible attainment of human subjectivity for Black being, other than being maimed between the enforced alternatives of social death or physical nonexistence in proto-Hegelian suicide.

The Promotion of Slavishness, or Nietzsche's Contempt

In every country of Europe, and the same in America, there is at present something which makes an abuse of this name a very narrow, prepossessed, enchained class of spirits, who desire almost the opposite of what our intentions and instincts prompt. . . . [T]heir two most frequently chanted songs and doctrines are called "Equality of Rights" and "Sympathy with All Sufferers"—and suffering itself is looked upon by them as something which must be *done away with*. We opposite ones, however, . . . believe that . . . the dangerousness of his situation [Nietzsche here refers to "man" in the most general sense] had to be increased enormously . . . and his Will to Life had to be increased to the unconditioned Will to Power—we believe that severity, violence, slavery, danger in the street and in the heart, secrecy, stoicism, tempter's art and devilry of every kind,—that everything wicked, terrible, tyrannical, predatory, and serpentine in man, serves as well for the elevation of the human species as its opposite.

—Friedrich Nietzsche, *Beyond Good and Evil*

Accordingly, we must learn to identify as a cruel-sounding truth the fact that slavery *belongs to the essence of a culture*. . . . [A]nd even if it were true that the Greeks were ruined because they kept slaves, the opposite is even more certain, that we will be destroyed by the *lack* of slavery . . .

—Friedrich Nietzsche, *On the Genealogy of Morality*

In the introduction to the Cambridge Texts in the History of Philosophy edition of *Beyond Good and Evil* the editor, R. P. Horstmann, ventures a preemptive admonition against possible "misreadings" of Nietzsche's oeuvre. While allowing for different and much more critical readings of Nietzsche, Horstmann warns potential readers against what he conceives of as unsophisticated misgivings against Nietzsche's originality:

He speaks of perspectivism, the will to power, of human nobility (*Vornehmheit*) and of the conditions of a life liberated from the constraints of oppressive tradition. . . . [O]ur evaluation will depend on the amount of tolerance and sympathy that we are prepared to mobilize towards Nietzsche the person. . . . If we are not convinced of the soundness of our normal views, . . . a book like *BGE* might be considered illuminating and even helpful. . . . In questioning not the normality but the objectivity or truth of such a normal worldview, Nietzsche's writings can have the effect of making us feel less worried about our inability to account for some of our central convictions in an "absolute" way. (vii, viii, ix, xxviii)

I have quoted at some length because this analysis amply illustrates philosophy's white agnotology. This sentence's appearance in a Cambridge University Press introduction, which will likely be standard college reading material, shows that studied ignorance (Mills) holds its ground over and against possible anti-enslavist critique. Contrarily, I am not reading Nietzsche's work as a trained philosopher, let alone as a Nietzsche specialist who needs to do justice to Nietzsche's work in its potential complexity. I do not want to understand Nietzsche charitably but rather want to read his ideas about the slave and slavishness literally enough to foreground Nietzsche's contributions to late nineteenth- and early twentieth-century epistemic anti-Blackness, without being seduced by the mystifying splendor of his prose or by his pre-postmodern rejection of Enlightenment's teleologies. Accordingly, the questions are these: For whom could Nietzsche's musings about slavery and the slave be "helpful"? Who is the "we" that will have the freedom to read beyond Nietzsche's contempt of slavishness without being addressed by it? What function does the slave serve in Nietzsche's argumentation? What does it mean that Nietzsche's ruminations have reintroduced the slave into Western philosophy for the twentieth century, given the widespread positive reception of his work throughout the last and into the present century by Marxists, Feminists, and Poststructuralism alike? What relation does his use of the slave as a figure of thought entertain to actually enslaved beings in the history of transatlantic slavery, and, even more urgent, to postemancipation late nineteenth-century Black life? Why does the slave have to survive in white anti-modern philosophy of the twentieth and twenty-first century, if the intellectual brilliance of Black knowledge must be seen as an interruption of any such freewheeling metaphorizing of the slave? And how does it happen that well into the twenty-first century, intellectually literate readers may be asked to understand argumentation as "helpful" which relies on the identification of the slave with slavishness—over and against decades of Black witnessing to freedom struggles in literature, arts, and historiography? Once we no longer read Nietzsche's work to gain ever greater finesse in interpreting his contradictions and ambiguities, once we refuse to take his potently verbalized abhorrence of Western modern "decadence" and his ironical rejection of humanist orthodoxies as an ally for projects of poststructuralist deconstruction, a very different picture emerges. One can see his texts as an influential philosophical mobilization of white subjects against Black being.

To say that Nietzsche promoted slavishness might sound counterintuitive at first sight, given his obvious contempt for the meekness of what he called "slave moralities." His arguments in both *Beyond Good and Evil* and *On the Genealogy of Morality* rest on his thoroughly contemptuous troping of the slave and slavishness, borne by Christian and Jewish docility, ressentiment, and betrayal of any human creativity and of the power to live as a "noble" subject. Nietzsche's purportedly antagonistic critical reckoning with Western pre- and post-Enlightenment philosophy in fact shares with Hegel's allegorical project the white position of making slaves responsible for their enslavement. It also maintains common ground with (post-)Aristotelian abjection of the slave from civil society. Neither did this trope remain in the realm of philosophical abstraction, where it, as has been broadly argued, could do no harm to actual slaves. Even if one did accept it, though, as a purely metaphorical intervention, it reproduced Black fungibility and redisseminated a theoretical speculation about the slave's lack of human will, and the slave's serviceability, docility, and malleability. That is to say, a metaphoricity of slavishness has been resurfacing in entirely unquestioned ways. On high ground—that is, in white philosophy, as in de Beauvoir's allegorical anecdotes of old slaves in the American South who preferred the safety of enslavement over a struggle for freedom—it mobilized affect against submissiveness; on the low ground of white interpellation—as in generations of Microsoft computer users not being startled in the least by their technologies' use of "master" and "slave disc"—it trained white vernacular in complicity with mastery. Nietzsche's work and its reception strengthened a white habitus for which it is essential to distance one's own will, competence, and agency from the slave's complete lack of these human qualities. The afterlife of slavery also resides in the indifference and unwillingness on the side of philosophical and vernacular knowledge production to see in the very image of the slave's slavishness an articulation of anti-Black abjection, which became the lasting legacy of Black being.

Blackness is lived under the bane of white judgment of its existence always already emblematized as slavishness. White circular thinking transfers its metaphorical objection to the hateful state of slavery to white contempt of (post-)enslaved being as deplorable and hateful. In this way, any philosophical and moral responsibility for white abjectorship, which has forced Black being into ongoing subjection, becomes displaced into both facile and anti-Black metaphor. Even in progressive thought of the twentieth and twenty-first century, as the long-lasting effect of Hegel's and Nietzsche's allegories, the epistemic equation between the slave and all kinds of wanton serviceability persists and has been extended to castigate Black life until today. For white people, the slave, and by extension his progeny, Black being, has always been the party that submissively did things oneself did not want to do, or that passively suffered things one did not want to have done to oneself. Consequently, the slave was that being the human could do everything to, and with, without any possible redress. This goes for violence of all kinds (see also, most poignantly, Sharpe, *In the Wake*). It includes practices running the gamut of inexplicable terror, without redress, which Black scholarship and activism has fought *and* archived for centuries. It also, much closer to home, pertains to academic scholars' disacknowledgment of Black intellectual labor without even having to anticipate a chiding: fungibility on a continuum, as Hartman and others have pointed out. Persistent twentieth-century notions of the slave's slavishness have been constitutive and indispensable for wide-ranging operations of "n----ization" (Walcott; also Judy) in the wake of enslavism, as Christina Sharpe argues. Thus, even the very debate philosophy has conducted as to whether or not one should understand, reject, or even champion Nietzsche's views on slavery as a satirical inversion is a practice of anti-Black abjection, because it uses the default post-enlightened human being's pejorative distance from the slave to make its point.

Accordingly, it does not matter if Nietzsche may or may not be read as bending towards the slave and ennobling the slave by making him the one that knows suffering and wants freedom from it. Even if that were the case, and if his argumentation could be read as kind of reverse satirical compassion, such reading functions only on the basis of anti-Black assumptions about the enslaved and by making Black being into a figment of white imagination. However, I do not agree with a reading of Nietzsche as making some shocking space for the slave's subjection as an education of the "human spirit." Because Nietzsche is at no point speaking from the perspective of the slave, but consistently from within the parameters of the truly free human subject, such reading is impossible to me. His extended employment of the slave and "slave morality" makes sure to contrast the slave's prerogatives with those of the "noble" mind:

> I found certain traits recurring regularly together, and connected with one another, until finally two primary types revealed themselves to me, and a radical distinction was brought to light. There is *master-morality* and *slave-morality*. . . . The distinctions of moral values have either originated in a ruling caste, pleasantly conscious of being different from the ruled—or among the ruled class, the slaves and dependents of all sorts. In the first case, when it is the rulers who determine the conception "good," it is the exalted, proud disposition, which is regarded as the distinguishing feature, and that which determines the

order of rank. The noble type of man separates from himself the beings in whom the opposite of this exalted, proud disposition displays itself, he despises them. . . . The cowardly, the timid, the insignificant, and those thinking merely of narrow utility are despised; moreover, also, the distrustful, with their constrained glances, the self-abasing, the dog-like kind of men who let themselves be abused, the mendicant flatterers, and above all the liars. . . . The noble type of man regards *himself* as a determiner of values; he does not require to be approved of; . . . he is a *creator of values.* . . . In the foreground there is the feeling of plenitude, of power, which seeks to overflow, the happiness of high tension, the consciousness of a wealth which would fain give and bestow. . . . [T]he noble man honors in himself the powerful one, him also who has power over himself, who knows how to speak and how to keep silence, who takes pleasure in subjecting himself to severity and hardness, and has reverence for all that is severe and hard. . . . The noble and brave who think thus are the furthest removed from the morality which sees precisely in sympathy, or in acting for the good of others, or in *desinteressement*, the characteristic of a moral. . . . A morality of the ruling class, however, is more especially foreign and irritating to present-day taste in the sternness of its principle that one has duties only to one's equals; that one may act towards beings of a lower rank, . . . in any case "beyond good and evil." . . . [A]ll these are typical characteristics of the noble morality. . . . It is otherwise with the second type of morality, *slave-morality*. Supposing that the abused, the oppressed, the suffering, the unemancipated, the weary, and those uncertain of themselves should moralize, what will be the common element in their moral estimates? Probably a pessimistic suspicion with regard to the entire situation of man will find expression, perhaps a condemnation of man, together with his situation. The slave has an unfavorable eye for the virtues of the powerful; he has a skepticism and distrust. On the other hand, *those* qualities which serve to alleviate the existence of sufferers are brought into prominence. . . . [I]t is here that sympathy, the kind, helping hand, the warm heart, patience, diligence, humility, and friendliness attain to honor; for here these are the most useful qualities, and almost the only means of supporting the burden of existence. Slave-morality is essentially the morality of utility." (*Beyond* 153)

According to Nietzsche, the "slavish" desire for freedom (along with democracy and equal rights, one of the modern Western demands to have ruined European societies in the wake of British liberalism, abolitionism, and working-class movements, in *Beyond Good and Evil*) was stilted in its futility; consequently it became "ressentiment" and has, by way of mental and physical miscegenation corrupted the European mind. The trope of slavishness contains descriptors, which for Nietzsche add up to his strongest pejorative, his synonym for Western modern degeneracy of mind and spirit: "slave morality." This morality, as opposed to the spirit of masters and the "gay savants," accrues from a compression of traits endemic to and paradigmatic for the slave: moralistic righteousness, inauthenticity and deceitfulness, relations of utility, prostration, and will-less subservience: "The Greeks have no need for conceptual hallucinations like this, they voice their opinion that work is a disgrace with shocking openness. . . . Nowadays it is not the man in need of art, but the slave who determines general views: in which capacity he naturally has to label all his circumstances with deceptive names in order to be able to live" (*Genealogy* 165).

The point I am making with these very partial readings of Hegel and Nietzsche is twofold. For one, and in support of recent scholarship by Italian Nietzsche scholar Domenico Losurdo, it is long overdue to abandon what Losurdo calls the poststructuralist, postmodern "hermeneutics of innocence" vis-à-vis Nietzsche (as well as other [re]canonized European philosophers (see Broeck, "Never"), as manifested in, for example, Deleuze's reading. Losurdo's magisterial monograph (see Rehmann) demonstrating Nietzsche's political investments in actual enslavement, thus counterwriting a history of Nietzsche reception which has read the slave in Nietzsche as purely and usefully metaphorical, makes obvious that Nietzsche's articulations of slave morality and its desire for freedom are entirely a function of his contempt for this morality itself, but also for the enslaved's actual struggles. The study reconstitutes much-needed historical contextualization to Nietzsche's pronunciations on slavery, placing his views squarely in referential connection to transatlantic slavery, and abolitionist movements in the United States and Europe. To wit, Keith Ansell-Pearson in his *Nietzsche contra Rousseau: A Study of Nietzsche's Moral and Political Thought* also quotes Nietzsche's contemptuous throw-away remark about Harriett Beecher Stowe, albeit only in passing (45–46).

Therefore, my reading also contradicts Judith Butler's discussion of Nietzsche, which shares with thinkers like Derrida, as well as Deleuze and

Guattari, a fascination with Nietzsche's "fables," with his narrative "inauguration of values" by way of what she considers a creative speech act:

> You may remember that although it seems that for Nietzsche the genealogy of morals is the attempt to locate the origins of values, he is actually seeking to find out how the very notion of the origin became instituted. And the means by which he seeks to explain the origin is fictional. He tells a fable of the nobles, another about a social contract, another about a slave revolt in morality, and yet another about creditor and debtor relations. None of these fables can be located in space or time, and any effort to try to find the historical complement to Nietzsche's genealogies will necessarily fail. Indeed, in the place of an account that finds the origin to values or, indeed, the origin of the origin, we read fictional stories about the way that values are originated. A noble says something is the case and it becomes the case: the speech act inaugurates the value, and becomes something like an atypical and atemporal occasion for the origination of values. Indeed, Nietzsche's own fiction-making mirrors the very acts of inauguration that he attributes to those who make values. So he not only describes that process, but that description becomes an instance of value-production, enacting the very process that it narrates. ("What")

This fascination with what is being read as Nietzsche's anti-teleological intervention screens Nietzsche's explicit philosophical contempt of slavishness as the emblematic morality of decadent modern society; Butler's opaque reference to a fable of "slave revolt" evades the fact that Nietzsche saw the modern ursurpation of morality by the "slavish mind" as a contemptible triumph of power for anti-aristocratic degeneracy.

My second point is to again foreground the implications of the ongoing revivification and recirculation of the slavishness trope in white Western thought, however much its employment is being justified by its purely metaphorical use value. It is precisely that use value which should be at stake. Every time the trope of slavishness is set in motion, and thus allusions to its referential ground, the Black (post-)enslaved are being activated, an archive of Black death is being restacked. Another act of abjection has taken place, mobilized by the fungibility of a term. I see no reason for the perpetual restaging of the trope—one could talk about submissiveness in so many different ways!—other than an intergenerational, pervasive, and unshakable habitus of what Saidiya Hartman has called the white "enjoyment" (*Scenes* 1–17) of anti-Black contempt, masking itself as innocence.

Enslavism and Abjection

The absence of enslavism in white critical reflection, including gender studies, thus dominates even postmodern critique and still binds white philosophy and theory to a "hermeneutics of innocence," to quote Losurdo again. By contrast, modern enslavism needs to be analyzed as the major propeller of modern capitalist mental and psychic constituencies. If commodification and propertization, the learning, grasping, and materializing of the world as ownable, have been generally acknowledged as the characteristics of (post)modern capitalist society, then the white abjection of Blackness, the violent making of thingbeings, of packageable, shippable, transportable, and possessable, and as such usable, itemizable, and fungible bodily entities, was its constitutive practice. As the primary site of financial networking, crediting, speculation, insuring, profit, and calculation, as we know most graphically from Ian Baucom's *Specters of the Atlantic*, the practice of enslavism must also be considered as the primary psychosocial and cultural, collective, and individual training site for capitalist white human sociability. To learn, directly and indirectly, how to commodify an always already resistant being needs to be considered the primary threshold exercise for the modern human to become, to empower him- or herself as, subject. If a human society could achieve that kind of transport and handling (in the physical and metaphorical sense) of more than ten million sentient beings as things, and then could manage to abject this practice successfully from a collective memory of the history of human freedom, it must have passed the test of its own emerging system's demands in the most generic way, and nothing could stop that sociability from further world commodification. This must be considered as the founding practice of the human subject: the global transactioning of a shippable sentient species. It (pace Patterson) differs fundamentally from other traditions of human bondage; it not only created social death, but also the globally negotiable, transferable, and competitive profitability, for the human, of Black social death in a generative way. The crucial difference between, say, warlords that kept prisoners as slaves on their grounds, and the transatlantic modern production of social death was the achievement of an abstraction of nonpersonalized property, item mobility, and thus global marketization and the capitalist inheritability of social death. One could, as a human, inherit social death as capital—financially and otherwise, directly and indirectly—as one could inherit other forms of wealth, which of course entailed a constant and structural reproducibility of Black socially dead sentient beings.

The question I am asking is, what epistemic and affective capacities the human, as a group, trained itself to exert, to be able to carry out such a historically crucial endeavor, and which role has gender struggle played in it? What needs to be stressed in this context is the structural impasse of comparison, the impossibility of analogy, between modern enslavement, on the one hand, and forms of colonial or patriarchal and classist subjugation, domination, or conquest of the Other by which the a priori humanity of population groups was called into question and suppressed, on the other. That impasse lies in the purposeful and concerted production of accumulation and fungibility, to use Hartman's terms (*Scenes*), of Blackness as, literally, something which categorically lay outside the realm of the human, without land, without gender, without a position within the nexus of free labor and capital, an enforced state of sentience next to the human world without a relation to and within it. It lies in practices of abstract and concrete marketable creation of Black serviceable flesh, as Spillers has argued ("Mama's Baby"). That impasse worked in enslavement, as well as it has been working in its enslavist afterlife, as Christina Sharpe has forcefully argued in her most recent book, *In the Wake*.

If one acknowledges enslavism as a white supraindividual practice, what has it meant for white European empowerment across gender divides, not just in the economic, political, or social sense, but also in the psychocultural, and psychohistorical sense? The problem is how to figure that out in retrospect, particularly if it has functioned as one of the best kept inner sanctums of white (postmodern) consciousness. What we need is a (psycho)analysis of the meaning of abjectification, of white abjectorship, as it were, in the sense of the race-fiction based itemization and the absenting of human relationality for Black sentient beings, for the white European subject across gender, who has used the very results of those practices of abjectification, perversely, as the threatening border of his or her own entitlement to self-possession. Thus the most ubiquitous European post-Enlightenment liberation metaphors— "We don't want to be slaves!" or "I am not your n----!"—mark that white horizon precisely. What I mean to get at is the challenge to think about white self-possession as learned, trained, acquired, and (ac)knowledged not only in a process of defense and advance against feudal interpellation by the powers of the aristocracy and church rule, that is, as a cluster of ideologies emblematizing the European subject's liberation from overwhelming and restrictive powers—which translates in the nineteenth and twentieth centuries into further rebellions against subjectivation by the state, the factory, patriarchal power, and the tyranny of the symbolic. Instead, from an anti-enslavist perspective, these discourses and practices become visible as learned, trained, acquired, and (ac)knowledged in the collective direct and indirect production of sentient Black social death.

My notion of abjection here has drawn, first, on a rather literal, *OED*-like definition of the "abject" as that which is rejected and outcast, unworthy and threatening. Second, I have been going back to Kristeva, but want to historicize her, as it were, and twist her notion of the abject. This move follows Saidiya Hartman's suggestion in "Seduction and the Ruses of Power" from 1996, David Marriott's *On Black Men*, and Sharpe's recent employment of the term in *In the Wake* addressing the abjected enslaved and thus transferring Kristeva's notion from psychoanalysis to history, as it were. For Kristeva, abjection is the key term for the human subject's hauntedness by that which cannot be assimilated with one's notion of a self—bordered in its psychic integrity. Thus, the abject is that phenomenon, moment, or being which irritates and disturbs the subject's psychic coherence, and which subjects have to disavow if they want to maintain agency *as* human subjects. I am not, however, interested in a quasi-ethnographical description of Blackness as abject; quite to the contrary, I mobilize the term abjection here—pace Kristeva, and encouraged by Hartman's historicizing of the term—to speak of abjection as a white practice of making subjectivity, as that which renders Black being abject in order to be. Thus, my interest is in the work of abjecting, which remakes white power and anti-Blackness on a daily basis, individually and collectively. I argue that the splitting off of the enslaved Black and of enslavism itself from the symbolic order was an act of successful externalization of allowing the white Western subject to engage with internal objects-to-be-subjects (as in gender struggle) but literally leaving the abjected *outside itself* and its parameters of subjectivation. Physical thingification of Black being grounded abjectedness as a Black legacy—in that Black beings were literally, and consequently philosophically, thrown overboard by the modern constitution of subject-object boundaries which fixed both of those positions as white, internal, language-able, and protected against the social death of anti-Black enslavism. This is a crucial break in thought and methodology: instead of white speaking about Black suffering—which must be seen as a, however postmodern, return of white-on-Black ethnography—I address white doing, as a cultured, sanctioned, embodied, and inherited practice against Black being. This takes its cue, again, from Hartman's discussion of "white culpability" (*Scenes* 83), which she employs as a referential term for both the direct material, legalized violence enacted on Black life and the second-order violence contained in (post)humanist discussions of the slave.

In both the processes of producing social death and of re-abjecting Blackness, gender played a crucial role, even and especially so in the object-protestations of white female would-be-subjects self-cast into a post-Hegelian logic. I read the subject as the incarnation of the masterful will to subjectivity which, indeed, did not conceive of a Black "other," since Black humanness did not exist, was entirely abjected from any human relationality.

To rephrase, I am interested in the labor white subjects, as humans, extend vis-à-vis Black being to constantly render it antagonistic to human life in all aspects of its production and reproduction, and antagonistic to their own subjectivity. This labor shows, if one wants to look, not only in aggressive racism of the militant sort, which is easy to disown from a liberal or radically critical point of view, but also in the seams and margins of white everydayness, its cultural, social, and political "normalcy," including its artefacts, literatures, and epistemologies. As recent work by Black scholars and activists—as in the campaign Black Lives Matter—have demonstrated again and again, this white work of abjection did not end with formal emancipation of the slave, but has been an unbroken continuum to this day (Sexton, "Social Life"; Broeck, "In the Presence"). In the field of gender analysis, this is owed to the persistence of the woman-as-slave analogy pioneered by Wollstonecraft, de Gouges, and others in what is generally accepted to be the foundational moment of feminism, that is, the founding moment of a binary anti-patriarchal discourse.

White freedom and subjectivity have not been perceived, in white gender studies, as social, cultural, physical, and virtual frames for which enslavism has been constitutive, so that they need be considered as always already saturated with their proper anti-Blackness. Accordingly, how has gender as a term, and consequently gender theory, figured in these pervasive practices and discourses of anti-Black abjection? I turn to another scenic reading, this time of a white feminist novel, Valerie Martin's *Property*, of 2008, which signifies gender as a practice of white abjectorship in risky, speculative, and quite drastic ways. This inquiry will take on paradigmatic function for the mode of anti-enslavist tracing I undertake.

White Abjectorship at Work

> Since the gendered female *exists for* the male, we might suggest that the ungendered female—in an amazing stroke of pansexual potential—might be invaded/raided by another woman or man.
>
> —Hortense Spillers, "Mama's Baby, Papa's Maybe"

The construction of gendered subjectivity depends largely on the successful management and controlled pursuit of a human being's libidinous desire.

But what does this easily acceptable sentence mean within the orbit of enslavism? How has the articulation of desire within the bounds of the human, and thus its complete and terrorist restriction to the white subject, succeeded in the face of pervasive day-to-day intimacy of white owners with enslaved thingbeings? The practice of white power, which was characterized simultaneously by a high degree of intimacy and an extremely rigid disavowal, carried within itself spectacular (Hartman, *Scenes*) unbounded practices of violence. The sexual nexus of slavery functioned in a way that excluded Black thingbeing from the symbolically legitimate circulation of desire; it did, as Louis Althusser would say, not interpellate Black being as gendered subjects, but worked so as to desubjectify them. What was white women's function in that game? How did white women function in a scenario with four positions, in which both "possessing the phallus" and "being the phallus" were seriously thrown into question by the presence of a second constellation of sexual available Black being, which either part of the white couple could freely access because of their ownership, or at least their capacity of absolute command. Accordingly, any sexual practice, gesture, command, or desire, which in the symbolic law of white patriarchal society would have amounted to self-endangering transgression, was affordable and realizable to white property owners. Enslaved Black being did not figure in this symbolic as a subject, not even as an object of possible resistance. As stipulated in, and enforced by the slave owner's law, Black life as thingbeing, as sentient property, did not have any capacity to demarcate a borderline of unviolatability against white use. *Property* addresses these issues headlong.

I am reading two crucial passages from Martin's novel—thus referring readers to a contemporary text that addresses the conundrum of gender and enslavism by way of a daring fictional reimagination of the master/mistress/enslaved entanglement. Martin works with the steamy props of antebellum romance (an almost gothic plantation setting, cruel and greedy white male characters, an assortment of narcissistic Southern Belles, wicked creoles, and self-indulgent splendor on display) but turns those props against the very genre conventions they conjure up. In her text, the enslaved organize for a successful uprising, the white master of the Louisiana sugar plantation, male protagonist of the novel, is murdered in the revolt; the light-skinned female "house slave," Sarah, who has been continually used sexually by the master, manages to run away in the fracas and to escape to Boston. Sarah is abetted by her lover/partner, a free New Orleans Black man, only to be apprehended by a slave catcher at the novel's end, not because of his detective intelligence but because, by a deus-ex-machina narrative twist, the enslaved's mistress, inheritor of the dead master's enslaved people and the estate, has a fit of female intuition, driven by the desire to reobtain her property.

With her, as Toni Morrison calls it in a back-cover blurb to the novel, "prised and clean-limbed" prose, Martin speaks to a void in theoretical conceptualizations of gender and anti-Blackness. Looking at plantation slavery as the constitutive American microcosm for gender articulation, her text squarely places property—that is, the existence of Black being as possession of human subjects—at the center of her text (see also Sharpe, "Lie").

Of course, my reading in this context does not claim to do the novel justice in terms of literary analysis proper; on the contrary, I am looking only at a rather select aspect of it, namely, its representation of the social, cultural, and psychic implications the material fact of property has for the positioning of Manon, the white mistress, and Sarah, the Black laboring thingbeing, and what it could mean for white gender studies to pay attention to those implications. Which is also to say that I do not in any detail trace the novel in its intertextual connectedness both to African American writing, theoretical and literary, about slavery and to antebellum white literature. What interests me is the problematics of the *splitting* of gender into white female human beings who have gendered subjectivity and Black enslaved women who do not; and the trans-aggressivity this splitting endows white women with, by way of enabling unchecked access to their slaves' physical and psychic existence as possession.

By way of constructing her tale as a first-person narrative of the white mistress, which does not allow for any changes of perspective beyond the protagonist Manon Gaudet's narcissistic reflections, Martin forces readers into an instructive but uncomfortable identification with Manon's position of white gendered subjectivity. The art of reading Gaudet's tale, Martin seems to insist, lies in the empathy a reader will need to picture the point-of-view of the enslaved by way of willfully positioning herself as possession of a white woman, and by, from that position, mentally responding to the questions a strategically ignorant Manon Gaudet keeps asking throughout her tale: "My husband is dead. . . . [W]hy would she run now, when she was safe from him? It did not make sense" (137). Being given the very last sentence of the novel, wondering at what good a free life in the North might have possibly meant to the now repossessed Sarah and her lover, Manon is allowed by the author to say, "What on earth did they think they were doing?" (209).

The two scenes I look at specifically are positioned at crucial points of the narrative's plotting. The first one is the novel's opening sequence: it establishes Manon Gaudet's position within the plantation orbit as a white possessor and, at the same time, as a subject at her master husband's mercy.

It also creates a voyeuristic white female gaze on white male violence and sexual exploitation of Black enslaved children that, by way of being voiced by the narrative's protagonist, envelops the reader in Gaudet's precarious oscillation between envious desire, repugnance, and a rather aloof disdain for male spousal misbehavior. This opening sequence is of strategic importance to the text because it already positions its heroine as a willing, though passive, participant/observer/voyeur, literally a spy through the looking-glass, in what she calls her husband's "games" which will in the course of the novel, slide into her active usurpation of the right to a deliberate masterful trans-aggression in her own sexual "game" with her enslaved servant.

I quote the pertinent passages from the novel at some length, in order to visualize the problematics for those readers who are not familiar with Martin's text. This is the first scenario: Gaudet repeatedly watches her husband—unbeknownst to him—at one of his favorite pastimes with his property. On the plantation's lake, he forces young Black boys to perform water gymnastics for him which entail their unconsensual sexual arousal and his brutal corporeal punishment of them as a consequence; the master, in turn, experiences orgiastic pleasure caused by both an enjoyment of the boys' forced sexualization and by the unchecked reign of his own violence which does not even have a need to be framed as illicit sadism, because its objects are things in his possession. Not only the boys themselves but also their enslaved mothers regularly have to bear the brunt of his desires, because they will be "punished"—in the white master's logic—for what he casts to himself, in massive disavowal, as their offspring's perverse performance. Manon Gaudet's very phrasing of that ritual reveals her own position as profoundly complicit with the masterful pleasure. What separates her interest from his is not any kind of empathy for the boys subjected to the ritual, or for the boys' families, but rather an angle of scandalized, envious fascination with the master's freedom which throws her own rights and claims as a presumably loved wife into sharp relief and subjugates her to her husband's moods and whims:

> They have to keep doing this, their lithe young bodies displayed to him in various positions. . . . The boys rub against the other, they can't help it. . . . [I]t isn't long before one comes out of the water with his member raised. That's what the game is for. This boy tries to stay in the water, he hangs his head as he comes out, thinking every thought he can to make the tumescence subside. (4)

Her next words give away Manon's conjugal implication in the master's pastime; even though she clearly recognizes the violence employed against the boys' integrity, it does not occur to her to question the enlightened racist prerogative on which it is premised: "This is what proves they are brutes, he says, and have not the power of reason. A white man, knowing he would be beaten for it, would not be able to raise his member" (4). She may call her own stance "incredulous" in the face of her husband's self-centered and willfully exploitative desire; in effect, however, Manon shares a gleeful satisfaction with him upon the execution of his fancies:

> He has his stick there by the tree. . . . Sometimes the offending boy cries out or tries to run away, but he's no match for this grown man with his stick. The servant's tumescence subsides as quickly as the master's rises, and the latter will last until he gets to the quarter. If he can find the boy's mother, and she's pretty, she will pay dearly for rearing an unnatural child. This is only one of his games. When he comes back to the house he will be in a fine humor for the rest of the day. (4)

The second scene under scrutiny here needs an attentive white reader to deal with her always already implicated awareness of white female titillation. The white master and husband having died, Manon Gaudet is enabled to follow her very own designs on and with her Black property, and the novel follows her vengeful dealings with Sarah and Walter (the half-wit, deaf master's bastard son with Sarah) in some detail. Time and again the text deconstructs its own premises, as it were, because behind Manon's narcissistic but shrewd readings of Sarah's righteous anger at the master's violence, it does allow readers to obtain glimpses of a possible line of joint gendered interests against the white patriarch. The text makes it very clear—drawing on a wealth of documentary material that Southern historians like Nell Painter have unearthed—that the ubiquity of white male so-called liaisons with Black females within the white plantation household was the crucial and unforgivable vexation for white women to drive them into opposition to the white male prerogative of freedom at their own expense (Painter, *Soul*). This deeply entrenched mad white female hatred of white male power to do what pleased the patriarch *might* have enabled a reconfiguration of gender so as to include African American female slaves within its claims of shared resistance, but this option was thwarted by white women's own possessive investments in their slaves, and the need to maintain the position of white ownership and control over and against a, however rare, potential of an alliance against propertization based on Black subjectivity and agency.

By way of a neat narrative ploy, Martin exposes that white female priority of interest. By having the master be killed in the slave uprising, and leaving Manon Gaudet as a propertied widow with the proverbial room of her own (based on the sale of the plantation, and the inheritance of her mother, conveniently deceased in a cholera epidemic in New Orleans), Martin has Gaudet find herself in the privileged and exceptional position of being able to master her own affairs. And master them she will. She will go to considerable, and financially unwarranted, lengths in recapturing the runaway Sarah to exert her ownership over the woman. Her ostentatious reason to have wanted Sarah back is the woman's competence as a servant on her white body, captured, tellingly, by Manon's statement: "No one could dress my hair so well as Sarah . . ." (206). However, the scenario I am going to discuss here reveals that Gaudet's investments in her property go far beyond the usefulness of being served and extend to a masterful enjoyment of trans-aggressive sexual freedom, which, at the beginning of the novel, she could but follow as a powerless voyeur.

After her mother has died, Manon is sitting awake in her house, being watched by the slave Sarah who is sucking her baby, wondering why her husband let Sarah keep her child, instead of selling it immediately. Watching Sarah's milk leak from her breast, it comes to Manon like a revelation: "It was for his own pleasure, I thought" (89). In a fantasy of wishing her husband dead before the fact, she takes on his position, assaulting Sarah by kneading her breasts, and sucking her nipples for milk. Having turned the tables on her husband she gleefully imagines that he, this time, is looking on "with an uncomfortable position that something was not adding up" (82). She thus successfully accomplishes the act of her own, gendered, liberation, by the trans-aggression of confirming and acting out the enslaved woman's splitting off of gender. The enslaved literally, in this scene, becomes an ungendered breast to fulfill the white woman's dreams both of power and of the physical comfort of body nurturance—which figures an ingenious textual signification on the hundreds of scenes of Black mammies feeding white babies in American cultural memory, as well as on Toni Morrison's scene of the white men taking Sethe's milk in *Beloved*.

Gaudet's sentences contract white freedom into a microcosm of pleasure, willfulness, possession and power: "I closed my eyes, swallowing greedily. . . . How wonderful I felt, how entirely free. My headache disappeared, my chest seemed to expand, there was a complimentary tingling in my own breasts" (82). One needs to be keenly aware of the fact that this is neither a scene of utopian women-bonding, nor of lesbian cross-racial desire, but entirely one of domination and violence:

> I opened my eyes and looked at Sarah's profile. She had lifted her chin as far away from me as she could, her mouth was set in a thin hard line, and her eyes were focused intently on the arm of the settee. She's afraid to look at me, I thought. And she's right to be. If she looked at me, I would slap her. (82)

The gendered subjectivation of the white woman, her freedom as an agent of her own desire, is literally sucked from the Black woman's body, contingent on the thingness-like availability and the degendering of the enslaved Black being who has become her serviceable flesh, as it were. As Spillers observed, slavery, under which gender and "the customary aspects of sexuality . . . are all thrown in crisis," provides "a realm of sexuality that is neuterbound, because it represents an open vulnerability to a gigantic sexualized repertoire that may be alternately expressed as male and/or female. Since the gendered female exists for the male, we might say that the ungendered female—in an amazing stroke of pansexual potential—might be invaded/raided by another woman or man" ("Mama's Baby," *Diacritics* 77).

This issue of gendered empowerment based on the enjoyment of one's property in a Black thingbeing already maintains an ambivalent and precarious status in Martin's novel, because text needs to be read from an assumed Black point of view to make its anti-Black violence palpable; however, that position remains conspicuously absent in *Property*, and the text relies—in a somewhat reckless gamble, I aver—on consciously anti-racist white readers to assume even the possible urgency of such perspective. Martin's gamble becomes even more obvious as such if one turns due attention to influential critical reception of the novel, which reconfigured Martin's oscillation and ambivalence vis-à-vis white gendered agency in enslavist terms.

In a glowing review of the novel, Joyce Carol Oates read the scene between Manon Gaudet and Sarah as a scene of coded lesbian love, claiming that "wordless scenes between mistress and servant, tenderly and sensuously described by Manon, are surrogates for romantic, erotic experiences" for both women (134). This is where the scandal for gender lies: How much agnotological *studia* must be preserved to be able to bypass enslavement in this scene? Not to be able to see that the white woman's freedom here is based on a theft of Black body (a theft of milk) and on the Black woman's absolute incapacity, as an enslaved thing, to respond other than with grim endurance? How much innocence vis-à-vis history must be held fast not to see that the response Gaudet rightfully fears has nothing to do with an oscillation between desire and shame in a constellation of incipient but secret lesbian attraction? To read this of all scenes as a germinal scene of even the possibility of women bonding across their "differences" entirely abjects the abjection of Black being that makes the sucking possible in the first place, and thus repeats the structural antagonism between woman's freedom and Black being's social death: Sarah, in this scenario, is not a human subject with anything to want for herself, but is made fungible for Manon's desire.

This is the horizon that gender studies needs to rethink and acknowledge. It means that modern and postmodern gender as a marker of humanness, that is, as a conceptual lever for white female human beings to be acknowledged as such, to expand their rights and subjectivities as free human subjects, and thereby articulate their structural opposition to slaves, has had a crucial syntactical function in the grammar of enslavism, and it thus belongs to a world that has to end, to use Wilderson's employment of Césaire's famous phrase (Wilderson, *Red*; Césaire, *Collected* 55).

Orphan Reading:
A Methodology of Tracing Absent Absence

Methodologically, my largest debt is owed to Morrison's notion of Blackness as ornate in its absence, as an absence screening a disavowed presence, developed most explicitly in *Playing in the Dark*. However, with respect to my discussion of gender's trajectory as a theoretical key concept, I need to push and expand her suggestion and rephrase it so as to speak of *absent absence* (see also Broeck, "Lessons"). Reading for textual absences which produce their own textual signification is of course not unique to Morrison; in fact, it has become—cast in Althusserian, Saidian, Butlerian, and numerous other poststructuralist, postcolonial, and feminist frames—an established practice of literary and cultural critical practice over the past twenty years. To transpose such a viable mode to a reading of theory against itself, therefore, will be considered an expectable transposition of a critical mode. However, my reading of white gender studies texts has produced another impasse, resulting from a moment of dense overlap between epistemology and methodology.

In texts that Morrison discusses in *Playing in the Dark* to amplify the present absence of African American impact on American society in canonical American literature, she finds, indeed, such *relation* between presence and absence: the literature she reads presents signifying clues of Blackness (characters, half-told stories, pieces of Black cultural memory embedded in white texts) that give occasion, in their ornateness, for tracing the absent larger story of America's racist past and present. American literature, she has amply demonstrated, has obscured the vital importance of African American contribution to American sociability on all possible levels, but it has not achieved a complete evacuation of Black agency. *Playing in the Dark* thus worked from the premise of a double layer of awareness on the side of white and Black American readers of literature: the shared referential horizon of the entity *American literature*, and the knowledge of the entity *African American history and culture*, at least on the most basic level. Her task, thus, was to foreground the relation between those two entities. What, however, if such a relation cannot be conceived of, because there is no possibly shared or shareable referential environment? What if, as in the case of the gender texts I will examine, the texts' implied subtext (a critique of patriarchy and the production of gendering and gendered oppression), its implied reader's interest (a person eager to understand and critique *gender trouble*), and thus the implied referential environment, excludes, by definition, any attention to that which lies outside gender and thus cannot produce curiosity in the reader?

One can say that a kind of closural pact works within gender theory to maintain enslavism's hold which lies precisely in the fact that white humans, including feminists and gender theorists, have decided that slavery has not been their story, their frame of reference, but has been a Black story. Enslavement becomes an absence that cannot have a presence visible to white readers in gender theory because no relation has been conceivable. The absence of enslavism as a white narrative remains a nonsignifying absence in the texts, because it has been a priori abjected from the texts' purview. This means that readerly identification remains hermetically closed and undisturbed, nothing in the texts creates occasion for tracing, because nobody expects, let alone needs, to be led to an absent larger story of relevance for the texts' purpose at hand. The occasions the texts might afford, one could say, are lost or wasted on the average white reader. By unacknowledged consent, by the closural pact of white identification, the absence of enslavism has been so enduringly fixed as *unavailable, unattainable,* and *undesirable* absence that there remains no void of missing; the texts' allure lies precisely in their seamless critical plenitude of critical presence.

My task, then, is to create an awareness of lack, to create a want to read the story of gender not as a story of (the struggle for) freedom, but as a story of abjection and abjectorship, and to make that grammar signify to white gender studies readers. I employ the notion of a grammar of gender here, to suggest that there has been a specific sort of white gender studies rhetoric that, contrary to its own pronouncements in which gender has been the blank, or the suppressed term of the Enlightenment, constituted gender as one of the levers to create a white internal, narcissistic discourse of the subject in Euro-American societies since the early modern disavowal of slavery in the late eighteenth century at the expense of abjected Black humanity. The subject of gender will be looked at not as one side in a binary male-female divide of subjectivity, but as a discursive construction of—at the same time that it subjected white women to a certain position of lack—woman's fullness as part of white modern human kinship by way of abjection of Blackness. I will discuss a history of denial of that development in the narratives of "becoming gender" that have been created in the feminist and gender studies deliberations in the wake of the second-wave feminist movement in the 1970s—a denial, which may be traced back to early eighteenth-century feminist formulations. Becoming a woman needs to be reread as a social, cultural, political, and material process which has entailed the unbecoming and degendering (Spillers, Mama's Baby; Carr) of abjected (post-)enslaved Black being.

Thus, I decidedly do not speak of the relation between "race" and "gender" but about the white subject of gender and its constitution in the historical abjection of Blackness, an engagement with the lacunae of our enlightenment legacy of gender. As I see it, the narrative of gender finds itself in a state of "referential debt," to paraphrase Felman (in Felman and Laub), to a disremembered history that doubles, as a second order of violence (Hartman, Scenes), the early modern abjection of Blackness as (post-)slavething, as not human. Feminism's and gender studies' racist agnotology and indifference has been widely critiqued by Black feminists over the last decades, as I have discussed in the previous chapter. I take this Black feminist theoretical critique "home," as it were, critiquing gender from within white gender, and I reexamine a number of white gender-theoretical key texts that have massively impacted the knowledge production of gender studies, transnationally and over the longue durée of the decades after the heyday of the second-wave women's movement. The selection and combination of these texts—Simone de Beauvoir's *The Second Sex*, Jessica Benjamin's *The Bonds of Love*, Judith Butler's *Antigone's Claim* and *Precarious Life*, and Rosi Braidotti's *The Posthuman*—suggests a genealogy of gender articulation that has in effect reproduced a specific form of agnotological, epistemic anti-Black violence that supported the enslavist form and content of critical world knowledge for generations. My point is that neither multi- and transculturalism's diversity agendas nor the poststructuralist turn to women's difference(s) and proliferation of racial and sexual "identities" of interest, nor the intersectional interest in the effects of interlocking modes of discrimination on multiply oppressed groups of women, as in "ethnic minorities," have addressed the issue that I see as indispensable to a critique of Western (post)modern, capitalist, corporatized, colonialist, necropolitical regimes of maintaining, formatting, regulating, and controlling human life, namely, modern enslavement and its afterlife. As I have shown, human life as Western post-Enlightenment societies have known it has been based on the continuous reproduction of nonrelationality between human beingness and Black sentience. Given this as a premise, the very installation of gender, in theoretical-philosophical terms, as the crucial lever to negotiate intrahuman relations in post-Enlightenment societies served the structural evacuation of Black thingbeing from human relationality, and thus, crucially, from gender. This book's task thus has been to devise orphan readings, as in readings that have not been properly "parented" by their immediate white family/discipline/ mentorship, that have been left to their own devices, separated from their white upbringing. These readings trace enslavist violence in textual strategies that become visible as textual acts of unwitnessing, silencing, and selective referencing, in the denial of intertextuality and epistemic agency of Black thinking, in the production of ontological blanks. They are white-on-white readings, however, that have been supported neither by available disciplinary interests nor by any critical density of political will.

To that avail, my close reading or tracing, owing some skill to my training as a literary studies scholar, pursues quite an eclectic and, in a sense, idiosyncratic array of foci. It will give attention, that is, to textual gestures, moments, and movements that to other readers might either appear not at all or appear inconsequential, minute, or peripheral, or, in other words, that might be textual elements that do not achieve particular signification other than the one implied in the closural pact. A methodological caution: I read the various paradigmatically selected texts in their respective vocabularies, taking seriously their own chosen frame of theoretical reference. So, I am engaging categories, respectively, that are mirroring a host of different theoretical approaches and intellectual loyalties, which I take up on their own terms.

Decidedly, the goal is not to do "justice" to the individual texts, let alone the wider oeuvre of their authors, in the sense of writing a more encompassing cultural history of gender's conceptual strengths and limitations. Borrowing my terms from Black feminist critic Hortense Spillers, I am after a kind of archeological "protocol" of gender's anti-Black "grammar," which requires attention to narrative syntax, textual "offs," and telling disputable details that have easily eluded or seduced the white gaze into identificatory reading practices. The following chapter, therefore, discusses paradigmatic white gender studies text corpora spanning the moment of de Beauvoir's inauguration of second-wave white feminism, the height of US-impacted feminism in the late 80s (see Benjamin, *Bonds*), and the emergence of gender and queer theory with Butler's work in the late 1990s and early 2000s. It asks how the white feminist affect of the analogy—that is, horror of abjection paired with an insistent maintenance of being human—grounded the discourses of man/woman, patriarchy/feminism, and masculinity/femininity, as well as of heteronormativity/queer desires, in short, the discourses of gender to the effect that these discourses of and within gender could be and *had* to be what discourses of Blackness could never be, namely, discourses of civil progress, discourses of free subjects' participation in social life, as opposed to discourses about social death. The persistence of those white affects as articulated in theory is what contains white gender studies in anti-Blackness, despite anti-racist protestations to the contrary.

Four

Abjective Returns

The Slave's Fungibility in White Gender Studies

De Beauvoir's Discontents, Feminism, and Enslavement

European white radical philosophy after the Shoah with very few political exceptions, did not respond to Césaire's claim that Europe was "indefensible" (see Césaire, *Discourse on Colonialism*). Whereas for white Western intellectuals the Shoah marked the absolute negative horizon of Western modernity's genocidal capacity, intellectual connections between the critique of post-Enlightenment twentieth-century modern social formation of capital, state, and citizen subject, on the one hand, and, on the other, the trenchant deconstruction of the colonial genealogy of modernity's regime—as tied to enslavement and to the subjection of so-called indigenous people— were missed. Even though Sartre—in exceptional clarity of the political moment—responded to Black liberation struggles with "Orphée noir" in 1948 (in Senghor), his response was not received widely as an exhortation to radically submit Enlightenment philosophy to a decolonial reading. Adorno and Horkheimer's *Dialektik der Aufklärung* foregoes colonialism and did not "meet" Césaire. Césaire's verdict on colonialism, which is not so much a postcolonial lament as it is a document of a massive decolonial destruction of the major tenets of European enlightenment as a white, Western knowledge formation, remained isolated; his indictment of enslavement as constitutive momentum of Western humanist societies remained an unanswered call for decades.

What does it mean, in this context, that Simone de Beauvoir, in what has become almost universally recognized as one of the founding texts of second-wave feminism, grounds her inquiry into the situation of "woman" in Hegelian allegory? The premise of her analysis rests on the seductive analogy of woman and slave that, in the long history of Western white feminism, dates back to early foundational texts like Wollstonecraft's *Vindication*. The facts that de Beauvoir, like many other cosmopolitan, transatlantic white intellectuals of that post-Shoah, as well as decolonial, historical moment, entertained regular contact and friendships with African, diasporic African, and African American intellectuals and that she spent an extended visit in the United States seems not to have impacted on her writing to the effect of rethinking the legacy of European enlightenment in terms of its enslavist and colonial biases. How did this epistemic bifurcation work, and to what theoretical and discursive effects? How did modern enslavement figure as a disavowed absented subtext to de Beauvoir's intellectual pursuit?

The motivation to reread de Beauvoir's oeuvre one more time arises in the context of a critique of feminism and gender studies, which have, however reluctantly, accommodated the talk about "race" and "difference" but remain characterized by a denial or a theoretical suppression of (post-)slavery, colonialism, and the function of white women within the coloniality of Europe and the United States. What appears to me as a severe limit to the conceptualization of racialization is its postmodern attenuation, its historically voided notion of race seen as a somewhat timeless and always presentist identifying feature of non-white people, marking difference on a lateral scale within racial variations of the human, without historical genealogy that, if acknowledged, would implicate white post-Enlightenment philosophy and theory, including feminism, in its implicit epistemic evasion or even explicit support of "New World" slavery's thingification of Black being. Thus, even the most recent incarnation of white theoretical address of difference, the transnationally disseminated paradigm of intersectionality, becomes, in white theory, an adjective to oppression. In those approaches— independent of an acknowledgment of their indebtedness to Black feminist criticism—it appears that, in general, non-white, non-Christian women have been oppressed by overlapping axes of subjugation: race, class, gender, and religion. Magically, however, white middle-class Christian women seem to have only one problem, and that is their gendered discrimination and marginalization. If anything, for gender theory influenced by Marxism, class might enter into the social description, as might age, sexual orientation, or regional restrictions; much of intersectionality studies coming out of gender theory, however, lacks a conceptualization of white, middle-class

Christian women as racialized. These approaches have until most recently remained uncognizant of the international Black critique of the last decade, which has severely implicated Western modern and postmodern societies, their ideologies, practices, institutions, and formations—such as gender—in a position of structural responsibility for enslavism. Even gender theory, which has striven to realize race as a component of gendered subjectivity and agency, has more often than not foregone the necessity of such historical reckoning. As Barnor Hesse, thus alluding to the longue durée but also the unacknowledged history of our modern imaginaries, observed a few years ago:

> Contemporary discussions of essentialism and social construction-ism that usually surround the designation of race have tended to neglect the historicity of its pragmatic colonial imposition, discursively and materially engraved in a protracted and complex intellectual and institutional process that endured from the late fifteenth century to the eighteenth century. What emerged as the colonial distinctions assembled between non-Europeanness and Europeanness, across and within the metropole and the colony, remains the basis of contemporary popular, social and pseudo-scientific racial classifications. In other words, beyond its institutional modalities, race is inherited as a modern imaginary that consecrates the difference between a distinctive Europeanness and the regulation of its designated non-Europeanness, provid-ing both with a colonial rather than a biological heritage. The importance of this imaginary lies in its provision of a "horizon" that "structures" the social "field of intelligibility" [Hesse is here quoting Laclau], facilitating and limiting the conceptual condi-tions under which it becomes possible to perceive, think, and feel things and relations in particular ways and not others." (298–99)

The concepts of feminism and gender have been crucial levers to constitute the field of modernity's intelligibility for white European and American subjects. A post-enslavist critique of gender, then, involves a hermeneutics of epistemological suspicion, in order to grasp a complicated architecture of overlap, contradiction, and interdependence of modern white subject positions with the abjection of Blackness, both in the metropolises and on the so-called periphery, the thick description of which has been hampered by an articulation within the (post-)Enlightenment debates about subjectivation. Contrary to the post-Enlightenment, post-Hegelian assump-tions of a controlling, universal binary conflict casting subject and other/

object as the motorizing power of modern development, modernity needs to be reevaluated as the dynamic locus of relations between the unequally positioned free subject and object in mutual negotiation, on the one hand, and, on the other, as a site for the production of the abject located beyond negotiation (the enslaved and her progeny). Both white women's feminism and gender as a theoretical concept have played a crucial and productive role in the trajectories of negotiation and abjection to wrestle for, articulate, and produce power. The amnesia of critical theory, including gender studies, has functioned largely as a kind of epistemic screen to bar controversy with the camps of decolonial and Black critique, a phenomenon that we have seen to be interrupted only in the last few years, largely as an effect of Black feminist theory and feminist subaltern theory (see, for example, Cornell; Spillers, *Black*; Hartman, *Lose*; Khanna; Spivak; Sandoval; Mohanty; John; Williams, *The Alchemy*; Hill Collins).

In this context, to investigate de Beauvoir's feminist advances in the post–World War II period criticizes gender theory's implication in what one might call a postmodern racially innocent ethics of anti-oppression which de Beauvoir ingeniously mobilized in advance of gender. In order to achieve this advance, de Beauvoir's work, I argue, partakes in the postwar decolonial moment, in which, however, she does not engage Black critique; instead, she capitalizes on that moment to reinscribe the white female subject into white Western philosophy and critical theory.

As Pal Ahluwalia has recently demonstrated in *Out of Africa*, the "colonial question" needs to be brought back to, or brought to bear on, the thought of European intellectuals of the postwar period, particularly in France, thus excavating the colonial traces of the poststructuralist, postmodern argument, particularly the Algerian violent resistance, but also West African or Caribbean colonial contradictions. His project, following the clues laid out by Robert Young in his earlier, pioneering publication *White Mythologies*, delves deeply into the textual, political archives of Fanon, Sartre, Camus, as well as the later Althusser, Cixous, Derrida, Foucault, Lyotard, and Bourdieu to suggest that "it might well be that the border intellectuals who questioned the universality of European modernity are intimately connected with the colony itself. . . . [I]n fact the post-structuralist and post-modern project has its deepest affiliations in the colony. It is in Algeria that we find the most radical disjuncture between the promise of European modernity and the reality, which demonstrates the very pitfalls of the universality of those ideas. It is here that the very antecedents of the critique of European thought can be located" (14). While I don't agree with Ahluwalia about his implicit claim that European intellectuals could not have developed a critique of colonial universality before the signs and practices of Algeria began to haunt them—which would suppress enslavement and early colonialism as formations which might have impacted on white modern philosophy—I am referring to his text because it pictures in all vividly detailed clarity the enmeshment of white European critical intelligentsia with the colonial project, and forcefully argues against the white amnesia screening it from more recent, presentist inter- and intratextual discourses.

De Beauvoir does not figure in Ahluwalia's book except as Sartre's companion, but one shall of course assume that the intellectual and political networks in radical response to the Algerian War of Independence must have challenged her budding philosophy just as well. While Ahluwalia's book lays open the North African connection, as it were, both *Race after Sartre* (Judaken) and *Race and Racism in Continental Philosophy* (Bernasconi and Cook) investigate Sartre's and de Beauvoir's (among others like Merleau-Ponty, Levi-Strauss, and Arendt) connections with Négritude proponents like Diop and Senghor, as well as with the radical Caribbean caucus in Paris around Fanon, Glissant, and the Césaires, foregrounding the impact those exchanges and collaborations had on the formulation of anti-racist and anti-colonial argumentation, and political stances in Sartre's oeuvre. Again, one should safely suppose de Beauvoir's more or less active involvement in this anti-hegemonic ferment. While this moment of postwar intellectual history awaits further archival research, thus adding to the more recent recuperation of crossover contact between European Marxist and Jewish and postcolonial intellectuals after the Holocaust (Rothberg, *Multidirectional*), a third strand needs to be added to the scenario of de Beauvoir's artistic, philosophical, and political environment, as Michel Fabre, among others, has repeatedly stressed, and that is the mutually challenging relationship between African American intellectuals, like Richard Wright, in Parisian exile and their Enlightenment schooled, humanist, existentialist philosopher friends, like Sartre and de Beauvoir (Fabre 159).

Slavery and Ambiguous Interventions

The problem is, of course, that in France in the late 1940s and 1950s, among white philosophers, the notion of slavery, if anything, would have had an entirely Hegelian/Kojèvian horizon. There was no slave trade historiography that had made its way into a wider discourse, no Black studies departments or professorships that could and would exert demographic and political pressure on white subject positions. This is a good argument to anticipate, and it does indeed explain much of the white isolation of postwar intellectual debate—except, and specifically if one looks at Paris in the postwar period and at the ways in which the city had become a meeting place for early Francophone decolonial intellectuals, if one factors in the personal relationships Sartre and de Beauvoir had with Black intellectuals like Fanon, Césaire, and most of all Richard Wright, the question seems noteworthy and worth further reflection why that intellectual contact never led to a reexamination of de Beauvoir's own epistemological location. How does her writing, in its insistence on a creative reemployment of Hegelian allegory, then, obscure rather than illuminate a positioning of the subject of gender vis-à-vis its colonial and enslavist implications in the history of modern Europe?

At this point I will detour into the *Ethics of Ambiguity*, because that text antecedes *The Second Sex* in a much clearer, more strongly interventionist self-contextualization in the political moment, without placing an emphasis on the issue of gender or women at all. Even though *The Second Sex* is crucial for my analysis in its function of creating and widely disseminating the very notion of a philosophy of gender, *Ethics* should be read as a kind of ante-text, establishing de Beauvoir as the visible and respected ethical narrator of a political, cultural, and social crisis of demanding urgency. In that postwar moment of crisis, how does she create the imperative notion of transcendence in the face of life's ethical ambiguity which then will evolve into her interest in the position of woman as a kind of secondary subject (or object, in her terms) that clamors for fullness and citizenship, strives to take center stage? What is the relation de Beauvoir creates between "woman" and other existentialist agents of freedom?

Ethics of Ambiguity is actually a direct political intervention, making a strong argument for a leftist political stance beyond Stalinism, for the necessity of an anti-colonial, anti-racist, and anti-fascist ethics that surpasses political opportunism, narcissistic heroism, and any kind of operational, bad-faith-based careerist kind of political engagement that mires the subject in the realm of the serious, as de Beauvoir calls it. It precipitates from very abstract musings at the beginning to swift detailed argumentation, densely packed with examples pressing the political moment in which its writer was embedded. The specific manner in which the text engages that moment, its selections and stresses, its placement of urgency, its choices of where to take a stand, and the delicacy of its positioning of the speaking and, indeed, narrating I, all deserve our attention. Over and against reading the text as a document of purely intraphilosophical speculation of the depths of existential freedom, there is a drive towards a very mundane concreteness to the essay that its philosophical claim tries to marginalize at the outset but which keeps coming back for massive interference in its discussion of "situations," of dilemmas of ambiguity, in her miniature narratives of existentialist court sessions. Contrary to most critical readings, I venture to say that the text does not stay within the boundaries of discussing ambiguity as an uncontingent abstract sign of the problematic boundaries between self and other, of the tension between transcendence and immanence, and of the complications of ethical action in the face of this tension. Rather, it is full of narrative, politicized episodes (a rather unkosher trait for philosophical inquiry proper), which build up her articulation of the subject of transcendence. Crucially, the text does not explore the relation between transcendence and immanence as a hybrid of interchangeable, permeable, reciprocal, and flexible locations; its empathy privileges the subject's given, even transgressive, desire for freedom, as opposed to clearly separable human bearers of unfreedom and immanence. It not only positions those poles as ontological givens, but also has them, in a series of anecdotes that relate historically identifiable occurrences, acquire a social and historical materiality. Those episodes naturalize those positions so that, structurally speaking, it appears as if the struggle of transcendence versus immanence is a necessarily inevitable binary human vexation, for the spectacle of the subject, in its ascendance out of immanence, to unfold. The narration of this spectacle of the subject's desire leads us to the question most urgent for de Beauvoir's moment: the question of ambiguous violence in the human articulation of freedom, without which the desiring subject may not be free, but will remain in the realm of the serious or other modes of false consciousness. "Thus one finds itself in the presence of the paradox that no action can be generated for man without its being immediately generated against men" (*Ethics* 99), de Beauvoir maintains. The challenge I see here is that the text, repeatedly and without duress of its own logic, brings historical contingency to its surface in its very anecdotalism. Stalinism, colonialism, lynching, women's oppression, French collaboration with Nazism, and the resistance are all narrativized in nutshell narratives, more or less explicitly, situation by situation. Instead of bypassing the issue-ladenness of this essay, then, as most of the commentary has chosen to do, one needs to engage it emphatically within the context of this very particular engagement. The general allusions de Beauvoir presents about women's and about the slave's suffering come to matter in a striking way: in contrast to her rather direct references to the contemporaneous French and European political and social scene, woman and slave figure in this text in a tellingly vague, unspecific, and ahistorical manner. The suffering of woman and slave, that is, are rhetorical levers for *Ethics of Ambiguity* to characterize situations oppressive to the human spirit, situations that demand agency as transcendence, because immanent reaction would mire the subject in what de Beauvoir, in quite a Nietzschean vein, discusses as slavish consciousness.

Thus, in *Ethics*, her extended meditation on subjectivity and on the ambiguity of an ethics of free human choice, de Beauvoir turns repeatedly to situations of blockage of freedom: by way of incursions of power against the particular human being, on the one hand; or by immoral human acceptance of immanence, on the other. In those situations of blockage, the gesture of freedom, the human subject's extension of itself towards the—however finite and contingent—future as "ontological possibility of a choice," will be neither articulated nor enacted. Her characterization of oppression, which in *Ethics* always needs a human interaction, interestingly hinges on the way tyranny in various constellations makes human beings into things, which effectively robs humans of the possibility of achieving transcendence:

> Only man can be an enemy for man [whereas, as she argues a page before, "material obstacles may (only) cruelly stand in the way of an undertaking" (81)]; only he can rob him of the meaning of his acts and his life because it also belongs only to him to confirm it in its existence, to recognize it in actual fact as a freedom. . . . It is this interdependence which explains why oppression is possible and why it is hateful. . . . [I]f, instead of allowing me to participate in this constructive movement, they [men] oblige me to consume my transcendence in vain, if they keep me below the level which they have conquered and on the basis of which new conquests will be achieved, then they are cutting me off from the future, they are changing me into a thing. (82)

Against this annihilation, revolt is not just ethically justified, but demanded, as she thoroughly explains in the chapter "The Antinomies of Action"; in fact, for her, the question of good and evil appears to be settled despite the ambiguity of violent resistance that always already threatens to dehumanize the agent of resistance himself: "We have to respect freedom only when it is intended for freedom, not when it strays, flees itself, and resigns itself. A freedom which is interested only in denying freedom must be denied." And, clearly departing in this instance from Hegel's life-and-death antagonism, for her the recognition of human freedom is a demand *prior to* any particular struggle: "And it is not true that the recognition of the freedom of others limits my own freedom: to be free is not to have the power to do anything you like [which would be the enactment of transgressive masterful desire]; it is to be able to surpass the given toward an open future; the existence of others as a freedom defines my situation and is even the condition of my own freedom" (91). No postmodern equivocations about the impossible decidability of judgment or about the contingency of diverse subjects' instantiations of freedom claims for her—freedom reigns absolute, even in the ambiguity of its achievement. It is *because of* this unconditional insistence on freedom via human transcendence that in de Beauvoir's judgment the passivity of human immanence, or slavish consciousness in its various manifestations, becomes the object not only of her criticism but also of her radical contempt. The slave, thus, becomes the figure of suture, but also of dramatic slippage between emblematizing the victimized human oppressed by factors beyond his own agency, on the one hand, and the ignorant, submissive, dependent existence that has forsaken human agency, on the other. While *Ethics* rather graphically describes situations of enslavement, its argument repeatedly slips back into the arrogant Hegelian assumption of the slave's slavishness.

The rhetoric of slavery in *Ethics*, despite its rebellious impetus, actually serves to hide the actual resistant agency, which enslaved peoples—not the rhetorical figure of the "slave" in post-Enlightenment philosophy—have had in European and New World history. In de Beauvoir's argument, the slave is a static metaphorical figure, not a human being enslaved; her text remains strategically ignorant of the fact that it was the enslaved's (and their diasporic progeny's) resistance which came to formulate the most radical critique of the Enlightenment emancipation she endorses as her legacy. That radical resistance could have been very present to a French intellectual in the rupture of the Haitian revolution, which marked a clear break with white Enlightenment, but also in the exposure to Black epistemology available to de Beauvoir in the late 1940s and particularly the postwar years in Paris. However, drawing on de Beauvoir's knowledge of actual New World slavery—presumably acquired on her travel to the United States and in her acquaintances with (African) American intellectuals—the text breaks the philosophical mode of her deliberations to introduce the example of "old negro slaves" in the Carolinas "who were bewildered by a freedom which they didn't know what to do with and who cried for their former masters" (85). Since the text does not at any point offer bibliographic sources, one must take de Beauvoir at her word and extrapolate that this reading of the assumed slave's consciousness derives, by whatever route, from the "good case" of the "proponents of slavery" of the Old South against "false liberation," which, according to them, could only necessarily "overwhelm those who are their victims as if they were a new blow of blind fate" (86). De Beauvoir's chutzpah appears breathtaking, and I wonder if and how African American and anti-colonial African intellectuals might have possibly responded to it. For one thing, by what ethical right does she assume to know "the Negro's" consciousness so authoritatively? And, for another, how does one explain the utter lack of self-reflexivity that does enable her to ignore the chasm she aggressively opens with this argument between herself as a free agent in full possession of knowledge and agency and the slavish slave, a stock figure of racism if there ever was one? Not only does she draw that distinction but she compounds it by claiming an unquestioned hierarchic relation between an unnamed instance of responsibility and oversight, and the "ignorant slave" who must be "furnish[ed] with the means of transcending his situation by means of revolt, to put an end to his ignorance" (86).

Obviously, de Beauvoir does not realize the masterful contempt implied in what for her is the quintessence of existentialist argument (Simons 115): that somebody's unfreedom requires the intervention of the free moral subject to act for liberation. *Ethics* operates within the emblematic modern post-Enlightenment split between a free voice of articulation, on the one hand, and embodied but unvoiced suffering of unfreedom, on the other, in which (white) philosophy is per definition on the side of the free subject, able to speak a freedom in universal terms which the slave per definition cannot even conceive of. Slavery, or more precisely, the slave, thus becomes the free person's intimate burden. While this has mostly been read as an appeal to empathy, implicit in its call for freedom as an undivided human claim, which requires everybody's responsibility (86), from a post-slavery perspective, the assumptions about the slave inherent in this train of thought are disturbing, to say the least. The slave, that is, is characterized precisely by what Nietzsche named "slave morality," that is the incapability of even registering a desire for, let alone the willingness or competence to formulate a radical critique of unfreedom. Instead, the figure of the slave in *Ethics* remains entirely under de Beauvoir's rhetorical control, and never acquires any of the epistemological, political, social, and symbolic agency as his own subject, which de Beauvoir would call moral freedom (see Arp 115–23). It is only in the limited and somehow isolated context of the slave community, "enclosed" in "his ignorance" like his slave friends, that the slave might "live as a free and moral man *within his world*" (de Beauvoir, *Ethics* 85; italics mine). The slave's assumed ignorance in de Beauvoir's view is his lack of consciousness about his condition as man-made and, as such, as un-doable, which results in acceptance of his slavery, in a "resignation of his freedom" (to be a subject in the real world, one assumes) to his condition, "since he cannot even dream of any other" (85).

Only if the slave has been woken up from the "sleep of slavery" (96), has been "furnished" with means of transcendence—only, one presumes, if he has been put in the company of (post-)enlightened European intellectual philosophy, which bears the responsibility for but also has the right to articulate freedom (86)—will he (I am using the masculine, following de Beauvoir) be able to understand his own subjection, and act accordingly. Acting, in de Beauvoir's consequence of Hegel's argument, involves risking his life, because only in that risk lies the potential for emancipation. I will come back to the issue of martyrdom, but first one needs to dwell on the issue of "furnishing." This strand of argument obscures a number of problems: first, what about the instance that "furnishes," how could that instance be marked, and why would that demarcation be missing in her argument? If the slave has to risk his life for freedom, does that entail that the instance who puts the slave next to freedom has previously also risked life, and why would that narrative not appear in the text? Or would the lacunae about the one who furnishes imply that there are different structural locations to occupy vis-à-vis freedom, so that there are always already free subjects, who can then put the slave next to a freedom, which is, as a sine qua non, immediate to themselves? Where, then, would that consciousness of freedom originate? How would the given existence of the free voice be structurally contingent on the voiceless slave, because it appears quite strongly in de Beauvoir's text that in the same way that transcendence is not thinkable without the foil of immanence, free articulation needs the slave as its other figuration to be thinkable as progress and existentialist achievement. De Beauvoir, in a manner anticipating her elaborations in *The Second Sex*, uses her reading of slave consciousness to characterize woman. The oscillation of *Ethics* around the figure of the slave carries over into a series of tenuous deliberations about women's situation; in *Ethics*, she already begins to put in place the slave's symbolic potency to discuss women's oppression, which she will extend into a full-blown allegory, and thus empower considerably, in *The Second Sex*.

Let me come back now to the existential value of life and death, and de Beauvoir's quite literal endorsement of slave suicide in the case of an imposed blockage of transcendence. In quite Hegelian manner, she requires that moral freedom must be the transcendent absolute (*Second Sex* 131), to be arrived at, if necessary, by the risk of life: "There are limited situations where this return to the positive is impossible, where the future is radically blocked off. Revolt can then be achieved only in the definitive rejection of the imposed situation, in suicide. . . . Freedom can always save itself. . . . [I]t can again confirm itself by a death freely chosen" (131). Remaining as a slave, also means remaining in the realm of the serious, which in turn means, in de Beauvoir's existentialist judgment, not to rise to the challenge of a moral freedom, to forego, that is, one's subjectivity. I have no argument against this kind of philosophy of the revolt, as long as it merely describes emphatically the conundrum of desperate and impossibly tragic choices oppressed people have had to face in history. Paired with de Beauvoir's absolute critique of what she considers slavishness, including her employment of an imagery of the immoral and dependent slave, however, de Beauvoir's ethics here, if put next to the historical experience of mass enslavement in the Middle Passage, becomes rather a reckless moral imperative. The affordability of raising the bar for a moral life, in the existentialist vein, to require the martyrdom of mass suicide of millions of people in order for them to be considered moral subjects, even in hindsight, seems a white position to boot, one that entirely ignores the historical reference of its episteme.

Rhetorical Slavery and the Distinction of Gender

My reading, as has become obvious, entails a kind of retroactive hermeneutics, a reading for potential epistemological controversy that the text contains but does not foreground. Clearly, even though in the second part of *The Second Sex*, de Beauvoir recapitulates parts of Engels's, Bachofen's, and other's historiographies of gender relations, as well as the role of women in various so-called premodern, and modern societies, and even though in the last part she almost excessively makes way for graphic details to document the situation of white French middle-class women like herself, the text's goal is to establish a philosophical positioning of woman in the most universalizing and general sense, to counter the white patriarchal mythology of woman as lack, absence, nonsubject, and, at best, as ornamental and empirical. De Beauvoir's argument derives from the premise to understand femininity and sexuality as a patriarchal construction—whence the most notorious sentence of *The Second Sex* that one is not born but made a woman. Even though she uses history and the empiricism of her own example to detail the making of the feminine mystique, she needs to turn away from that detail in order to create a counterspace, as it were, for woman as a general and universal subject position that philosophy would recognize. De Beauvoir's ultimate goal, that is, was not to create some kind of counter-ethnography of a certain group of women in a certain historical, cultural, social, and political *situation*, but to enter woman into philosophy.

At this point, the slave enters the picture again, because de Beauvoir's text needs the figurative value of the slave's situation to generate an allegorical figure to emblematize women philosophically, beyond history and the contingency of class, age, region, and other factors. In a swift anti-patriarchal rhetorical move she explicitly appropriates Hegel's master-slave analogy, claiming that slave consciousness, slave labor, and slave dependency are the ultimate signifiers of women's situation.

Much feminist de Beauvoir reception has read this as an innovative strategy, and the rhetoric of woman as slave to patriarchy resonated through the various transatlantic articulations of second-wave feminism in the wake of *The Second Sex*, from de Beauvoir to Kate Millett to Marilyn French (Broeck, *White*). However, this analogy is actually a replay of early modern feminist protestations, reaching back to the arguments of Wollstonecraft and Olympe de Gouges. To juxtapose woman as the absolute Other to man as absolute Subject is a philosophical premise that, in the tradition of Wollstonecraft and early modern feminism, displaces the early modern foundational triangle constellation of (white) *subject*, (white) *object*, and the Black male and female enslaved *abject*. By rhetorically positioning woman as slave to patriarchy, while in fact the white woman under the name of "slave" learns to position herself as an object struggling for civil recognition within modernity, the category of hereditarily enslaved Blackness and its perpetuated nonrelation to the Western human subject is erased. White men come to prototypically figure human embodiment, and white women (subjected to being a lesser version of the human species, like a child) make it the business of their accumulating freedom to fully enter all the privileges of the human. At the point at which de Beauvoir takes up the analogy, we are, after 200 years of feminist struggle, definitely talking about an intrahuman conflict between transcendent and immanent human embodiment.

There are at this point a series of publications that recast de Beauvoir and the history of the discourses surrounding *The Second Sex* between its original publication, its first American publication in 1953, and the recent revival of interest in her mid-twentieth-century articulations of women's "situation" and gender trouble. In the wake of Moi's groundbreaking biographical and theoretical recovery of de Beauvoir's life and oeuvre, a number of renarrativizations have emerged recently. A most decisively anti-racist reading was published in 2014 by Black feminist philosopher Kathryn Gines in "Comparative and Competing Frameworks of Oppression in Simone de Beauvoir's *The Second Sex*," speaking back to Spelman's pioneering text from 1988. Its main arguments run parallel to my own reading (Broeck, "Comments"), as witnessed in the symposium on Gines's work, published under the title *Commentaries on Kathryn T. Gines*. White feminist publications crucially do not recast de Beauvoir as an unproblematic feminist ancestor in any hagiographic sense but do engage critically and in very sophisticated ways with her pioneering theoretical contributions around a complex variety of issues including embodiment and materiality, sexuality and gender performativity, political engagement and human rights, and her philosophical reconfigurations. Very recently, a small number of these narratives have begun to discuss de Beauvoir's major texts in terms of their discourses of race, mostly in terms of an acknowledgment of de Beauvoir's indebtedness to African American intellectualism, directly via her friendship with Richard Wright and indirectly via her relationship with Nelson Algren and the Myrdals (see also Simons).

Paradigmatically, Penelope Deutscher's reading of de Beauvoir's take on the so-called race question views de Beauvoir's analogical discussions of race as one of her sustainably productive critical contributions in terms of adding radical political momentum and the force of transcultural transposition to the feminist agenda. In Deutscher's introduction to her *The Philosophy of Simone de Beauvoir: Ambiguity, Conversion, Resistance*, one of the magisterial studies to be circulating in the most recent wave of transatlantic academic de Beauvoir reception, she summarizes:

> The writing of *The Second Sex* in 1949 by a French philosopher and novelist has been interpreted from many perspectives: biographical; Beauvoir's personal resistance to the confining conventions of bourgeois femininity; her affiliation with existentialism; her background in the writings of Hegel, Husserl, Heidegger and Sartre. To be added to this list is a further lever Beauvoir used to rethink the making of the sexes: a theoretical approach and methodology she had encountered in analyses of race relations in the United States, including the work of Richard Wright and Gunnar Myrdal. "Just as in America," she repeated a formulation attributed to both Myrdal and Wright, thereby transposing a discussion of race to a discussion of sex, "the problem is not with blacks (*il n'y a pas de problème noir*), rather there is a white problem, just as 'anti-semitism is not a Jewish problem: it is our problem'; so the woman problem has always been a problem for [or of] men." (2)

Deutscher clearly sees this as a worthwhile, overdue and generative move of great importance, going on to ask: "Further, what of Beauvoir's transpositions between race, sex, and generational difference? How might a language generated to address race have to be modified in its possible application to class, sex, or age differentials? How do ethical and political formulations change as they modulate between differing forms of alterity?" (3). Thereby returning her (presumably) feminist reader, as did de Beauvoir's 1949 text, to an epistemological default orbit of women's interests in which Blackness, by force of the transposition, does not factor. Deutscher argues quite convincingly that de Beauvoir developed her critique of patriarchal social stratification by way of direct comparison with US race relations, derived from, and ideologically and methodically impacted by, the Myrdals work; Alva Myrdal had actually produced a five page appendix to *An American Dilemma* (G. Myrdal) called "A Parallel to the Negro Problem" which likened woman's situation to that of racist discrimination and which de Beauvoir must have obtained through Nelson Algren (78; see also Simons 170). Deutscher, reading *with* de Beauvoir stringently, recapitulates in positive terms de Beauvoir's acquisition of knowledge about African Americans' racist subjugation for her productive analysis of women's subjugation as a social construction, as documented in the germination of arguments from *America Day by Day*, through *Ethics of Ambiguity*, to *The Second Sex* (Deutscher 74–93).

In a similar vein, German feminist Doris Ruhe, in her "Simone de Beauvoir, Sartre und Fanon," positively notes the remarkable influence of African American experience—through the mediation both of de Beauvoir's own experiences during her stay in the United States in the late1940s, well prepared by her immersion in Myrdal's *American Dilemma*, and of her friendship with Richard Wright—on the theoretical framework of *The Second Sex*. Ruhe clearly approves of de Beauvoir's analogization of woman's experience with the Black experience of slavery and post-slavery discrimination; she suggests that de Beauvoir's conception of *être* versus *devenir* finds its grounding in her observations of the American negro's plight (184), as much as de Beauvoir's critique of "separate but equal" as a racist denial of white power hegemony and oppression will mutate into the argument that women ought to fight for human transcendence just as men should, instead of resting smugly in their feminine difference.

I do not doubt the validity of those observations, but beg to differ in terms of an evaluation. My interest, by contrast, is to engage this transposition as a problematic epistemological ground, to interrupt the theoretical satisfaction evident in Deutscher's and Ruhe's readings. Elisabeth Spelman in *Inessential Woman* had looked at de Beauvoir's textual investments in the "race question" in a more skeptical vein.

My argument is in dialogue with Spelman's and Gines's suggestions, but I need to backtrack into recontextualization, again, of de Beauvoir's textual traces. As I have argued above, there has been growing interest in the post–World War II, post-genocidal moment as a potential window of opportunity for the creation of sustainable alliances against genocidal modern formations, as well as for mutual philosophical challenges for various agents in the social, political, and cultural spectrum (see Rothberg, *Multidirectional Memory*; Khanna). The condemnation of the Holocaust—in the writing of Arendt, Horkheimer, and Adorno; in the early testimony of survivors; in the media coverage of the trials in Germany; in the post–Nazi occupation revival of European democratic politics in France, Italy, and the other liberated European countries—could have been self-aligned with early decolonization (with Fanon, Césaire, the Black surrealist intellectuals, and early Pan-Africanism; see Judaken; Sharpley-Whiting), with the resistance in Algeria and Indochina, and it might have met the roots of 1960s civil rights unrest in the United States in the disillusionment of the returned GIs with American racial hypocrisy. But French intellectuals' decolonial resentment, stirred up as it was by mostly Caribbean scholars and artists in Paris, did not develop into a fundamental anti-racist theoretical articulation of French metropolitan society much beyond Sartre's engagement, nor did it entail a decolonial theoretical questioning of Enlightenment among the white philosophical circles of the École normale supérieure. Manifold mutual personal and collective exchanges, friendships, and collaborations between, and arguments across camps between, various strands of Négritude, African American civil rights discourse, post-Stalinist Marxist analyses, psychoanalysis, late surrealism, anti-fascism, progressive ethnography, and Jewish post-Shoah ethical critiques of the collapse of Western civilization developed in this historical moment. However, a possible relentless deconstruction of white capitalist colonialist modernity did not emerge from those crosscurrents.

However, it seems crucial in this context to note the absence of patriarchy, and how it may be related to, impacted by, and constitutive of the modern world system of the colonial matrix of modernity as it had come into view in the 1940s in Eric Williams's *Capitalism and Slavery*, even if it would only much later be radically reformulated (Quijano, Wallerstein, Mignolo, Blackburn, Baucom, and Linebaugh and Rediker) as one of the essential targets of critique. It remains a desideratum to reconstruct the discursive processes and the political agency by which the politics of decolonization evaded an address of sexual difference (Khanna). Transnational and postcolonial feminist studies have thus of late undertaken a critique of the misogynist flaws and limitations of postcolonial thinking, mostly by way of a critical return to Fanon, but also in Sharpley-Whiting's work on the intellectual avoidance, elision, and disremembrance of Suzanne Césaire's early feminist decolonial advances and on the political and philosophical contributions of Négritude women (Sharpley-Whiting), but the question remains far from having been settled. This male leftist and decolonial denial worked to the detrimental effect of eliding white patriarchal hegemony as well as Black macho posturing, and obscuring *the situation*, in banal and in existentialist terms, of the post-enslaved, Black, colonized woman in particular (for the parallel African American context, see Hull et al.; Wallace). Opposite the male left and anti-racist liberation movements, the early articulation of white middle-class feminist interests in their concentration on male power and privilege at home separated itself forcefully from the wider anti-capitalist and decolonial struggles—a bifurcation that was announced and prefigured in the upheaval of de Beauvoir's discovery, as it was perceived, of the first-person female. In the midst of postwar political, cultural, and theoretical ferment in Europe, which we are only now beginning to reread in its unprecedented and unequaled interconnections, overlappings of critical philosophies, and potential for alliances beyond racialized, sexualized, or nationalized subject positions, de Beauvoir realized herself as a *woman* intellectual and decided to follow up on her early intimations in *The Ethics of Ambiguity* to make space for the subject position of "the second sex."

The signifying and repertoire building power of Simone de Beauvoir's texts has, by way of their continuous dissemination and reception, preordained feminist epistemology until today. The crucial lever of what appeared at the time as a new philosophical prefiguration was actually a reconfiguration of a very old allegorical trope with a very long history, namely, the rhetorical construction to cast woman as slave in opposition to man as master.

For de Beauvoir, as for post-Enlightenment thinkers in the Hegelian tradition, the subject is thought of as such, because it masters the other who is thus structurally always already in the potentially submissive slave position; thus, if de Beauvoir wants to install woman as the primary antagonist to man, she has to signify her as Hegelian type slave, that is, to narrate her figure as emblematic of the species slave by giving woman a situation and a consciousness of the slavish—even though world history, even the history of European white women de Beauvoir has had access to, does not bear that out at all. But Hegelian allegory, and Western modern philosophy in its wake, knows subjects only as masters. There is no subject model in Western thought that would not require a subject that is one precisely because it masters its objected other, which in turn may dialectically strive for becoming a subject, making it into its object. This binary opposition, however, could and can only work because of its unspoken third term: the position of being abjected from this struggle, namely, the early modern position of factually enslaved African-origin people. This triangle, however invisible, enables the notorious Hegelian opposition: the position of the abjected is the one that any given object may differentiate itself against, thus aspiring to or actually becoming a subject (however "lesser"). That has been the actual dynamics of modern Western history; that is how transatlantic modernity has functioned: it is not that the object overturned the subject and dethroned Man, or reversed and sublated the binary, but that the object woman learned to partake in the abjection of the third term and thus has accumulatively gained grounds towards recognition of subjectivity. The position of the abjected was necessarily taken up first by the enslaved thing—that which the object at the cost of a future successful self-definition and empowerment avoided at all costs to be, or even to be seen as—and then as a hereditary legacy of the slavethings' progeny, Afro-diasporic people interpellated into the position of nonhuman Blackness. To create a gender binary thus in a perverse way benefitted politically and philosophically from the propagandistic threat of abjection that the signifier "slave" evokes, which, however, functioned necessarily to distance the object, as lesser but human, from the threat of its delocation. That leaves the actual slave and, by the logic of inheritance, Black people as things, outside of the contention altogether, because a thing and its successors do not have human characteristics by definition. White feminism, with de Beauvoir and others, actually succeeded in forcefully installing woman as quintessential modern post-Hegelian aspiring object other to the subject man.

Post-Hegelian philosophy called this object slave, which was not the word Hegel used originally, speaking of Knecht, and referring to inner-European class conflicts. Hegel's philosophy, even though Susan Buck-Morss is right to refer the ongoing contemporary debate about the master-slave dialectic to an acknowledgment of the Haitian revolution, ignored the modern global enslavement trade and actually evaded an address of the annihilation of Black humanness in New World slavery. For feminism, and gender studies, to follow the modern subject rhetoric, which has consistently positioned the slave as the subject's object-antinomy, was a rather productive and generative move, as much for Wollstonecraft and de Gouges, as for Simone de Beauvoir, because being slave became the horizon of degrada-tion from which the object-subject negotiations about rights and freedom could be differentiated successfully. The slave, thus, is claimed in entirely rhetorical fashion; de Beauvoir's analysis remained anchored in a philosophy of binarism, which does not have any critical interest in thingification of the enslaved in actual modern, enlightened history.

In the process of metaphorization of slavery for all kinds of miserably oppressed states of human beings, slavery was emptied out of any reference to enslavement and to the originary modern violent mass commodification of human beings. Using the analogy becomes an endless inter-textual return of metaphor to previous metaphor; creating a mental repertoire of slavery among white intellectuals, and specifically within early modern, modern, and postmodern European-American philosophy, which equates slavery with the status of *humans* being made miserable, overworked, without rights, without pay, and dependent on other humans as masters. This figuration is what actually allows post-Enlightenment philosophy in its various strands, including Feminism and Marxism, to mobilize the analogy as a negative foil to demarcate a political limit for white Europeans and Americans and to be able to claim compensation and justice, and a wider range of freedoms on the grounds of actual or threatening transgression of that limit. The issue of hereditary abjection of Afro-diasporic progeny of slavethings was thus elegantly sidestepped, as was the issue of the historical *Taeterschaft* of white Europeans and Americans for enslavement. The metaphor of slavery in (post)modern allegory, one could say, knows no responsibility for the historical transgression of early modern transatlantic enslavement of Black people; and the respective white social agents being rhetoricized into slaves (as in women, the proletariat, entire nations, addicts, and other clientele) thus, generation for generation, unlearned to remember white subjects as mediate and immediate agents on the masterful side of that transgression.

One particular issue remains to be raised. De Beauvoir's specific argument hinges on her idea of the woman being enslaved by her body or, more precisely, by her reproductive function. However, while it is true that the mind-body dualism and its gendered connotations have indeed been one of the cornerstones of modern white male self-empowerment, there are two objections to make: one is that the position of body within this dualism which was relegated to woman, and which actual women have made it their point to either reject or to occupy with a vengeance, must be considered a position *within* the human, because not even the most strident male philosopher would renege on the fact that a human is because of a particular physical embodiment, even though, as opposed to animal life, mind and maleness become the privileged features of that specific modern subject embodiment. A thing, however, has neither, and that is what has abjected the slave, and "its" descendants, male and female, from Western dualistic philosophy, as well as from the successful competition for subjectivity that has played itself out in post-slavery Western modernity.

The second objection is that it seems rather a reckless metaphorical operation to claim that one can be enslaved by one's own body. In fact this figure of speech but adds to a litany of self-victimization of the Western subject, which constantly has had to position itself, rhetorically, in a struggle against enslavement in order to be. The metaphoric operation displaces any conscious agent of enslavement. Individual social actors, a social institution (the state, an autocratic political system, a colonial power, an economic corporation, or all of the above), and its beneficiaries may be immediate enslavers, and of course there are a host of individual and social actors indirectly connected to and benefiting from enslavement, but no inert physical body or any of its functions, like want, desire, reproduction, can enact enslavement. The metaphorical operation to let a universal, unmarked notion of body speak for a system of social regulations and interpellations, like white European motherhood, which have indeed positioned Western women in distinctly disadvantaged, othered and oppressed social positions, screens and suppresses the blatant difference between being a human interpellated into a particular social position, like a white woman being subjected to motherhood and being a thing, or the abjected progeny of thing existence.

The relationship de Beauvoir's text entertains to slavery is one of fetishistic avowal—the text depends on it to make its point—and disavowal—it cannot really engage actual New World enslavement and (white) women's relation to it, because that would incapacitate her argument. This double bind haunts not only de Beauvoir's text, but has impacted on feminism and gender theory to lasting effect. By mustering the anti-colonial sentiment of her political moment in order to strengthen a white female critical intellectualism, that is, by way of radical participation in the renunciation of authoritative Western power discredited by the Holocaust, as well as by colonial atrocities coming to Western consciousness, *The Second Sex* aligns gender struggle parallel to and by way of the analogization, in inevitable competition with the decolonial struggle. Critical cultural capital in Western metropolises, after that moment, will be had only by way of entering that prefigured competition between subject positions clamoring for attention, response, and acclaim—this parallelization occasions the possibility of acknowledging the epistemological leadership of Black women's subject position for a poly-axis coalition between white and Black women aiming at the deconstruction of a modern system of thingification and abjection. White women, however, had different options for liberating their subjectivity than Black women, structurally speaking, and their very chance at having their gendered subjectivity acknowledged was linked to the differentiation from Blackness. What would have been demanded from white women is a surrender of exactly those particular rhetorical claims to "enslavement" which de Beauvoir's rhetoric aggressively installed in favor of actively seeking out solidarity with Black women and men. De Beauvoir's argument, for generations to come, foreclosed the recognition of the colonially globalized power mechanics of gender, and, in consequence, of that cross-racial alliance.

Only the rhetorical logic of women's victimization guarantees the very appeal of de Beauvoir's argument. In a repetition of Wollstonecraft's eighteenth-century claims, woman had to be written into early modern negotiations as an aspiring object-to-become-subject in order to finally mobilize fuller participation, equality, and subjectivity (or, in existentialist vocabulary, transcendence) for white women within modernity. Because *The Second Sex*'s metaphorical system, however, uses and reduces slavery, again, as/to a signifier for white woman's purposes, any epistemological opening out on to and thinking in solidarity with the position of the abjected hereditary Blackthing becomes precluded. De Beauvoir's protestations of empathy with the slave in both, *Ethics* and *The Second Sex* thus speak from a position of a subject "arrivée," bending towards, but also contemptuous of, the slave woman it/she shall never be.

Jessica Benjamin: Gender and Bondage

[The ego] is not only the ally of the id; it is also a submissive slave who courts the love of his master.

—Sigmund Freud, *The Ego and the Id*

This book is an analysis of the interplay between love and domination. It conceives of domination as a two-way process, a system involving the participation of those who submit to power as well as those who exercise it. Above all, this book seeks to understand how domination is anchored in the hearts of the dominated.

—Jessica Benjamin, *The Bonds of Love*

Benjamin's dedication is to a feminist post-Hegelian theorization of human intersubjectivity (Yeatman), contending with patriarchal monologic subjectivity models characterized by female dependency and submissiveness in human relations, but also rejecting models of feminine narcissistic subjectivity in reverse, as it were. Her argument hinges on a critique of the modern psychosocial and cultural patriarchal structure in the Western symbolic, which invites the female in a relationship to the male to enter into a kind of self-inflicted bonding, or sometimes even bondage (in the sense of dependency), for which the compensation is extracted vis-à-vis enjoyment of a masochistic drive, a lustful subordination. That structure ordains that only in that subordinated position may acceptance and, even if thwarted, some form of recognition be gained for the female. Her point in creating inter-subjectivity models of mutual recognition as a counter to female submission has been, as an analytic, greeted enthusiastically in gender studies, including Butler's late commentary ("Longing"). However, none of the critical parties involved with Benjamin's work have taken on the assumptive logic of her argument's frame, its political syntax, and its metaphorical semantics. This logic is a replay of the Nietzschean "slavish slave" via a critical reading of Freud. Its circularity runs like this: women in patriarchal societies are (educated to be) submissive; submissiveness is a necessary requisite of slavery; therefore the slave is characterized by and embodies submissiveness as such; submissiveness is lived by women, therefore woman is a slave—to men, to her passion for men, to her dependency on men. This implied argumentative chain creates anti-Black, racist affect by way of pervasive and persistent social metonymy: woman's submissiveness is slavish, the incarnation of slavish life is Black existence, all Black life forms originate in slavishness, so slavishness is Black; thus, if woman wants to reject submissiveness, she has to reject being identified with the slave and its afterlife in the Black. The white feminist affect mobilized against slavishness registers in effect as anti-Black sentiment, even if that is not a purposefully racist maneuver. This becomes manifest in Benjamin's writing on various levels: crucially, in the use of *Story of O* (Réage) as a framing device. In the 1965 English edition that was available to Benjamin, this frame is meta-framed, as it were, by the introductory addition of a quasi-historiographical account of Barbadian ex-enslaved Black people in rebellion against the British imperial governor, because they want to be re-enslaved, not being able to bear their sudden freedom. Women, as *Story of O* implies, may enjoy a deeply masochistic relation to men, as slaves enjoyed their enslavement to their white masters. This is a very specific racist historical lie with respect to slavery and its abolition in Barbados, and one cannot but wonder about the level of indifference that enabled Benjamin to look past this framing foreword of the first English edition, and still go on to use *Story of O* as her organizing device. As a metaphorical operation, it is pure anti-Black contempt, implying either mass Black masochism—slavishness indeed—or mass Black stupidity, or both. To use *Story of O* as her paradigmatic metaphorical landscape to discuss women's subordination and disabled subjectivity in bourgeois nuclear families and heterosexual relations, signifies unquestioning acceptance of the white mythology of the slave's slavishness, and a willingness to disseminate it. The same holds for the organization around and the saturation with tropes of enslavement of Benjamin's own text, which altogether displace the Black enslaved and the history of white enslavism from view in their semantic fungibility. This willingness shores up both an epistemic and an ethical problem in the text's ostentatiously disinterested and strategic employment of the discursive apparatus of enslavement to discuss white (by default) women's psychosexual entanglements with patriarchy.

In 2000, Jessica Benjamin, feminist professor on the faculty at New York University's Postdoctoral Program in Psychotherapy and Psychoanalysis, engaged in a public letter exchange with Lester Olson, professor of communication at the University of Pittsburgh. The subject of their correspondence, published in *Philosophy and Rhetoric* (Olson), was the charge of ethnocentrism leveled against white middle-class feminism of the post–civil rights decades by Audre Lorde and other Black feminists at the history-making 1979 conference to honor the legacy of Simone de Beauvoir's work for US and international feminism. The conference, entitled *The Second Sex* Conference, was supposed to offer a forum as broad as possible to engage in issues such as the making of gender, the role of the body, feminist consciousness and its relation to European-based philosophy, (homo)sexuality and radical emancipation, and other questions de Beauvoir's work has called forth. Olson had recalled this charge in his rhetorical analysis of Lorde's famous speech at that conference, "The Master's Tools Will Never Dismantle the Master's House," in which Lorde strongly criticized white feminist racist ignorance of Black feminist work and called upon the emerging gender studies of the moment to reconsider their political and cultural analyses so as to direct attention to the differences among women and to include the specific contributions made by Black women, and particularly Black lesbian feminists—facing multiple oppression by factors of race and gender, and discrimination against their sexual choices—in order to improve not only their anti-sexist reading of the world, but also anti-patriarchal politics against "the master's house." As Loeb has observed about the controversy:

> Benjamin not only rejects the substance of Lorde's observations about the whiteness of mainstream feminism and academia, but Benjamin also blames Black feminists and other feminists of color for refusing to work with the conference organizers, and more generally, for dividing and detracting from the socialist cause. . . . Disturbingly, Benjamin asserts in her published remarks that Lorde's commitment to race and group difference detracted from and potentially destroyed the political base of feminism by diluting its socialist base with concerns grounded

in mere "identity." Benjamin blames feminists of color and queer feminists for continuing the "opposition" between "cultural feminism" (which Benjamin implicitly derides), and the more properly "political feminism." (Loeb 41; Benjamin, "Letter")

Benjamin's argument becomes interesting in my discussion of her work in this chapter, specifically of *Bonds of Love*, but also *Like Subjects, Love Objects: Essays on Recognition and Sexual Difference.* Her late twentieth-century feminist intervention consists of a body of book-length texts and a great number of essays, published between 1988 and today. Benjamin has located her project at the crossroads of a revised post-Hegelian and Post-Freudian subject-object psychoanalysis and various strands of feminist critiques of the nuclear family, which she places in mutual interrogation in her writing (for a thorough discussion of Benjamin's project, see Yeatman).

Bonds of Love mainly attempts a critical psychoanalysis of the feminine, whose position in patriarchal society is one of submission, fixation in self-sacrificing motherhood, and absence of a desire that can reach beyond masochistic gratification. Women, so her argument goes, have been bound into the patriarchal system by being primed to enjoy the pleasures of "slavish" submission. Her point is that this desire for/in submission needs to be owned, and not shamefully disavowed, so that it may be critically examined and, eventually, given up in favor of a greater diversity within heterosexual relationships, as well as more balanced equitable emotional and sexual attachments between women and men. She claims that both intimate and social gender relations between "male" and "female"—conceptualized by patriarchy as essentialized versions of self and subjectivity—may and should be reconstructed by way of consciousness-raising and psychoanalytical intervention, so as to allow for more fluidity, mutuality, and exchange particularly with regard to child raising, in order to interrupt and break the oedipal fixation the traditional gender binary has been based on, in permanent and subconscious repetition. In her second monograph, *Like Subjects*, Benjamin continues to investigate the conundrum of relation between "self" and "other"; the book figures largely as a response to various interventions from poststructuralist and constructivist angles engaged with psychoanalysis, which have fostered a shift in feminist theory towards deessentializing and differentiating notions of "women" and femininity. Benjamin's oeuvre has developed a major argument that has sustained her work into her most recent publications: by way of a reconstruction of psychoanalytic tenets, she arrives at her key concept of intersubjectivity, carried by the figure of "the third," which supposedly becomes the motor of a possible transcendence of fixed gendered subject positions, and allows for mutuality of desire and recognition of agency between selves, based on a shared reference to a common object (see Yeatman, again).

My interest is not to participate in this debate on its own premises, but to examine it for its obvious and not so obvious momentum of anti-Blackness, to which her exchange with Olson alerted me. In none of her texts does Benjamin engage in any directly analytical or even observational address of Black feminist interventions. This is astounding as a fact in itself, because the decades between 1979 and the end of the century saw an unprecedented upsurge of Black feminist work in various disciplines, taking on white feminist indifference and racism in various arenas, including literary studies, sociology, history, film studies, women's studies and emerging gender theory, and psychoanalysis as a field (see Sherri Barnes's full-fledged bibliography, again.) A timeline of selective publications to mark the most important controversial interventions pertinent to Benjamin's field and interests reads as follows:

1977 *Combahee River Collective Statement*
1981 *This Bridge Called My Back*, edited by Cherríe Moraga and Gloria Anzaldúa
1982 *But Some of Us Are Brave*, edited by Akasha (Gloria T.) Hull, et al.
1983 *Pleasure and Danger*, edited by Carole S. Vance, which includes articles by both Jessica Benjamin and Hortense Spillers
1987 Spillers's "Mama's Baby, Papa's Maybe"
1988 Benjamin's *Bonds of Love*
1992 Conference Psychoanalysis in African American Contexts: Feminist Reconfigurations, essays published in Abel's collection *Female Subjects in Black and White: Race, Psychoanalysis, Feminism*
1996 Spillers's second article, "All the Things You Could Be by Now If Sigmund Freud's Wife Was Your Mother"
1995 Benjamin's *Like Subjects, Love Objects*
2001 Jean Walton's *Fair Sex, Savage Dreams*

The year of the de Beauvoir conference at Barnard, 1979, is two years after the Combahee River Collective's Black feminist proclamation of an epistemic and political manifesto on behalf of Black women. It is hard to underestimate the volatility of Black and white feminist relations at this point in time. Breines's discussion of the period in *The Trouble between Us* is very useful in terms of its recuperation of this controversial phase of women's and, indeed, feminist US history; even her rather upbeat reading of the potential for and practices of Black and white alliances in the 1960s and early 1970s, however, has to concede the growing ethnocentric indifference of a movement for white middle-class women's self-empowerment, poised at the threshold of entering academia and other social arenas, like business, media, and politics, to gain and stay in positions of power. This volatility is what Lorde picked up, articulated, and intensified with her speech, which needs to be read as one of the key moments in the history of encounters between US Black and white feminisms.

As Benjamin rightly observes in her reply to Olson, Lorde's speech marked a turning point for feminist theories of gender in that white feminism's notion of an uncomplicated, transparent binary divide between patriarchy on the side of power and women qua being women on the side of the powerless and oppressed, and therefore in radical insurgent opposition to systemic discourses and practices, could not be sustained. Thus, as Benjamin maintains, the move into 1980s and early 1990s identity politics, and the multiculturalist acceptance of differences among women in theory and political practice was inevitable; and the emergence of "race" as a marker for difference eventually became the established discourse. What interests me in Benjamin's reply to Olson—two decades after the crucial event—is, for one, the mode and tonality of her description of the differentiation within feminism, her political defensiveness, and, most importantly, the disjoint between her obvious awareness of those controversies' urgency and the absence of any response to it in her own work.

I had come to a rereading of *Bonds of Love* and Benjamin's later work with the expectation to find, if not a working through of the importance of racism for psychoanalysis at its juncture to feminism, at least a taking into account of the most directly pertinent contributions concerning "race" in Benjamin's own professional and disciplinary environment. Not finding anything, at least not on the surface of her writing, complicated my task, because I did not want to let the matter rest with a resignation to this obvious absence of "race," typical of Benjamin's and other work of those decades (Walton), because in contrast to that absence, slavery and the slave are hyper-visible in *Bonds of Love*, albeit in an exclusively metaphorical register. The question arises, then: What does this combination of absence of Black (feminist) work on "race," on the one hand, with the symbolic über-presence of the slave, on the other, tell us about epistemic anti-Blackness? How does Blackness trail and haunt Benjamin's work even in the mode of its denial? How does the intimacy of her utter silence on "race" with aggressive pronunciations of the slave create effects of anti-Blackness, notwithstanding Benjamin's denial of racist purpose, or even ethnocentric limitations, in her 2000 letter to Olson?

My analysis reads Benjamin's work as a paradigmatic moment. As Jean Walton has also observed, white feminist psychoanalysis could have opened a window on the racist psychic interpellation of white subjects, but chose not to. My close reading examines Benjamin's intricate coupling of the slave to a negation of the historical psychology of US racism, which, for American critique from whatever camp or discipline, cannot be considered but as crucial to the making of subjects, so that an attention to this void in psychoanalytic theorization of gender still and again remains a desideratum.

This is not an issue of kvetching with hindsight knowledge: Black feminist insurgent energy was militant, outspoken, and ubiquitous in the last decades of the twentieth century, as the conference uproar, among other incidents, makes clear. On the contrary, it needs to be argued that to ignore those contributions has required a special kind of screening, the fixing of an innocence vis-à-vis gender. My reading here traces how this fixing proceeded to produce a segregation of white feminism, even though the decades between the late 1980s and today have seen expanding theoretically sophisticated acknowledgments of *difference*, and accumulating concessions that white feminism and white gender studies cannot speak for all women. Hardly has there been any white acceptance of Black feminist epistemic ability and power to address gender issues beyond the province of Black women's intersectional oppression. However, it has been a constitutive Black feminist demand early on to claim the relevance of Black knowledge for a formation as basic to gender theory as psychoanalysis has always been. I want to go against the grain of a white response that has kept responding with a resigned "Well, what do you expect?" as if there is a kind of magic inevitability to white epistemic isolation, with the intention of recovering the scandal of Benjamin's silence and evasion, which has only strengthened the whiteness of psychoanalytical feminism. This isolation, as Jean Walton realized in 1995, needs to be called out; her project to "put race back into psychoanalysis," however, still goes unnoticed in Benjamin's work after *Bonds of Love*. It becomes important, therefore, to think of Benjamin's work in its longue durée not as an act of idiosyncrasy but as a kind of insistent projection of white feminist ownership of psychoanalytical discourse.

Benjamin's first book successfully transferred de Beauvoir's work into psychoanalysis. It stands at an important transitional moment for feminist thinking, which begins to move from conceptualizing "woman" to thinking about "gender" and gender relations—a progression which, however, remained largely within a binary, and essentialist framework, until the advent of post-structuralism, constructionism, performativity, and queer theory—the impact of which Benjamin will respond to in her second book, *Shadow of the Other*. *Bonds of Love* in 1988 became an instant, *New York Times*–reviewed bestseller, was immediately translated (at least into German), and was canonized in women's studies classes; it garnered a wide, if controversial reception that allows reading of the book as one of the signature texts of the late 1980s to which following generations of scholars, including Judith Butler, have kept returning. In her later work, Benjamin has extended her argument, seeking for ways to disable gender dichotomy in its psychic effects on the individual, as well as in its social, political, cultural ramifications, pleading for acknowledgment of "thirdness" and the force of intersubjectivity, to overcome the volatile gender polarity ascribed to psychic instantiations of masculinity and femininity, as well as the violence and breakdown of private and social communication resulting thereof. However, she never interrogates the individual or social psychic implications of a possible racialization of (inter)subjectivity. Her work bespeaks to me a massive, if veiled, investment in anti-Blackness; first, by the very fact that it insists, in 1988 and 1996 respectively, in the face of twenty to thirty years of Black feminist interventions onto the discursive scene of "woman" and "gender," on ignoring Blackness and instead enshrining women and men as immutable and untroubled psychic positions unencumbered by racialized social practices, let alone structural differences seen from an ontological perspective. This creation of Black absence shores up a white abstinence from the social, cultural and political apparatus of racialization, which interpellates every subjects' symbolic, as well as imaginary. The evacuation of Blackness and racism's psychic machinations from her purview are not a negligible oversight, a kind of regrettable but minor irritation nonincidental to the exploration of subjectivity, but a crucial and strategic act of delaying and in fact deferring psychoanalysis's attention to racism. *Bonds of Love* stages a repetition of Black abjection, over and against the lively and stirring interventions of Black feminism at the time, and thus results in a transposition of Black social death onto the scene of gender-oriented psychoanalysis. In remooring feminist and nascent gender studies in the orbit of its default "race"-free subjectivity, *Bonds of Love* subscribes to and pushes an epistemology of gender enabled by the writing out of Blackness. In its mainstream acceptance—even though her work has always been controversial among gender theorists—Benjamin's work may be and needs to be read as paradigmatic instance of white knowing that cannot be left to its assumed psychoanalytic universalism, which gets to be confirmed even in criticism, or in theoretical rejection of it. In her equation of "mastery" with patriarchal desire and cognition, she leaves the mastery of white supremacy, upon which modern and postmodern subjectivity has hinged, out of the very range of her questioning, thus referring her universalist assumptions back to a white frame of reference, in which any possible attention to the psychological investments in and the labor of becoming white gendered (instead of, in the Freudian or Beauvoirian frame, "man" or "woman"), that is, to the psychic racialization and white subjects' interpellation into anti-Black abjection, becomes abandoned to disinterest and silence.

Even though she ignores "race," the trajectory of her argument derives much affective force from her—presumably white—readers' abolitionist pre-suppositions: slavery is compromised and morally discredited. Thus, basing an argument about the female subject's psyche as constituted in masochistic desire on an extended metaphorical employment of slavery, provides a palpable amount of both titillation and taboo breaking both for the psychoanalytic profession and for *Bonds of Love*'s white feminist readership. This employ-ment feeds off of Black enslavement but does not have any interest in it, and thus constantly re- or deroutes her readers' epistemic progress back to white subjectivity. The anti-Blackness here lies specifically in the fact that Benjamin's imagery arsenal of feminine submissiveness as desire, and desire as submissiveness reinscribes slavishness as the assumed phantasma of the slave's psyche. According to this logic, a given enslaved being does not act submissively in contingent, limited circumstances, but the slave, ontologically speaking, is and exists only as submission. It is submission as practice that makes one a slave, a practice not structurally equitable with the position of human subjectivity, so that submission has become the sole property of the slave, and the property only of the slave. That line of reasoning, implied but never owned up to in *Bonds of Love*, ends us in a paradigmatic anti-Black human cognition: that being a free subject requires its opposite slavishness as its springboard and foil, and that, as a consequence, only self-possessing individuals can have autonomy and a mature psyche. The Benjaminian subject can, with psychoanalytical guidance, learn to know and thus own her masochistic desires, and this ownership of desire marks the necessary distance to the submissiveness of the slave, taken as a given: the achievement of this ownership functions as passage through voluntary debasement and subjection into transcendence. This might be a white psychic economy that psychoanalysis has encountered. As a narrative that implies and seeks social relevance as a feminist argument in debates of gender, it, again, inscribes the Black/slave—if readers seek for her at all—as cynical grotesque, and installs a gesture of utter contempt for the Black/slave: How would somebody who is not legally, socially, and culturally a free individual to begin with, seek transcendence in bondage? But the psychic life of the Black/slave doesn't appear in Benjamin's register of human gendered development, except that the slave's fungibility to prop any kind of human argument successfully bolsters the economy of affect *Bonds of Love* relies upon.

If thus the actual Black/slave is successfully evacuated, indeed barred from *Bonds of Love*'s considerations, what benefit does the analogy accrue for a psychoanalytical discussion of feminine subjectivity? If woman has femininity, that is, if she acts out masochistic desires—which is Benjamin's point of departure—it marks her as a human, because she is entitled to own (even if in all patriarchal conflictedness) an economy of desire in the first place—as opposed to the sentient thing, which cannot know desire and historically has been coerced into the procreation of generations of sentientness—a reproductive practice of unsubjectivation for which Black/slave desire did not play any role at all. The Black/slave being has been supposed to have no human properties, certainly no "desire of one's own," and, accordingly, no masochism or sadism to feed into the psychic drama of withheld or given recognition that engages Benjamin. However, the very psychic site for the ability of femininity to be acted out within a binary opposition to masculinity in the first place, lies in the referable-to-existence of the psychic no-man's-land of the Black/slave who functions but as the horizon of a debatable submissiveness, so that the feminine can attain to various registers of active and passive desire.

Benjamin's further focal concern is with the constellations of male and female subjectivities brought on by the psychic installation of "mother" and "father" as external social and interiorized psychic instances of interpellation and formation of the child. In Benjamin's post-Freudian discussion, those positions are not only essentialized in terms of gender polarity, which has been a source of response and debate by poststructuralist theorists like Butler. They are also driven by a kind of color-blind universalism for which the positions of mother and father, and the sexual division of their roles and functions in society are being taken up by nominally and factually adult, mature, and free subjects who, it goes without saying, are thinkable only as by default white. In critical opposition to this avoidance of seeing mothering, fathering, and being a child other than in terms of the white nuclear middle-class family, Black scholars (for a Black feminist response see Gumbs et al.) have repeatedly drawn attention to both the historical formations of Black family life produced by (post-)enslavement (Painter, *Soul*) and the inability of Freudian analysis to recuperate an analysis of possible Black interiority of psychic constellations (see Marriott, *On Black Men*, "Inventions")—which, of course, white society has not allowed to exist in its midst in the first place.

I want to turn to a series of textual instances, including the title and her recourse to *Story of O* in *Bonds of Love*, where the history of enslavement and thus Blackness make resistant, if almost negligible, appearance at the same time that they create, as absent presence, some excessive overreach both in Benjamin's framework and in the course of her argument. I am reading, as it were, back from these moments into the text, instead of reading in identification with the text's obvious surface. By making these instances the paradigmatic lever of analysis, it will become visible that *Bonds of Love* homes anti-Blackness in a way that the text's own trajectory does not own up to. This will require a palimpsestic method to recreate layers of intertext that are conjured up to support *Bonds of Love*'s trajectory even if they are not explicitly discussed; other intertextual instances will appear only by way of a critical reading from a Black perspective, because they are entirely disavowed and silenced, as for example the Black/white ongoing controversy surrounding the issue of Black motherhood in the United States—a debate that should have been crucial for her argument about mothering and its social, political, and cultural implications. Conjoining both of the levels of visible and invisible intertext with the surface level of *Bonds of Love* opens our perspective on Benjamin's cultural imaginary of anti-Blackness: it reaches back to key modern texts outside the repertoire of psychoanalysis (which is Benjamin's claimed framework), like Nietzsche's *Genealogy*, Hegel's "Lordship and Bondage," and French post–World War II intellectual elites' philosophies of various political loyalties, from de Beauvoir to Jean Paulhan, which exult in enshrining, as their particular horizon of philosophical contempt, the figure of the slave.

Benjamin stands at the feminist end of a long line of philosophers and psychoanalysts for whom recognition is a one-to-one human relation. It is taken as a given in that framework that the master always needs recognition from the slave, which results in an impasse because the slave in her or his slavishness can only give submission. The slave side of the dialectic is equated with a slavish surrender of will, of action, of negativity, of transcendence, in other words, with the impossibility of a subjectivity that could give recognition. The position of the human (in other words, the subject/master, which is the position white philosophy has been agonizing about) is always already one of self-pitiful unfulfillment, because the slave does not deliver what the master desires, because submissiveness can never be the same as a free subject's acknowledgment of one's humanness. The pornographic fantasy of *Story of O* answers this presumed lack with the omnipotent fantasy of the slave's voluntary, orgasmic hyper-conscious, and performative submissiveness into the hands of the omnipotent master, which enables both master and slave to transcend the futility and impossibility of antagonism; it is in the joint transcendence gained by slavish submissiveness to the extreme that the master may obtain pleasure from the slave's performance, and the slave's pleasure may be grounded in her pain which signifies voluntary surrender to another's pleasure drive as bliss, an enjoyment of the master's pleasure, as Paulhan's preface to the novel amply demonstrates. Paulhan's intervention, which was part of the 1965 New York edition that Benjamin's bibliography cites as her primary text (Réage), constitutes the immediate intertextual frame not only to *Story of O* itself, but also, if entirely unacknowledged, to Benjamin's employment of the erotic text as her focal point of reference for *Bonds of Love*. Given the fact that Benjamin's 1988 book was an intervention, first and foremost, into American feminist theoretical debates of its moment, her silence on Paulhan's address of *Story of O*'s special brand of eroticism, which establishes an explicit connection to New World slavery, needs to be read as a strategic evasion. To enter into a universalizing theoretical speculation about feminine submissiveness in terms of slavishness by way of reference to a text and its intertext, which both capitalize on "happiness in slavery" (the title of Paulhan's framing essay), amounts to quite an agnotological achievement.

That essay of Paulhan's explicitly, right from its subtitle, "A Revolt in Barbados," onward, demonstrates an awareness of the parameters of actual New World enslavement. Posing with great intellectual authority (which Paulhan, while controversial, actually enjoyed among French intellectual elites in his time), his essay *invents* (see Beckles for the historiographical record of Barbadian post-slavery history) a historical incident, ornately endorsing it with enough historiographical factualness (names, dates, people, and places) to make it appear as the true story Paulhan claims it to be. He cleverly, and quite tongue-in-cheek, claims there was a document of the incident, which was lost to the deadly conflagration he is reporting to us. The point of his story is to represent the newly freed slaves' yearning to be re-enslaved because, in his telling, they prefer "the happiness in slavery" to the burdens of freedom (Réage xxi, xxii, xxiii).

The rhetorical brashness of this fiction demands very close attention, lest the reader either get lost in its confident, predicative sweep, or dismiss it too easily as a crazy white male fantasy. Given its first (French) publication in 1954, it needs to be read as an assertive gesture on Paulhan's part. Paulhan who is known as a staunch defender of France's colonial claim on Algeria, in the face of the Algerian War of resistance not just claims interpretative patriarchal authority over O's narrative, but also carves out enslavist space in his intellectual field. Both in the postfascist and postcolonial moment of its originary French circulation and in the post–civil rights movement and post–Black Power point of its publication in the American English edition of 1965, to publish this pro-slavery allegory that exhorts white feminine submissive desire may only be seen as a provocation of sorts. The strategic lie of a pro-slavery ex-slave revolt in Barbados counts recklessly on white readers' historical agnotologic ignorance and disinterest, and their active, always already operational willingness to imagine the enslaved as "slavish." As a matter of fact, the history of post-slavery Barbados was marked by massive Black resistance to the reinstallation of racist regimes of exploitation and violence (Beckles).

The rhetorical symbiosis of happiness and slavery in the first place, but, moreover, its charge with referential value by talking about it not only in a recognizably metaphorical register but staging this fiction with all the props of historiography, makes contemptuous purposeful mockery of factually enslaved Black being in Barbados. Ornamentally bolstering truth claims with historically verifiable colonialist details (like the organization of workhouses, the substitution of prison cell for slavery's lash, and the law to punish ex-enslaved apprentices' in cases of illness), Paulhan, without any expectation of Black reprimand, presents himself as the necessary white patriarchal authority to sanction *Story of O*'s narrative as ethically viable and to chastise all possible objections to its pornography as philistine. White libertinage feeds off Black people's unfreedom with a sound measure of glee, preposterously displacing the violence of enslavement onto the slaves and their revenge against being freed. Inconsistently, he admits, though, that slavery was not the happy affair his story has tried to advertise. His reference to both Hegelian dialectics and the Christian prophecy that "the last shall be first" demonstrate an awareness of slavery's injustice and violence; this becomes smoothed over with the rhetorical twist to lay the responsibility, again, at the enslaved's feet. Toppling the regime of slavery too soon was unwise on the part of white owners, because the slaves were not ready for accepting the new law, preferring to expose themselves to known forms of violence, over and against possible freedom. It is that twist which enables Paulhan to turn away from Barbados and investigate the erotic fantasy of submission. He casts his invented story as a forerunner to *Story of O*, a kind of necessary ancestry to boost the illicitness of female masochistic fantasy. Equating the rigorous white female enjoyment of masochism to voluntary submission of the slave to violence gives *Story of O* both the social relevance of heresy and a heft beyond its reach as a feminine sexual fantasy. Freedom, in this argument, becomes a selfish pleasure that the slaves had the superior and mystic wisdom to forego. The slippage here from slaves to lovers and mystics must be noticed: the slaves become at the same time perennialized as disappointed devotees to masters and lionized as mystic, almost otherwordly, sufferers, a model for the subject to emulate. Of course, only in the free human imaginary could this ever develop as a hyper-charged wistful metaphor for the subject's omnipotence to suffer what he or she desires. It must also be seen as quite a swift white patriarchal maneuver, having discredited both actual anti-slavery struggle (not an unimportant success at a time of rising anti-colonial struggle in France) and possible feminist resistance to masculinist sexual fantasies in one bold stroke. In fact, Paulhan's text must be read not just as a justification of enslavement but—if combined with *Story of O*'s textual obsession with the props of anti-Black violence, as in the enforced wearing of Black clothes, the mules/shoes, the overwhelming mulatto presence—as a melancholic racist pornography: as the recuperation of enslavement as an erotic site, the unhampered access to which abolition and the legal termination of slavery had ruptured.

At this point, it might strike the attentive reader that this allegorical operation functions as a recurring trope of French postwar liberal intellectu-alism: obviously, Paulhan's happy slaves are a replay of de Beauvoir's crucial imagery of the "old Negro" whimpering to be taken back to slavery. While feminist de Beauvoir uses the trope to signify what she considers despicable submissiveness, it is just that quality which Paulhan's eulogy of the feminine quality of transcendence by surrender exhorts. In both cases, though, the metaphoric's inappropriateness, its rhetorical opportunism overrules the specific referential context. It is even more striking to see how smoothly Paulhan's framing device traveled into an American context without caus-ing an uproar and could even function as a taken-for-granted, unprotested subtext to a feminist inquiry like Benjamin's. One needs to linger on the fact that Benjamin does not see any need to unravel this narrative from the point of view of enslavement—if at all agreeing to take on the *Story of O*'s narrative and rhetoric as her framing device. An acknowledgment of enslavement's history would have challenged her to disequate voluntary submission with slavery, and thus with the slave. What if one turns the whole thing around? What if the slave *refuses* recognition? What if the slave, knowing herself as a being made into a thing by acts of free human will, despises that human will and creates other forms of freedom? What if the slave is not slavish, neither in the post-Hegelian sense of having surrendered and offered subservience, nor in the Nietzschean sense of "slave mentality," displaying cunning cowardice and making a superior virtue out of meek-ness, nor in any white psychoanalytic sense of eroticized submission. What, in other words, if the slave is the one with knowledge of the world, not in the Hegelian sense—because she labors on and in it, which enables the dialectic turn for mastery over the master—but of the entire human world of possession, mastery, freedom, subjectivity, and will; because she or he sees the masterful subject from the position of being the targeted abject of this human will? Why has white philosophy clung to the assumption that the slave's want, that which marks her lack, is always already to be master, or to be "free," which would entail being a replica of what she sees as the motor of her abjection? (See Gordon; Mills, *Racial*.) Had Benjamin engaged any of these questions, I contend she could not have incorporated the *Story of O* as a morality tale into her argument. The fact that she has not should not be read as understandable, if maybe deplorable, limitation of her argument, but as symptomatic of the strategic white deployment of the slave.

The psychic formations of masculinity and femininity that Benjamin's critique hinges upon are structurally exclusive of Black being. As Frank Wilderson has argued ("Vengeance" 21), the Black/slave does not stand in a dialectical relation to the symbolic order of subject and intersubjectivity, but has been absented, or, as I call it, abjected, from it. Blackness exists in the repetitive continuous legacy of Black beings' thingness, as Hartman has pointed out: "The subterranean history of death and discontinuity informs everyday practices in myriad ways. . . . If repetition 'continually cuts back to the start,' or is homage to an 'original generative instance or act,' as Snead argues, then what is returned to is the inevitable loss or breach that stands at the origin and engenders the Black 'New World' subject" (Hartman, *Scenes* 75). To understand the unbroken continuity of a white imaginary of Black/slave consciousness that has consistently construed any possible psychic interior history of the Black/slave as a blank, overwritten by the racist splitting between free human subjectivity and Black slavishness, would require an acceptance of enslavism as constitutive. A reckoning with Black psychic interiority would ask white subjectivity to disappear, instead of to continually unfold and hyper-entitle itself—a process in which a feminist psychoanalytic conceptualization of gender plays an active part.

To propel this unfolding, Benjamin surges into an extended argument in favor of the female, and particularly the woman's ownership of her desire, or a desire of one's own. The coupling of desire to ownership leaves desire in the exclusive domain of the human, because for the Black/slave, being herself property (Davis, "Don't"), or a post-enslavement fungibly useful being without a human life of its own, neither ownership of self nor desire could become a prerogative. Gender and feminist theory, consequently, ought to respond to this conundrum by pushing itself beyond the white limit of talking about subjectivity and desire in terms heavily indebted and starkly resonant of the eighteenth-century liberalism to which they owe their existence. Instead, Benjamin's recirculation of the feminist standard trope of self-ownership partakes in the economy of thingification, because white women's self-possession in the United States has been depending on the assumed nonexistence of Black women's claims for subjectivity, which, if ever acknowledged, would antagonize the humanist premises of feminism as we know it. Ownership of the self as a claim has been unthinkable without the a priori acknowledged claim to the subject's possessive being in the world as a human entitlement (see Broeck, "Never"). For human society to acknowledge Black desire, the notion of ownership itself would have to be abandoned. Ownership as a concept—socially, legally, or psychoanalytically speaking—ends us back in an anti-Black imaginary, in the structural cognitive willfulness that freedom and autonomy of the subject lies in antagonism to the slave. At the same time, though, the slave needs to be the subject's springboard, hence the need for the thingified Black/slave to enflesh the possessable, so that possession could be marked as progress and the human achievement of autonomy. This autonomy, of course, entails the right to all kinds of worldly enjoyment (in Hartman's terms); it extends, thus, to the entitlement of owning submission to male mastery as one's desire, and to stage ownership of that form of subjectivity publicly in anti-Black terms. Benjamin's employment of *Story of O* without any degree of skepticism repeats this abjection in theoretical terms.

The Subject, Desire, and the Question of Violence

The stakes of this for Black people are tremendous, but not in the ways academics might think. There has been a mistaken investment in analogizing Black "subjects" to subjects in the Lacanian sense. This is incorrect for several reasons, perhaps the simplest of which is that Lacan was wrong. Not all subjects are created by the same lack. Lacan's sense of lack, after all, includes within it a theory of structural positionality: a theory called the oedipal triangle of subject-mother-father. But, prior even to the very possibility of that particular schema of structural positions, another framework of structural positions has already seen to it that some people lack subjectivity itself, because they are created collectively as nonsubjects as such, slaves—prior to their creation as individual subjects—by the violence that placed them in the collectives where they are in the world in the ways that it did. And, of course, this means that it concomitantly created other subjects collectively as those who are *not* positioned by the violence of slavery (Ricks, *On Jubilee* 31).

The voiding of any historical reference to enslavism from Benjamin's deployment of the term slave enables a metaphorical maneuver that only agnotological readers can appreciate, because it is contingent upon a sharing of both author's and readers' distinctness from the slave in her argument. Benjamin's very terms of address thus leave Black being abjected from the practice of mutual human (re)cognition that the text wants to enable. However, the trajectory of her argument derives all of its affective force from her (presumably white) proto-abolitionist readers' predispositions. It thus feeds off of a white antislavery sentiment but reroutes readers' epistemic progress back to an articulation of woman (by default white) as the potentially |(self-)enslaveable subject in question. Thus, in a repetition of earlier white feminist allegorical rejection of slavishness, she queers the motto with a psychoanalytical approach in order to critique female masochistic desire while at the same time acknowledging its social and individual force. But the question that nobody has asked of *Story of O*, or of Benjamin, because the seemingly transparent usefulness of the metaphorical installation is naturalized entirely in a white sexual imaginary and erotic vocabulary, must be this: Why would white people fantasize themselves into a game of slavery, or, on a meta-reflexive novel, theorize a psychoanalytic scene of free human subjects as a scene of slavery—never mind which position, the sadistic or the masochistic, they are taking up or addressing critically? What is the fungible value of the game as such for a feminist intervention in the late twentieth century?

In Benjamin's gender-focused reading of O's story, the anti-Black effect lies in even pondering an erotics of enslavement. Who can use those terms freely and with abstract cognitive jouissance, but from an enslavist perspective? Imagine asking the enslaved to read this aggressively generalizing sentence: "[This book] conceives domination as a two-way process, a system involving the participation of those who submit to power as well as those who exercise it. Above all, this book seeks to understand how domination is anchored in the hearts of the dominated" (*Bonds* 4). Domination, however, becomes clearly, and doubly—by O and by Benjamin's use of *Story of O*—framed as domination over the slave, who serves as key signifier to represent the psychic momentum of voluntary submission, or slavishness. She bases this point on a critical, Foucault inflected reading of Freud's notion of civilization. She criticizes Freud's concept of repression, for which "the rule of authority is preferable to the war of all against all. An unflinching scrutiny of human destructiveness convinces him that the repression demanded by civilization is preferable to the ruthlessness that prevails in the state of nature" (2). In Benjamin's view, his "monumental theory of psychic life and its interaction with culture" (4) seems to be hard to challenge, but does require a correction. Taking her cue from Foucault, she maintains that "this (Freudian) opposition between instinct and civilization obscures the central question of how domination actually works" (4). In her turn to Foucault, she uses his theory of power as a ubiquitous force that works by manifesting itself in and traversing across all social agents, not in the form of a clearly oppressive imposed structure, but as settled within the subject, as disabling and enabling, as oppressive and productive, as an inclusive and selective distribution of agency. Thus she makes her point about the psychic "yes" to power located both in individuals and in social groups, as the slippages within her text between individual and social psychology will show. She quotes Foucault: "If power were never anything but repressive, if it never did anything but to say no, do you really think one would be brought to obey it?" (4). Foucault's very question here disappears the violence of thingification from purview: if power, as in enslavement, entails to destroy a being's agential capacity to become a human subject in the first place, obedience, indeed, will be plainly and absolutely enforced. Even the very term itself, obedience, semantically implies another choice; the word only makes sense if the possibility of nonobedience is precalculated. This is a kind of agency that the thing was not supposed to have; as it was, Black being remained outside power's productive interpellative capacities. It requires a human to be a possible locus of desire, and thus to exert even a claim to power. Any actual practices of the slave that secured survival and reproduction must be theorized, as both Wilderson and Moten did in different ways, outside the orbit of post-Enlightenment theories of agency. As Hartman has demonstrated in *Scenes of Subjection*, even the spectacular forms of amusement and diversion enforced on the plantation, which circumscribed Black enslaved sensory experience beyond labor and reproduction for the plantation system, can only be seen as another form of violence on Black being. Those entertainments recast the enslaved's abjection from a human range of social, cultural interaction as a perverted kind of bestowed pleasure. Power, in a site of enslavement, does not in fact diffuse to the Black enslaved; it remains squarely possessed by the enslavist. The only way to enact power, was the option to disown the master of one's being by way of flight or death—in both cases, though, these acts reestablish the very absence of an interactive relation between Black being and human society. Accordingly, if one wanted to work through questions of social relations, agency, and desire by way of mobilizing the allegory of slavery, Foucault needed to be critiqued for a crucial limitation.

As an answer to Foucault's question, Benjamin instead lets loose a chain of significations: instinct/repression/obedience brought on by love for first powerful figures/civilization/self/aggression/submission. And by using the metaphorical concept "bonds of love" for this entanglement, she intends to address a challenge that she sees for psychoanalysis as well as for feminism's study of "gender domination" (*Bonds* 7): how to analyze and possibly transcend the dominated position of women in Western societies if and when women remain submissively connected to patriarchal power in intimate ways, as daughters, wives, and relatives of men they love. In a psychoanalytic replay of de Beauvoir, she takes de Beauvoir's rhetorical use of the Hegelian master-slave metaphor and pushes it to a bizarre level of anti-Black signification (7). The rhetorical reference to establish a wider social impact for her critique of subject-object relations is the postwar urgency, for psychoanalysis, to theorize the phenomenon of Germans' mass ecstatic hysteria for fascist power, and their voluntary and total submission "to the hypnotic leader." This phenomenon, to her, cannot be adequately described without recourse to what she considers as the primary structure of authority and obedience, domination and submission: the "gender polarity" that to her "underlies such familiar dualisms as autonomy and dependency, and thus establishes the coordinates for the positions of master and slave" (7). The slave here stands allegorically for both feminine dependency and the majority of Germans in thrall of the dictator. A turn to American history, instead of German fascism, however, would have called for an altogether different perspective on "domination" and "mastery," and would have disabused Benjamin of the ease with which the slave, again, appears in its multipurpose functionality for the human. For the thingified and shipped enslaved Black being, of course, there was not even the faintest hint of, however hysterical, choice, which insight completely disables the allegorical value of the slave for the points Benjamin wants to make. This opportunistic use of the metaphor, however, has become so naturalized in critical theories of the human that her argument can count on being shared by feminist white readers without objection.

The way I see it, Benjamin's reference to German fascism is not a haphazard or innocent textual strategy; it allows her not to look at the enjoyment of anti-Black abjection as a practice of the human subject, which might have troubled her approach. Her focus on eroticized submission in gendered terms screens an abyss of violence in American society, which lies outside the human subject-object (equals male-female) recognition mechanics she endorses:

> The fantasy of erotic domination embodies both the desire for independence and the desire for recognition. This inquiry intends to understand the process of alienation whereby these desires are transformed into erotic violence and submission. What we shall

see, especially in voluntary submission to erotic domination,
is a paradox in which the individual tries to achieve freedom
through slavery, release through submission to control. Once
we understand submission to be the *desire* of the dominated as
well as their helpless fate, we may hope to answer the central
question, how is domination anchored in the hearts of those
who submit to it. (*Bonds* 52–53)

This dense sentence raises a host of questions: Where does Benjamin draw a
line between individual fantasy, fantasies as psychic illness or perversion, or
even as acted out fantasies between individuals, on the one hand, and the
factual material social realm of "freedom and slavery," on the other? If she
uses those terms explicitly, she has to bear that question. Second. why is it
that white people can speculate as to what goes on in submissive psyches
by way of using an equation with the slave for that purpose? Submissive
human individuals do no doubt exist—but the eroticization of the slave's
domination is always already a projection, a historical densification of practices of actual enslavement in which it fell to the master to create today's
social, cultural, and literary legends of slavishness? The eroticized willingness
of the dominated has been the dominator's prevalent fiction passed on by
transgenerational transmission as the potent disavowal of the pleasures of
anti-Black abjection for the subject (see Hartman, *Scenes*; Broeck, "Legacies").
What then is the referential value for feminism of a piece of libertarian
pornography that repeats all the standard images, positions, gestures, and
commands of the notoriously brutal *Mastery, Tyranny, and Desire: Thomas
Thistlewood and His Slaves in the Anglo-Jamaican World* (Burnard) but is
being used as an innocent framing device?

What is the anti-Black implication of the suggestion to "overcome"
feminine dependency and "bondage" by way of taking an active part in
regimes of the subject's desire? If the female has femininity, that is precisely
what marks her as human: she is part of an economy of desire in the first
place; she is not a slavething. For Black being there has to be no interior
psychic life, no properties, certainly no desire, and thus no masochism to
feed into a game of withheld and given recognition, as long as the human
subject persists in its narcissistic theorization. As Frank Wilderson has argued,
the Black/slave does not take part in the psychic constellations of Oedipus.
A sexual history marked by unlimited sexualized use value and by being
the occasion, the affording site, of human titillation does not permit any
privatized, nuclear family initiation into the oedipal drama, where the worst
shock is watching "ma and pa doing it." For the Black/slave the threat of

castration has never been metaphorical, but a matter of life and death. The triangled constellation Benjamin assumes as universal human condition, in which the child's psychosexual formation unfolds behind the closed doors of a home insulated from agents, discourses, and practices beyond the home's reach, displaces the history of Black being's enslaved reproduction onto the scene of nonhumanness.

Benjamin quotes Freud: "[W]ithout the restraint of civilization, whoever is more powerful will subjugate the other" (*Bonds* 54). Based on Freud and his analytic legacy, American psychoanalysis has not taken "civilization" to include Western modernity's history of abjection. If one assumes it, with Freud, as self-evident "that the slave must grant recognition to the master," as Benjamin does, in an also quite explicitly Hegelian use of the individual slave's surrender to an individual master, then where does that leave American history? The desire for allegory, again, overwrites any psychoanalytic interest in the role that the sites of "n----ization" (see Judy) have played in the psychic life, and lives, of white society. The allegorical perspective keeps reenabling a willful ignorance (Mills, "White"), the ability not to see that (post-)enslavement racial formation has created a white interiority, a white capacity for abjective desire, a psychic life always already white gendered, a psychic life for which mastery and enslavement were not played out in an exclusively metaphorical register of power and submission, but were the life-and-death decisive factors of white and Black existence in the United States (Broeck, "In the Presence").

If Benjamin says, "This authority [of the master] is what inspires love and transforms violence into an opportunity for voluntary submission" (*Bonds* 64), then one might look at this sentence with some incredulity to begin with; as soon as the "opportunity for voluntary submission" becomes yoked to the figure of the slave, its meaning cannot be contained in a quasi-innocent framework of neutral description of sexual practices universal to the human psyche. By opening the frame of her argument to make statements about "civilization," in Freud's sense, and not just about the psychic maladies of individuals, her text invites the context of a particular American symbolic. However suppressed, its taken-for-grantedness by her implied readership cannot be divorced from the incontrovertible abjection of Black being, over and against all efforts at disavowal. However, Benjamin is interested not in abjective desire as social violence, but in the destructive effects omnipotent desire has on the subject himself, as long as the subject does not encounter and realize resistance of another subject's free desire (67–68). She constantly slips in and out of clinical scenarios of sadomasochism into an articulation of social crisis—by way of allegories of domination based on "real life persons" (68, 89), for which, however, racist violence as a factor does not at all figure. Sliding from child psychology (77) to "Western thought" and to "Western versions of individuation," *Bonds of Love* manages to reinscribe a critical version of Western patriarchal formations of the human psyche that entirely ignores the racist, anti-Black character of patriarchal domination. This cannot be seen as inevitable or as a lag in knowledge, but is strategic. The text figures within and against a concerted effort of Black feminist interventions to force white feminism to listen, and thus reinstalls the centrality of gender antagonism by its very use of the slave analogy:

> [E]rotic domination, for both sides, draws its appeal in part from its offer to break the encasement of the isolated self, to explode the numbness that comes of "false" differentiation [from the mother]. It is a reaction to the predicament of solitary confinement—being unable to get through to the other, or be gotten through to—which is our particularly modern form of bondage. The castle of Roissy [in *Story of O*] marshals the old forms of bondage—the ritual trappings of male domination and female submission—as if they could redeem us from the sterility of modern rationality. (83)

Story of O's phantasma of slavery is rejected in favor of a vision of human (inter)subjectivity freed of the "numbing" enclosure of patriarchal bondage—but for this operational trope to function, even in Benjamin's critical take on O's story, the horizon of slavery must rhetorically be available in the first place without having to address the structural antagonism between human life and Black enslavement, and its afterlife.

Mothering

As has become visible in her remark about the modern subject's failure of differentiation from the mother, a critique of the mother as a bourgeois formation essential for the nuclear family, of motherhood, of mothering, of mother-infant relations, then, is of course central to Benjamin's suggestion to create a different kind of intersubjectivity that allows subjects to differentiate from those "numbing" primary attachments (which she sees as "our modern form of bondage") and, on this basis, to be able to "get through to the other" (*Bonds* 83). This transformation will need a different figuration of gender roles and functions, which will require first a different kind of psychoanalytical observation of and ascription to "the mother" and "the father," and subsequently a different kind of pedagogy as well as a feminist social, political, and cultural change of expectations of gender. What needs to be overcome, in her view, is the patriarchal fear of "the mother" as archaic and primitive force that will keep subjects bonded and in static dependency, which, as feminist theory has amply demonstrated, has been prevalent even in classical psychology and social theory. Instead, she envisions a change in gender relations and in gender psychology that would enable overcoming of the stifling impact of the nuclear family and create the possibility of more liberated and equitable intersubjective relations for individual members of society, but also for society as a whole, in which one person's subjectivity would not have to come at the cost of someone else's; and thus ultimately society would not anymore be stuck in sadomasochistic structures of human relations. One of the images she conjures up in this discussion is the adage of the "dark side of maternal power" (*Like* 107), criticizing the blatant sexism of this trope but entirely disregarding its racism. That is the point that the following passages will engage.

Benjamin argues in favor of "reforming polarities" (of the maternal-paternal binary) into productive "tensions" (*Like* 108), instead of either "counteridealizing" (107–08, a term taken from Kristeva) or denigrating the mother, because by "opposing [her] power, one remains connected to it, borrows its charisma, and is ultimately seduced by it" (108). Accordingly, she needs to argue against the "feminist repudiation of the father" (108), and against feminist theory that "seeks to restore a lost maternal or feminine order on the margins of culture and to avoid the darker side of maternal power." In order to achieve that point, she assumes intense factual power of the maternal within both the individual and social life of subjects, even though it remains within oedipal binds and needs a patriarchal frame, as it were, to be experienced as power in the first place: "[I]s this not the unconscious flip side of a woman's embrace of maternal power the mother's own feeling that she is a monster? Her terror of her power over her child, of the hatred mothers necessarily feel, inspires a wish to be controlled by a male counterpower" (107). She further elaborates:

> As I have stated, the girl's Oedipal position entails no less chauvinistic contempt, no less a repudiation of the masculine. Indeed, the Oedipal girl's insistence on being the "little mother"—better known in kindergarten as the role of "little boss"—runs counter to the passive adoration of the male object and may be used to transform femininity into a triumphant assertion of superiority, a more successful way to capture power than the boy's identificatory

love of the father. The unwillingness to relinquish the fantasy of maternal omnipotence, particularly when it is linked to the image of the sexually tantalizing, feminine object (*as it tends to be in Latin or African-American culture* [italics mine]) is readily apparent in women's defense of their traditionally exalted power to give and sustain life. And perhaps, as Dinnerstein argued, women's allegiance to maternal omnipotence plays a part in their acceptance of social submission—not in the sense of historical cause so much as its current inspiration. For without question, those who most idealize motherhood are those who most loudly defend the values of the paternal familial order. (107)

"[A]s it tends to be in Latin or African-American culture": the casualness of Benjamin's aside is the racist punctum here, which motorizes the force of her argument, as it is the specific function of concrete examples to do. This is particularly so when a given text can assume an always already shared understanding, with its readership, of the example to deliver up a naturalized fact. Without ado, Latin and African American women are swiftly aligned here as backwards, patriarchal agents, holding on "traditionally" to the twin "exalted powers" of maternal "omnipotence" and their power of sexual seduction. I cannot address the issue of "Latin" culture at this point, even though the very term in its stereotypical generality is an insult in this context. My interest is in the massive agnotological and nonchalant anti-Blackness of this throwaway remark, which now, but also, and more importantly, at the time of the book's publication, flies in the face of decades of Black feminist theory and the historiography of New World slavery. What gives one pause is the lack of any critical response in the ongoing and lively debate Benjamin's books have mobilized. Said sexual prowess and alleged "matriarchal omnipotence" of Black mothers, in fact, were the target of the most irate, articulate, and extended wave of Black feminist articulation at the time of Benjamin's publications. In the very same selection of the key feminist texts of the decade in which Benjamin's "Master and Slave: The Fantasy of Erotic Domination" a prior version of *Bonds of Love* appears, Rennie Simson outlines the contours of Black female sexual identities in historical perspective as a castigation of this mythology. This collection, *Powers of Desire*, did contain contributions which amply articulate an antiracist *and* antisexist critique of Black women's enforced trajectories during and post-enslavement in the United States. However, instead of turning to this work, Benjamin's argument rehashes one of the most insidious attacks on Black women's integrity within Black communities and beyond: the point of Black female licentiousness, on the one hand, and, on the other, that of their destructive matriarchal power over Black communities, as was made in 1965 by the notorious Moynihan Report (*Moynihan Report [1965]*). Arguably, that report could even be said to have been one of the crucial causal factors for the explosion of Black feminist energy, organizing and theorizing in the wake of its public controversy. Benjamin's parasitical relation to this, shared with a wide readership, bespeaks a feminist racist politics of lingering, persistent repertoires of anti-Blackness. I use the term "lingering" because of the passive-aggressive quality of these troping practices that go out of their way to appear as neutral, certainly never racist, theoretical pronunciations; instead, they are made to rest inconspicuously, but recognizably, in the marginal space of white arguments purportedly out to make other, universally theoretical points. But they are also aggressive, in that they quietly recirculate—through and within various disciplinary discourses and critical formations—the dense sediments of anti-Black articulations, dating back to enslavement, that white American feminism has never proactively renounced, let alone invalidated. This point is essential not only because it asks for a political critique of Benjamin's dismissal by explicit naming of Latin and African American women as agents of patriarchal tradition, but also because it poses a theoretical problem. By the twin strategy of calling our attention to Black women's existence by way of disappearing her in the pejorative manner of this mention, Benjamin's text recapitalizes on the energy of well-established tropes of Blackness for analogical purposes as a late twentieth-century replay of the slave metaphorics of earlier texts. One must ask why the text needs this side reference to the Black woman, given the obvious fact that otherwise the text has no interest in engaging Black women's psychosexual history or any of their anti-patriarchal interventions, and it has no clue as to the actual political, cultural, and social abjection of Black women and men by white society, or else to speak of a "paternal order" of Black communities would forbid itself.

As a refrain of earlier white feminism, Benjamin's theoretical work on gender differentiation and her critique of gender roles needs the figure of the Black woman as a foil. The alleged backwardness of Black women—the loudest defenders of the paternal familiar order, in Benjamin's book—embodies the regressive horizon of dependent subjectivity Benjamin's feminism projects to reject and overcome. The allegorical value of the bracketed remark far exceeds its seemingly marginal position in the text. It reinscribes Benjamin's late twentieth-century urging for a necessary change in the psychoanalysis of gender into a tradition for which the freedom of gender and the prerogative to theorize it has only become thinkable as a formation set *against* slavishness; the nonchalance with which Benjamin brings the trope into state-of-the-art gender studies by way of a direct referential transferal from Black slave to "Black women" in and of her contemporary context cannot but be considered a dare to Black feminists.

Her intervention concentrates on giving back to the mother a desire of her own, without which no subjectivity of the female could be recognized, an intervention within psychoanalysis in order to weaken the analytic explanation power of the phallus as "overvalued emblem of desire" (*Like* 132). The human subject (male or female) needs to be brought up to enjoy its unencumbered possibilities of being in society, not a negativizing post-oedipal separation from the mother, so that a space of freedom (126) can be created for subjects and objects to meet and mutually install each as such. Both positions, of *mother* as well as *father*, in the oedipal triangle, she suggests, should be reformed so as to create more space for the female subject's self-realization to overcome compulsory and exalted practices of mothering, and to enable more productive practices of fathering, allowing less antisocial subjectity for the father. For Benjamin, because it is the lack of fatherly contribution to parenting and family reproduction that underwrites and supports the sadomasochistic patterns at work in society as a whole and in individual psychology, "again, it is not absence of a paternal authority [as other theories had it]—'fatherlessness'—but absence of paternal nurturance that engenders submission" (146).

Trying to bring this apodictic approach to bear on the history and presence of Black life—which should be possible given its universalist pretension—results in absurdity. Fatherlessness, and the deplored "absence of paternal nurturance," in the context of American enslavist history, resonates in a register entirely abjected from the oedipal triangle. As Black historiography, political and social studies, and critical Black psychoanalytical contributions have amply demonstrated over a span of a century, Black family reproduction has never been given white society's respect; in fact, the law, as well as institutions of higher education, welfare, and policing have excelled in a political, social, and cultural abjection of Black right to and capability of nuclear family parenting.

Adrienne Davis, Patricia Williams, Nell Painter, and Hortense Spillers, most importantly, have drawn attention to the fact that mother- or fatherhood was an impossibility for enslaved Black being, whose children did not belong to biological Black mothers or fathers, or to improvised families, but became white owners' chattel property (even and especially so if the "chattel" was sexually reproduced by the master himself). This deliberate bastardization and orphanization of Black children had dire consequences: the triangularization and oedipal identity formation within the family triad mother-father-child, set as the universalized standard by the white bourgeois family unit and theorized by psychoanalysis, became an imposed impossibility for generations of enslaved life, which Black communities have fought against consistently. Black people's enforced legal, social, cultural, and political banishment from proper (by white standards) human development of free subjects registered in the white mind, including the white scientific mind, as lack, or disability, or aggressive refusal to perform in accordance with the nineteenth-century Victorian and later twentieth-century post-Freudian normativity. Surviving way into the later twentieth and the twenty-first century, this racist assumption of Black improperness has created a collective white psychic legacy of splitting human subjectivity from Black individual and social modes of existence, so that psychoanalytic attention to subjection formation, self, and identity (terms varying with the changes in scholarly repertoires), and the importance of gender in relation to those concepts, could confidently rest on analyses of default white family constellations. In fact, while white ownership of Black life has required ongoing psychological, mental, and social acts of compensation on the part of Black communities, starkly different from the gendered task of white middle-class legitimized conjugality and parenting, in order to counter the constant imposition of white patriarchal theft of reproduction from Black kinship structures, and the destruction and denial of both Black fathering and female mothering subject positions, there has been almost no interest on the part of white psychoanalytic theory to scrutinize their abjective assumptions. This politics of avoidance makes sense within a white supremacist framework: any acknowledgment of (post-)enslavement's impact on the psychic life of the white nuclear family, which prevails because of its perpetuated history of a very early splitting within the white child's psyche into "mom, dad, and myself," on the one hand, and entirely ungendered, undifferentiated Blackness on the other (see Katz) and thus of purifying white subject formation from interferences by Black claims to oedipally organized life would necessitate far reaching theoretical compensation about subjectivity and gender differentiation. Black reassessment of the assumption that white family constellations may be universally and productively constitutive for social and individual reproduction, and thus a) nothing outside a binary white gender purview might require theory's interventions and b), consequently, the violence of the Freudian paradigm might continue to go unnoticed, has been consistently ignored (Broeck, "Gender," as well as "Property"; Wiegman). Hortense Spillers's work has most clearly addressed the effects of slavery's impact on psychic constellations of Black communal life in American history, especially focusing on the position of Black women, as I have discussed in previous chapters.

Benjamin addresses what she sees as an imbalance in the theory's repeated turns to the phallus, and thus to the male principle, as it were, as the sole guarantee for a child's entry into "reality." The oedipal superego *falsely* "represent[s not only] the paternal law of separation. It also leads the child into reality—the reality of gender and generational difference," because "the phallus, once the token of sameness [for the boy] now also becomes the sign of difference [prohibition to become the father]" (*Bonds* 150). She is therefore concerned with rectifying an analysis of the subject's sociability by way of an acknowledgment of male and female mutuality and complementary in functions of nurturing and support for individuation uncoupled from the gender binary.

However, the human symbolic has both disallowed the Black *father* to embody the law of the symbolic, and forced the Black *mother* to be the omnipotent—even if despised—supermom for an entire nation, as Spillers has observed ("Mama's Baby"). I am introducing here the notion of *enracing*, a human acquisition and inhabitance of the white default position without which the oedipal triangle could not successfully take effect in enslavist societies. The oedipal constellation also produces, confirms, procreates, and demands the occupation of racialized positions. The historical fixation of the conflictual dualism of gender within human society has been based on a hidden but haunting suppressed structural antagonism; it entails that a subject's embeddedness in the human symbolic is being reproduced by an enslavist splitting into civilized and freely individuated subject and supposedly slavish flesh (Spillers), given to paternal authority through maternal submissiveness, which casts femininity (always already cathected with the Black metaphorized threat of slavishness) outside the (post-)enlightened symbolic. Consequently, white women in the wake of successful feminist movements have escaped this conundrum by having their whiteness trump their femininity, thus having claimed a chance for the realization of their own subjectivity and desire. Benjamin's work, by way of its evasion of this enracing, capitalizes on a white subject's affect against submissiveness. This affect has insistently cast Black life, in a vicious circle made fatherless over and again, as primitively submissive—in a state of nonsubjectivity being passed on through the line of the (post-)slave mother for generations.

The crucial question of the possibilities that this anti-Black affect affords white gender differentiation remains entirely understudied. For white humans partaking in the enslavist structures, anti-Black affect in US society may offer white male children the opportunity to enter into a forked oedipalization, as it were: holding on to an idealization of the (white) mother, while realizing the drive for subjectivation in the anti-Black violence to possess Blackness, without it being able to possess him, or stand in the way of his male free subjectivity. It may offer white girls an unthreatening, because non-oedipal, agency, not directed against the father, but enabling her to pursue a subject's aggressivity, a "desire of her own" (*Bonds* 163, 168) in racist differentiation. Triangularization, then, is a picture that needs complication by an acknowledgment of Black fungibility for the subject's emergence. I am quite aware that these are speculative suggestions to think through. Psychoanalysis needed to work through again the transitory moment of individualization into sociability by way of the child's entry into language and the symbolic, as a process that requires and secures humanization against slavishness as and for psychic subject formation. Benjamin's facile aside against Black women's alleged insistence on patriarchal models of motherhood entirely screens from view and displaces the problematics of white mothering, and fathering, as an enracing production of affect and desire. That feminist-inflected practices of parenting have been or might be productive of more socially just, participatory, unoppressive modes of subject life, mutually beneficial to both men and women because of learned intersubjectivity, might be borne out for progressive sectors of human sociability willing to undergo a process of regendering, as it were with a difference. However, if the driving motivation and motor force behind this change remains a charge of human subjectivity against slavishness, the enslavist production of human generations will continue to work its anti-Black violence.

The Suffering Subject

Benjamin's text works to shore up empathy with the human subject of suffering by way of analogy. With obvious Hegelian and Weberian undertones, she locates postmodernity's social crisis in the subject's enslavement:

> The separation of spheres intensifies as society is increasingly rationalized. As in erotic domination, the process replicates the breakdown in tension: the subject fears becoming like the object he controls, which no longer has the capacity to recognize him. As the principle of pure self-assertion comes to govern the public world of men, human agency is enslaved by the objects it produces, deprived of the personal authorship and recognizing response that are essential to subjectivity. (*Bonds* 185)

With a one-sentence sleight of hand she has thus catapulted her argument into a long line of post-Enlightenment debate which has bypassed the subject's history of enslavism by way of casting the subject as bonded and subjected. This becomes a prototypical rhetorical maneuver in which the critical gaze, fixed on the white subject, has only two poles of reference to evaluate the subject's situation: freedom and independence, or dependency on others. Benjamin, following Marcuse, wants to harmonize the subject's freedom with a vision of its relation to the other that does not render the subject "enslaved." There is no interest in her argument in an analysis of the jouissance the subject has taken in and from practices of anti-Black enslavism. Her focus is on the transformation of human subject-object relations into human subject-subject relations, but the role abjection of unhumanized Blackness plays in the momentum of this transformation remains hidden from view; her gaze is on the white suffering, and impeded subject that is always already pained by the disconnect and loneliness of a freedom unredeemed by intersubjectivity.

Anti-Black racism and its devastating creation of a sociability based on the abjection of Black life can thus not appear on her screen:

> As Marcuse points out, the denial of dependency is central to the bourgeois ideal of individual freedom: "Self-sufficiency and independence of all that is other and alien is the sole guarantee of the subject's freedom. What is not dependent on any other person or thing, what possesses itself, is free. . . . A relationship to the other in which one really reaches and is united with him counts as loss and dependence." The ideal of the bourgeois individual, Marcuse shows, is created by an art of abstraction, which denies his real dependency and social subordination. Consequently, his freedom consists of protection from the control or intrusion of others. It is a *negative* ideal of freedom: freedom as release from bondage, individuality stripped bare of its relationship with and need for others." (*Bonds* 176; Benjamin's ellipsis)

While part of Marcuse's Marxist argument, by its critical take on possession and the contingency of human freedom on self-possession would leave at least an opening for a discussion of the necessary anti-Black abjective effect of this logic, so that self-possession could be critiqued for its aggressiveness, not for its self-loss, Benjamin immediately slides into a critique of the subject's own negative ideal of freedom as a "release of bondage." She critiques this logic, of course, but only from the feminist point of view to suggest her model of intersubjectivity instead of dependency. For the female, cast as object, to be recognized as subject in her own right, so the argument goes, the male subject must overcome his notion of a male freedom possible only when pitched *against* that female object that, in the patriarchal phantasma, enslaves him. The female object herself, in turn, must replace the dependent feminine security guaranteed by her object status, must abandon the illusory power of her "slavish" bonds of love, to enable intersubjective interaction:

> It may be impossible to say where this cycle of real [male] domination and the fantasy of maternal omnipotence begins, but this does not mean that we can never break that cycle and restore the balance of destruction [of the idealized nurturer] and recognition. The answer awaits the social abolition of gender domination. And this means not just equality for women, but also a dissolution of gender polarity, a reconstruction of the vital tension between recognition and assertion, dependency and freedom. (176)

That the subject's practice of enslavism grounds both human misogyny and the possibility of human intersubjectivity is the absent presence of this argument; thus, readers' moral rejection of enslavement provides her argument's feminist energy, but only in a narcissistic way. Her project means to secure woman's place within a frame of possible recognition. Therefore, she needs to look past the fact that the subject's individualism and self-possession was, historically speaking, not at all an "art of abstraction"; the human subject's horizon of self-possession is the result of establishing self-possession for white subjects on the grounds of dispossession of the wider colonial object world and the enslavist possession of Black people. For Benjamin, following Marcuse, the patriarchal individual's abstractness lies in the male "denial of bonds," which intersubjectivity supposedly is able to transcend without just overturning the binary logic, whereas a post-enslavist reading needs to direct the attention to the subject's practices of bonding, of abjecting Black sentient beings shut off by human subjects in positions "male" and "female" from the status of a recognizable object (188). Benjamin shares a post-Enlightenment sadness for the subject—which extends from an analytic of psychosexual ego development to a social vision—with the Frankfurt school (190–91; see Broeck, "Das Subjekt"). Her vision for the creation of a world "through our connection to it" (193), instead of a domination of it that leaves the subject itself deprived and isolated, does not inquire into what Hartman calls the pleasures of anti-Black subjection (Hartman, *Scenes*) and therefore cannot see from the position of those who are structurally absent from relational intersubjective scenarios of connection. To the contrary, in a footnote that tellingly gives away her (at least passive) awareness of 1990s women-of-color interventions onto the scene of feminist anti-patriarchal negotiations, she lashes out against what in her view becomes an abject subversion of feminism, without brakes. In a slippage from mutual intersubjective recognition as value to a social agreement on the maternal valuation of social need and dependency, she reiterates her critique of the patriarchal valorization of abstract individualism, which insists on "the right of every individual to choose his values and pursue the fulfillment of his needs" (196). In a rather awkward jump of logic, though, she turns that argument against multicultural interventions by women-of-color against white racism and solipsistic versions of feminism: "The same groups that once embraced the idea of the unity of women based on their common essence then leapt to a 'new' awareness that differences of race and class were the real truth and that all universal categories only serve to deny such difference. In this turnabout there was no stopping point, no consideration of how to sustain the tension between universal commonality and specific differences." For Benjamin, the only "difference" worth theoretical address is gender: "By rejecting the false premise of paternal authority as the only road to freedom, we may recover the promise on which oedipal theory has defaulted: coming to terms with difference" (181). The "dualisms in Western culture" need to be abandoned in favor of a balance of different, but complementary forces: mom and dad, male and female, the great divide of gender having overcome by mutual intersubjectivity a world adjusted to a complementarity of reversible subject and object positions.

This kind of mutuality and intersubjectivity needs a deep cultural transformation of the politics of human desire to become inclusive of what has been suppressed: female desire. Such desire, then, in her argument, requires "ownership." The object may become a subject if it becomes possible to "recuperate what has been disowned." This liberation of a female/feminine desire could realize a less abstract, static, and oppressive and more agential subjectivity always already engaged in processes of mutual intergender negation and recognition in intrahuman interactions. To own feminine agential desire would enable a mutual acceptance of otherness and fluid positioning of subjects and objects, because "the attempt to psychically destroy the other is resolved through the other's survival" (182). As soon as the "other" establishes her own desire in the world, she can resist objectivization and the bonds of slavishness.

This scenario, by its structural contingency on the ownership of human desire, excludes the Black/slave who has thus never been afforded the potential of ownership, least of all an ownership of desire, actually having become a cypher for the very absence of self-motoring desire in Benjamin's very argument. Accordingly, some questions must be allowed: Did the "mother"/"woman" in American postfeminist middle-class culture survive because the Black did not? Could a psychic formation have evolved whereby a certain kind of rabid patriarchal misogyny has been displaced by way of transferring human violence onto the Black? Segments of American society could begin to accept a strong feminist impact on the making of subjectivity, to understand and to will changing forms of authority, mixed parenting, and other forms of "balance" and "intersubjectivity." Has this growing acceptance of feminism in white mostly middle- and upper-class segments been connected to an also growing passive indifference to Black death and to a collective abandonment of Black life by civic society after the relatively short interlude of white attraction to powerful Black movements for civil rights and Black Power? Which role might have feminism and psychoanalysis played in this process of creating a subject-object balance? As Benjamin says in an almost poetic vision of mutually reversible positions of activity and passivity, subject and object: "[B]y proposing that a symmetry is necessary in which both self [male] and other [female] . . . own the burden of subjectivity, . . . [w]e must not only recognize our tendency to destroy, we must survive for the other; and we must also ask the other to take on the onus of being a subject and surviving our destruction." She immediately goes on to stress "the social implications of realizing that the onus of subjectivity must be borne even by those cast in the position of the other, for they aspire to the subject position as well" (*Shadow* xix). This is a not quite verbatim, but most intricate replay of both Wollstonecraft's exhortation to women not be happily contended with being men's pets and Simone de Beauvoir's feminist rejection of femininity as "slavish." We are back in the Hegelian logic of dialectic overturn, with a specific Benjaminian twist that imagines agency, desire, and subjectivity through the reevaluation of the maternal, instead of its disavowal.

"There, however, it [the libido] was not employed in any unspecified way, but served to establish an identification of the ego with the abandoned object. Thus, the shadow of the object fell upon the ego" (Freud qtd. in Benjamin, *Shadow* 79). But there is no shadow of the Black on the white ego, because the Black does not qualify as an object. If, as Benjamin says, this approach helps us to understand "how the apparent boundaries of the self are actually permeable, how the apparently isolated subject constantly assimilates what is outside itself," if even "the self is constituted by the identifications with the other that it deploys in an ongoing way, in particular to deny the loss and uncontrollability that otherness necessarily brings" (79), how come, then, that Blackness has never inspired a sense of loss in the collective American psyche? If, secondly, the subject "is reciprocally constituted in relation to the other, depending on the other's recognition, which it cannot have without being negated, acted on by the other, in a way that changes the self, making it nonidentical," one can only conjecture, once more, that Blackness is no object, it cannot aspire, because it does not have the capacity to receive or give recognition, it has been beyond the pale of binarity. So, the play of "multiple differences," that Benjamin calls upon her readers to respect, that she is seeking a valuable position for, does not apply. Tellingly enough, this abjection repeats in the narratives of the theoretical controversies and debates she places herself into (postmodern, post-Lacanian feminism), from which any consideration of the Black/slave or even considerations of race are absent, being screened behind a rhetoric of differences and mutual respect for the "onus" of subjectivity (see 81ff.). Written into the raging debates about otherness and difference within feminism, gender studies, and women in general that marked her period, her formulations on otherness acquire a meaning beyond the staging of her own setting: "Nor can any appeal to the acceptance of otherness afford to leave out the inevitable breakdown of recognition into domination" (84), urging onto readers ominously that "recognition itself can go over the edge into knowledge as mastery." Sliding almost imperceptibly, but efficiently from a focus on the male-female binary into a debate called for by her political moment questioning a unified self of feminism, she proclaims the "challenge to the autonomous [male] subject requires more than deconstruction of the old notion of a centered unified self. . . . [I]t requires a notion of an inclusive subjectivity that can assume multiple positions and encompasses the Other within" (85). However, and here the subtext is double, no longer just the struggle between male subject and female object, as her engagement with Benhabib, Butler, and others demonstrates, but by way of absent presence, between feminism and its Others, "the negativity that the other sets up for the self has its own possibilities, a productive irritation, heretofore insufficiently explored" (85). This kind of productive irritation of the subject by the other, and the mutuality of acceptance of difference, is for her a psychoanalytic given, as well as an ethical imperative. Going back to Bataille's comments on the capacity of constant self-questioning in the subject, its awakening to this reflection on otherness as always already taking place under the sign of Auschwitz, its "stench and unalleviated fury," she names her project both a psychoanalytical venture and a moral obligation—thus, again, conflating the level of intraindividual psychology and the public sphere of the social, political, and cultural. She does not dwell on this, however, and, even more significantly, slavery and lynching are absent from her mind. At this point, she could have pursued the trace of abjection, but keeps it in a footnote (86, 88). Instead of going into materialism of history, she follows the metaphor once again as it offers a balance in its ideal vision: "But only the concrete outside other can break up the closed energy system [of the self], only the other who can be moved but not coerced by us can take on some of what is too much for the self to bear [in terms of the containment and ownership of desire]. There is no question that we need the other—the question is only, can we recognize her? And has not the master-slave problematic made clear to us that her otherness becomes vitiated if we fail to do so?" (91–92). The "abolition" of gender polarity, as Benjamin proposes, might indeed overcome the human subject-object positioning in its patriarchal configuration: the tension of gender having mutated into fully human reciprocal, recognizant complementarity, instead of remaining fixed as relation of male dominance over female dependence, coded over and again as slavishness. That dissolution of hegemony, however, does not result in an end anti-Black abjection, but actually in its fortification.

Repeating Abjection: Judith Butler Yet Again

In this section I move the discussion from feminist "classics" to state-of-the-art gender studies theorization and its relation to anti-Blackness. I argue that advanced contemporary post-identity gender studies (by which I mean turn-of-the-twenty-first-century critique), which have been more or less, and more or less explicitly, indebted to Judith Butler's advances in the conceptualization of gender as a performative practice, maintain a remarkable relation to enslavism. I have so far discussed the tropes of *woman as voluntary frivolous slave* (Wollstonecraft), *woman as dependent awakening slave* (de Beauvoir, following American nineteenth-century feminism), and *woman as sexual subject emerging from slavery* (Benjamin). These practices of feminist claim-making about and to subjectivity, in consequence, have reinstalled Black abjection.

What happens once the debate of gender moves into the reaches of poststructuralist anti-essentialism? On the one hand, one notes a rather sustained absence of engagement with historical transatlantic enslavement as one of the founding practices of the modern subjectivity which it has been gender studies' prerogative to discuss. Even though "race" (if oftentimes wrongly conflated with "ethnicity") has become an issue, most manifestly visible in last decade's debates about intersectionality, it has been severed from a historical-theoretical analysis of the inextricable connex between human subjectivity and Black enslavement. On the other hand, in theory's metaphoric register, slavery, and its ontological separation of human life as "freedom" from the threat of thingness, still and again seems indispensable. The poststructuralist discourse on the subject displaces the Black abjection that is the source of its own ability to articulate the human, however critically. However, this abjection keeps haunting the subject's (self-)reflection in its rhetorical expense of and allegorical investment in actual or threatening social death. The effect of this not quite successful theoretical labor, however, accrues to the white modern and postmodern subject in that it supports the subject's articulation of desire and recognition. The intense analogical energy spent on subjection as dehumanization (as in slavery), however, has not resulted in white theoretical interest in the abjected Black/slave's situation but keeps circling its attention back to the subject of human enunciation. Even in the hegemonic terms of the contemporary theoretical debate, which has also come to be crucial for gender studies, namely, "wasted lives," "precarious lives," "bare lives," any traces of the Black/slave's early modern, modern, and postmodern paradigmatic experience of thingification and death have been overwritten by an ontological interest in the human, which does not remember its genealogy based on the split of human from Blackness.

Rephrasing Butler's by now notorious gesture of "What does it mean to offer a critique?" (Salih 1), I want to ask, how does one critique Judith Butler's work without being immediately implicated in bad faith? Her thinking has been respected in almost all critical camps. Except for the ultra-reactionary fundamentalist institutions and individuals who have been spewing hate against her thinking and her person in various media for years, scholars and activists have cherished Butler's radically constructive insights which have offered, first, a massively productive intellectual rupture to reach beyond essentialism and facile identity politics, and, secondly, a paradigm shift within academia to seek out positions of ethical responsibility in a global frame beyond the postmodern indifference of her own formative years of philosophical training. Her interventions have traveled extremely well to multiple disciplinary sites and various international locations, and it would be hard to find a contemporary scholar in the humanities—of course, including myself—who has not been in some direct or indirect way affected by her intellectual labor and impacted by its implications. Why (and how to) undertake a critique of one of the most visible anti-sexist, anti-homophobic, anti-militarist, and anti-racist voices on the international scene of theory? At first sight, it appears to be a counterintuitive project. I want to pursue it, however, precisely because of the international hyper-visibility, preeminence, and acclaim her mode of critique has garnered, the wide and intense degree of identification her work has invited, and, last but not least for my argument, the success it has enjoyed in framing debates around intellectual and political issues of today. Butler's work, in its continuity over the last twenty-five years, has arguably produced its own school of thought; it has thus created sustainable intelligibility for some issues, and just as sustained unintelligibility for other questions. Despite, or maybe because of, what Salih approvingly discusses as her theoretical eclecticism, Butler's oeuvre in its particular hybridization of deconstructionism, post-Hegelianism, Jewish philosophy, European poststructuralism, psychoanalysis, feminisms, Althusserian Marxism, and phenomenology has not only corresponded with and across an array of otherwise separate intellectual discourses, but has drawn diverse theoretical constellations into engaged debates about the pressing issues of war, terror, and the precariousness of human life. Many Black studies and postcolonial studies scholars have engaged and worked with what amounts by now to a Butlerian hermeneutics. Her programmatic agenda has successfully combined critical readings of contemporary subjectivities, practices, and discursive formations as always contingent, non-identical, and performative constructions, which she holds to be undoable, with the political stance of a public radical intellectual. My critique, therefore, hinges on a very specific momentum of Butler's thinking which connects her argumentation with a long history of feminist/theoretical appropriation-cum-disavowal of the figure of slavery, specifically mobilized in her case by the metaphorics of social death.

In her turn to reconsider the issue of gender as a question of the human, which has taken her impact far beyond the realm of gender studies, even though she has not reneged on her affiliations with gender and queer studies, Butler has not penetrated the white screen of philosophy's anti-Black universalism. Even though her public interventions have become more and more radically anti-racist over the last fifteen years, in the antagonism her theoretical work suggests between the ontologically vulnerable human and the state, Black abjection from human society is rendered unintelligible. Thus, I read selected Butler text, across a number of publications, agonisti-cally, for its terms of address, its semantic strategies, its plotting and its content, its rhetorical maneuvers, and its silences. A nagging question has driven me: It is so abundantly clear, particularly in her later work, that her own labor is cognizant of and employs Black knowledge, so why would Butler's work not confront the scandal of enslavism as the progenitor of our modern and postmodern present tense, not in a merely allusive sense, but as the most radical negation of white philosophy and history as the Western academy knows it?

Because the horizon of enslavism frames my argument, I take issue with Butler's post-Kristeva notion of the abject. As I have already elaborated I do not discuss the abject as other, because the other may always be recuperated within a (post-)Hegelian logic of desire for recognition, potential mutuality, and reversion. I also do not see the abject as another's other—that would just endlessly defer the lines of conflict as potential. What I call abject remains as the *done to*, being outside lines of civic conflict, social claimability, and (post)modern sociability. Those lines, in actual fact of US and Western history, have been lines immanent to white societies, separating human from the Black/slave. I have been claiming that while gender as a framing category for subjectivity has enabled white Western women as a group, exceptions in the particular notwithstanding, to transcend the legacy of deeply entrenched misogyny most amplified by genocidal witchburning and to move successfully towards and into a location of civic and social claimant (see Federici). The eventual (neo)liberal success of gender's binary framework has been based on the cultural, psychic, social, and political installation of the state of slavery, and by extension the state of Black/slave as horizon of absolute rejection and ejection from the frame of the human, and thus of genderization. The (post-)Hegelian dialectics of binaries inherent to Western modern societies' self-conceptualization have needed a constitutive outside to their logic, which they found in the enslaved, against whom, then, violence could not and needed not be registered as punishment, transgression against rights, or psychosis. Even though, of course, Butler's work most prominently has opened up the debate of gender's performativity and of the vulnerable state of the human beyond the masculine/feminine either-or opposition in favor of assuming a rather more fluid and contingent performativity of one's gender and one's humanity, the status and function of gender as a term itself and its implication in the post-Enlightenment enslavist history of the human has not been examined.

In a series of permutations, the woman-as-slave analogy has made reappearances within feminism and gender studies, including in Butler's work, which have left the function of this specific rhetoric maneuver intact. Slavery still and again serves as the horizon of unspeakable abjection, from which human subjectivation needs to be distanced to be addressable as a question of gender, even in its dissolution, as in the figure of the queer. The provocation of gender, even as a performative, lies in its structural exclusion of the Black/slave's history and presence of abjection, which needs a double critique: one, it mires gender, and the human, in enslavist power; and two, it demands of Black feminism to remain structurally dysfunctional, in that the very notions of gender cannot recognize Black knowledge as epistemology of (post)modernity, only as ethnography of particular interest groups. It has to consign slavery to a safely melancholic transatlantic past—by way of recognizing the Black trauma, for example, in the reception history of Morrison's *Beloved* but disavowing it as the most radical critique of Western white philosophy and critical theory, including its own genealogy. For a theory of the precarious present to remain in gender, and thus in the human, that is, only replays a problem as old as Sojourner Truth's nineteenth-century exclamations by way of postmodern theoretical sophistication. Instead, the challenge is to read human gender as a white property, in both its possessive and adjectival connotations; it is a practice, a performativity that, at this point in time and after more than two centuries of feminist struggle, belongs to humans in as much as it defines them, but does not pertain to and consequently cannot be claimed by the dehumanized thingified Black/slave, or only at the expense of forcing Blackness into a realm of unsayability.

Thus, while the human owns gender, the Black/slave is fixed to race and contained in it. Race, as the complimentary to gender, has turned out to be a highly problematic category, and the theoretical shift in gender studies towards the difference of race enables, in an only apparently counterintuitive way, a compelling white theoretical conceptualization of universality in coalition, while it disables any white perception of the Black/slave's unreconciliation with the system of its abjection. Even if Butler's work eloquently argues for a revamped and progressive humanist universality, "proleptic and performative, . . . holding out the possibility for a convergence of cultural horizons that have not yet met" (Butler qtd. in Salih 96), which cannot be taken as a given, but which has to be achieved in a multisided common effort at care and shelter for vulnerable human life, adding race analogically (as an axis of difference additional to gender) to her agenda will remain a gesture of proto-abolitionist benevolence, as long as the historical impact of enslavism is not acknowledged in its structural relation to the prevalence of white knowledge and social practice. To talk about how "racial gender norms" illuminate "the limits of gender as an exclusive category of analysis" (Butler qtd. in Salih 95) as a "crucial intersection" (Butler qtd. in Salih 117) by way of a footnote allusion to Black scholars Hartman, Mercer, Spillers, and Fanon, makes race an understood signifier for Blackness as that which racializes gender by default, instead of seeing whiteness as part and parcel of racialized gender. It assumes that intersectional work translates into intersecting gender (white) with race (Blackness). This notion of intersectionality does not involve an examination of her own work's white positioning, even in post-Foucauldian terms of its fabrication and employment (analogous to the doability of modes of gender); instead, it shifts the issue towards a hazardous abstraction of Black being as *racialized difference* when a differentiation of gender obscures gender's very practice of abjection (Broeck, "In the Presence"). The historyless category of race, at the moments at which Butler discusses it directly, appears in exclusively psychoanalytical terms as a fiction of white paranoia of the police, the state, the media and its public, which of course leaves her own point of view unimplicated because of the intellectual distance her voice may and does assume vis-à-vis the kind of ultra-reactionary racism widely deployed by different actors in the Rodney King case. To respond with a clear anti-racist statement to the Rodney King beating (see Butler qtd. Salih 204–12), while it is obviously a valid act of public indictment, has not connected to an interrogation of the ways in which her own philosophical and critical trajectory has shared in the iteration of enslavism's intellectual screening acts.

This concept of race presupposes a conceptual bind between the assumption of (at least always possible) subjectivity and its ascriptions or deployments. Butler does not, of course, describe this bind in terms of priority or posteriority: human subjectivity being constantly made and remade in iterations of discourses and practices. However, the very possibility of iteration logically requires a human agency, even if that agency is never sovereign, but is at any point embedded in objectifying and subjectifying social, political, and cultural terrains, and thus contingent and available to different, even contradictory, interpellations. I see two problems with this approach, though. First, the concept of race in Butler's text—which actually contradicts her articulation of Fanon and Patterson—does not enable one to imagine the Black/slave's state of nonbeing, of an abject nonavailability to interpellation and iteration, to which enslavement and its (post)modern future have consigned the fungible Black/slave (Hartman, *Scenes*). Second, the notion of race, since it figures as a Black adjectival property, screens and avoids a pursuit of the question if and how human subjectivity has been structurally iterated, claimed, and negotiated, however controversially, as white property, and has been itself based on the splitting off of thingification and fungibility of the Black/slave (Salih 41). Consequently, by not addressing the issue of Black social death, on which Western modernity has staked any human life, Butler's interventions against the precarity, to which so much human life has been rendered, remain within the limitation of white benevolence. The very extent to which Butler has engaged Black knowledge has created a void of answerability in her address. This becomes most visible in the margins of her text: Butler's readings of Black (feminist) work are mostly embedded in footnotes, that is, evacuated from her principal theoretical address; this practice voids Black knowledge of its genealogy and makes it fungible, instead of recognizing it as interlocution. Thus, by turning purposefully away from seeking out the impact of enslavement, Butler's arguments forego the kind of negativity which might open out on a radical epistemic alliance with Blackness and Black knowledge beyond the notorious, dutiful, and ultimately white invested litany of race in line with class and gender.

Reading Abjectivation

Rereading Butler's work thus requires a hermeneutics of abjectivation, by which I mean the address of unmarked detail, which, however marginal to Butler's argument in its given position, girds her text in its power to secure a white readerly identification which always already refuses to engage the burden of white history. The inclusion of the textual chronotope of "social death" for Butler's work figured in obvious but not structurally acknowledged response to Gilroy, Hartman, Patterson, Wynter, Spillers, and some other scholars quoted only in passing—as a stepping stone on her way from *Bodies That Matter*, through *Undoing Gender* and *Antigone's Claim*, to the ontology of vulnerability (see Butler, "Rethinking") that she has been after in her later work, as in *Giving an Account of Oneself* and *Frames of War*. Butler's engagement with social death as threat for the human, by way of allusion to the extremes of dehumanization, might amplify theoretical constellations to seek out the implicatedness of white power and white knowledge (including modern and postmodern philosophy) in the historical production of dehumanization. However, Butler keeps nodding towards but always turning away from that option, in favor of reinstalling a repertoire of the philosophical universal and of an insistence on the unmarking of white subjectivity and power, most visibly in her recent work on the precariousness of the human beyond liberalism and identity politics.

To my knowledge, Butler has directly commented on enslavement and its ongoing force in the future it has created (Hartman, *Lose*) only a few times, and by way of employing slavery's rhetorical usefulness in passing. In the context of a debate about what counts as human life, she does acknowledge anti-Black violence: as a crucial example of whom the speaking "I" and "we" of her address should turn their empathy towards, her text points to the prison-industrial complex in the United States. In her conversation with Vikki Bell, "On Speech, Race and Melancholia," Butler mentions that this problematics is connected to the history of slavery, and offers a terse allusion to slavery with a reference to Saidiya Hartman's work. In her perspective, "race within diasporic culture" (Bell 170)—which, again, is her default signifier for Black being—is constituted as and in a limitless grieving desire for lost origins, a forced recognition of the impossibility of return, and thus as an "impossibility of essence" and a permeability to violence, which in turn then results in melancholia as a "kind of constitutive condition of Black urban culture" (171). The emphasis in this short passage is to muster a "racialized" example for her discussion of contemporary social and cultural melancholia.

Thus, Butler's work has offered a position against racism, but her work has evaded the issue of enslavism, white abjectorship, and, by extension, the implication of philosophy in it. Explicitly taking an anti-enslavist stance would involve reckoning with the modern and postmodern philosophic tradition she feels indebted to in order to point out its very own embeddedness in and responsibility for anti-Black violence. Butler's critique of racism relates to her intellectual biography and the formulation of a decidedly queer position, but cannot be articulated with postmodernity's anchoredness in a history and presence of enslavism. It would require connecting both her critique of human (gendered) performativity and her more recent attention to the material as well as psychic vulnerability of human life to a much more radical break from Western white philosophy than her projects have allowed. My reading therefore provides an object lesson for the peculiar effects the opacity of enslavism works on an apparently abstract and, as Butler's theory demonstrates, radically progressive train of argumentation. Butler's anti-racism, even though she has not explicitly acknowledged any such genealogy, works in the tradition of white US abolitionism of publicly grieving racism's devastation, the very posture of which has screened white power's exclusive possession of the status as human by its terms of address. Those terms have been characterized by an unmarked, default human subject position which bends towards Black being's suffering in particular instances of distress: in the last decades of post-multicultural identity politics, race has become a fungible demarcation, a meta-signifier for Blackness, so that the enslavist abjection of Black being becomes attached to it as an adjectival property. Race as a term has allowed the configuration of Black being's nonhumanness in terms of a seemingly neutral descriptive of differentiality, given from an Archimedian point of view. For white radicals like Butler, it has prevented a critique of the white abjectorship, which keeps producing this abjection in the first place. Race, in *her* texts and in the trajectory of their reception, has become synonymous with Black matter, as Salih confirms: "Since Butler's discussions of race do not make sense outside the context of her other theorizations of matter, I will deal with interpellation, performativity, and citationality before returning to the 'matter of race' " (139). In *Bodies That Matter*, Butler looks at Nella Larsen's novella *Passing* under the sign of queering, and asks "how sexual regulation operates through the regulation of racial boundaries, and how racial distinctions operate to defend against certain socially endangering sexual transgressions. Larsen's novella offers a way to retheorize the symbolic as a racially articulated set of sexual norms, and to consider both the historicity of such norms, their sites of conflict and convergence, and the limits on their rearticulation" (*Bodies* 20). The genealogy of passing in miscegenation necessarily appears as the departure for her argument; she asks the question of race, even of whiteness but refuses to address its enslavist violence. She does see the miscegenation taboo as a white practice to secure white gender maintenance as well as a "ritual of racial purification" (167, 184). However, this remains tied to an ahistorical psychoanalytical scene of the human, either "masculine" or "feminine," as taking place not only through a heterosexualized symbolic with its taboo on homosexuality, but through a "complex set of racial injunctions which operate in part through the taboo on miscegenation" (167). However, this phrase remains voided of the history of breeding and sexualized violence which constituted the grounds of the hysterical miscegenation taboo in the first place—a trope that has successfully hidden and neutralized the sexual fungibility of Black life, its unhumanness altogether, for white economic, political, social, and cultural purposes. Moreover, her argument gets stuck in a telling performative contradiction: she claims to reach beyond the assumption that "sexual difference is white sexual difference and that whiteness is not a form of racial difference" (182), while in fact she repeats this kind of white feminist fallacy by turning to a Black object (Larsen's novella) in order to talk about the materiality and, to that purpose, about the matter/ing of race.

Butler calls the symbolic "a racial industry, indeed [it is] the reiterated practice of *racializing* interpellations" (*Bodies* 18). However, for the Black/slave, social death is not the *result* of specifically contestable human practices of being hailed or constituted, but the grounds of his or her nonbeing, and thus constitutes the Black/slave's very non-addressability, non-interpellatability. The Black/slave is not being nameable as a "non-normative subject" for whom "living outside the norm involves placing oneself at a risk of death—sometimes actual death, but more frequently the social death of delegitimation and non-recognition" (Salih 11), but white society has been structurally dependent on Black death as literal commodity. Black being is not rendered socially dead, or actually killed, because of specific practices of "living outside the norm," but its social and actual death has enabled both the life of that human norm and its contestation. Consequently, any absorption of the figure of the Black/slave under the term of race, regarding racialization as Black as a human life outside the norm, misses the point: that the problem of the persistence of anti-Blackness is not located in a particular human racial difference and the attendant hysteria to contain that difference, but in the structural abjection from such very difference. The problem of the Black prison population is not that they are racialized, as are, for example, so many Asian minorities in the United States; the problem for the fugitives from the continent of Africa being left to die in the Mediterranean as a result of the Schengen Agreement and the Frontex border system is not that they are different from white humans in terms of their race, but that they have only existed as the progeny of enslaveable and enslaved things, as fungible, expendable forms of sentient being, by way of their structural fixation to the enslavist history forced upon them.

Similarly problematic is Butler's meditation on "white guilt," which Butler strategically distances herself from in an excessive and unwarranted footnote dedicated to it: "For the question there is whether white guilt is itself the satisfaction of racist passion, whether the reliving of racism that white guilt constantly performs is not itself the very satisfaction of racism that white guilt ostensibly abhors." I read Butler's indirect discourse on guilt, which she sees as a kind of undignified and unproductive self-flagellation and "paralytic moralizing," and rejects as intellectually disempowering moralist political correctness that remains mired in racism, as a response to the haunting of enslavism (*Bodies* 277). Butler's aggressive distance from guilt, which in fact is targeted at a white self-shaming which might not be politically productive but is nevertheless an index of acknowledgment of racist and anti-Black violence, becomes a highly charged screening device to contain enslavism and one's present relation to it in the form of disavowal. The text creates a rapport with its readership that symptomatically maneuvers theory and its dissemination/reception beyond, and into a denial of, a political and epistemic clamor of Black anti-enslavist intervention—white guilt, in her perspective, seems to be a white phantasma, which has no causal relation to Black critical agency. This seems to stand in direct contrast to Butler's well-known public opposition to hate-speech and what has come to be called racialized violence and her expressly forward alliances with queer anti-racist activism. One wonders, therefore, what the terrain of such articulation in a footnote—marginal but highly visible, conspicuous because of its ostentatious relegation to subtext—means to safeguard, if not just a personal aloofness on Butler's part. The honor that needs to be defended is not that of an individual politically indifferent subject. Rather, Butler's forward defense is built around the maintenance of an impeccable philosophical authority, which refuses to surrender the intellectual purity of its argument. That authority insists on owning the judgment of where, when, and how to address issues in question against claims by a moralistic mob bent on indicting modernity's regime of installing white humanity over Black abjection—a process in which philosophy and the theory of gender both played a crucial part. The history of enslavism which has caused white guilt to emerge as an individual and social practice in need of discursive compensation, returns in her work in rhetorical moves that draw attention to theory's indebtedness to Enlightenment philosophy, and thus to its abjections. These rhetorical moves consist of quite a classical post-Enlightenment retroping of the human subject as (always already, potentially) enslaved, as subjected to bondage, and of thus referencing slavery to sustain one's own argument. The fungibility of the slave for theory, indeed, has operated in two mutually complimentary ways. Either the human uses the slave to signify a horizon of abhorrence the subject does not want to suffer, or the slave is used to signify an abjection against which the subject's agency becomes recognizable—in both cases, however, the enslavist subject remains hidden from view.

Antigone and Fungibility

With *Antigone's Claim*, Butler's exploration of queer kinship and resistance, this fungibility makes yet another appearance. In Sophocles's original version of Antigone's story which Chanter discusses in *Whose Antigone?* the following sentence gives away Antigone's specific relation to the polis from which she is going to be ostracized. Protesting against the charge made to her of treason, Antigone rebuts Creon insisting that: "[It] was a brother, not a slave" whom she buried illicitly. In countless translations of the original Greek text as well as in its various literary incarnations this original phrasing has disappeared; only Chanter's recent work on Antigone, with which I have been in close correspondence, has refocused this crucial sentence. Translations for the buried dead vary between "criminal" (*Schurken*), "thief," "stranger," and other negatively connoted terms for persons who, in the eye of the state, would be lesser, but still human beings. The original sentence means to represent Antigone's loyalty to her brother as acted out in the burial, which in turn grounds any possible reading of Antigone as the maker of shareable ethical human claim, even though she acts against the ruling powers that be. Depending on point of view, this claim has been connoted—admiringly or condescendingly—in different translations, literary versions, and critical readings with *making a demand*, with *desire*, with *will*, and with *self-entitlement*; it has remained, though, the crucial anchor for any judgment of Antigone's controversial deed. Readings, one could say, have turned on an evaluation of this claim not to have buried a slave, but a brother, even if that context has disappeared underground for later versions and only manifests itself upon more extensive study of the play's textual history. Her claim thus insists on loyalty exclusive to Polyneices, a brother, and only a brother, which entails the compulsion to act according to sanctified rules of human kinship which ground and mobilize such self-endangering decision; it enables Antigone's unrelenting commitment. Because of this ethical commitment she is willing to take full responsibility for her deed, thereby gaining her notorious heroic quality. She accepts death as a consequence but refuses to accept the verdict of her guiltiness. *Antigone* may be seen, in the most literal meaning of the term, as a generative text: in a Barthesian reading, écriture/ writing, which bears and brings about more writing; also in that reading a text that is its own open signifier, as well as a text which became its own myth, mobilized for all kinds of cultural, political, and social interests, as in the case of Butler's reading of Antigone as an emblematic figure for her purposes of discussing queer kinship. From Hegel's readings on through to contemporary feminist theoretical discussions by Irigaray, McRobbie, and Butler, among others, which all in their own ways have circulated back to Hegel's intervention, the critical focus has been on Antigone's rebelliousness, her ebullient endurance, and her self-denying persistence. I am interested in Butler's deployment of the by now iconic rhetorical figure of Antigone, which has recentered the literary-historical and the critical-textual figure in contemporary politico-ethical debates about feminism, queerness, and resistance. Like Chanter, I am reading Antigone's claim to have buried "a brother, not a slave," not as a marginal detail, as which it has gone missing from feminist consideration, but rather as an excess which militates against smooth feminist containment. This excessive detail implicates readers in a crucial void of silence, a silence Toni Morrison has emblematically termed a "glaring" absence. The absence here is one of the missing trace of and to enslavism as the Western subject's constitutional practice. Because Sophocles's original sentence, which does draw attention to the thing beyond the frame of kinship, is not rehearsed in Butler's reading, one is again challenged to a hermeneutics of tracing absent absence.

As is well known, Antigone as a premodern and postmodern icon has been seen as the incarnation of feminine amorality, has been cherished or refused as an enemy of the state, and has become a feminist role model or an embodiment of oedipal entanglements eroding Oedipus's system from within. In all those cases, however, she appears as a figure and as a figure of thought, whose desire and practice is positioned in pronounced antagonism to the symbolic order (patriarchy, the state, antique and feudal tyranny, the law of Oedipus—depending on the critic's very own positioning). Generations of readers have received her as the voluntarist rebel, who breaks, undermines, or betrays male hegemonies of power. Butler too, in a critique of Lacanian absoluteness of the symbolic's power, resuscitates Antigone's claim as a kind of philosophical metaphor for an urgent possibility of destabilization. Her text conjures up patterns of queer and mobile, elective kinship which has the potential power to challenge the reign of patriarchal heteronormativity. Which is to say, Butler turns to reinterpret the mythical Antigone's fidelity to her sibling not as an act, which is always already normalized and sanctioned with oedipal family structures, but as an agential practice of creative kinship. In this reading, "brother" has the potential, then, to reference a relation of solidarity, mutual care and attention, and filiation in which every human being can figure as brother to another human beyond the heteronormative strictures of patriarchal rule or biological family status. Implying thus, with Antigone's practice of anti-state kinship, a horizon of resistance beyond the female anti-patriarchal subject, stretching her compassion to address *human* subjectivity beyond gender, Butler's empowering project is to supplement the Enlightenment's reading of the subject with a twist. In her version, attention lies not on Antigone as the isolated figure desperately and monologically speaking and acting out against Creon's / the state's powerful verdict, but on Antigone in community who has become an incendiary agent in the creation of self-willed elective affinity, that is, of a collective subject, for which kinship is the performative iteration of resistance to patriarchal interpellation. The point of resistance here takes one back to the modern subject's practice of enslavism which, precisely, is being voided by the disassociative focus of Butler's frame. By disassociation I mean the severance, in Butler's reading, of the position Antigone takes towards the slave and thus toward the practice of enslavement, from her claim as Butler frames it. In the original Sophocles version, Antigone actually creates a causal connection between her act of solidarity and the fact that this act was addressed to family. The phrasing that it was "not a slave" that she buried means of course that she would not have shown her defiant honoring gesture towards a slave, since the slave was not part of human family and kinship relations. Or, alternately, she or another human agent might display compassion towards the slave, but doing so would lift that agent herself beyond and outside of recognizable claims to human kinship that Antigone forwards here as a ground of protest against Creon / the state. The enabling antagonism her claim opens between her agency and the state, the symbolic order and the power of patriarchy to name her a traitor and criminal, rests on her insistence on this human kinship which binds the brother and her into obliging filiality, of which and in which the thingified slave can have no part. She can speak back here, if we were to employ Hegelian terms, to the subject in power as an object resisting its very logic. But this is possible only because the position of structural distance from the abjected slave, beyond subject and object, guarantees Antigone's human perspective, and her access to human terms of address at all. If her brother has honor as a kinship member, if *he* is not a slave, then it follows *she too* has that honor, or can and does claim it in her passionate struggle against Creon's strategy to isolate and neutralize her. I am reading this as a rhetorical move, which Sophocles allowed his heroine, effecting a space for female articulation for acts of speaking back to patriarchal power by asserting their nonslaveness. By not letting herself be silenced and by speaking back to Creon, Antigone, in myth, survives her death, as it were, and lives in collective memory as a figure to prove Western humanity's ethical consequence, which entails dying for one's convictions. By creating a female figure who can issue that claim, the story of Antigone keeps insisting on both, on the female agent's challenge to the symbolic, which is grounded, however, in her human kinship, and on her being not a thing. As a human, the struggle is opened for participation in and of the polis, of civil society, of Western culture. It is opened, though, precisely by creating the unbridgeable abjective border between kinship and enslaved thingness, which has consequently mobilized Western feminism. Of course, feminist claims were not immediately successful. As Antigone's death has paradigmatically shown to generations of emphatic critics, they have only been won in parts, and not in equal measure globally; achieved gains and positions have been lost. My point here is that the ability to make those negotiable claims in the first place was created by rhetorically and materially positioning the female object-to-become-subject as a possible and virtual agent of enslavist abjection. Only if the resistant actor can own herself in a way that enables its own terms of address may a human subject status be achieved; the recognition of human kinship is the urgently indispensable prerequisite for any political, social, cultural interlocution with the patriarchal state. It is a brother, not a slave I buried says, in other words, that I am not the sister of a slave: look at me, listen to me, I can speak, because I am as human as you, and you have no right, only the power, to judge my act immoral, criminal, unnatural, or in other pejorative terms. Antigone's otherness to Creon, to the subject of state power, becomes a contestable site of struggle, whereas the slave—essentially fungible for this rhetorical maneuver—remains a thingified entity without human claim. The modern and postmodern line of gendered argument that is opened by this argument shifts the struggle of who belongs to the polis from the antagonism between the power of the self-possessed subject and the abject slave to a confrontation between patriarchal subject and resisting human object, both operating within the realm of humanness.

This motif reappears in Butler's reading of Antigone, even if in veiled and transposed form. The continuity I see resides in Butler's suppression of the enslavist frame of reference the Sophocles original created; she takes up the notion of filial closeness to bolster and advance her intervention in favor of queer kinship without acknowledging the enslavist trace of a subjectivity contingent on abjection of the slave, now buried in the many recollective rereadings of the Greek tragedy. Antigone's queer agency, then, is emptied of its historical legacy and becomes an iconic human signifier of unburdened, presentist political mobilization.

Not surprisingly, the underside of Butler's textual voiding is the fungibility of states of Blackness rhetorically used for referencing human terror, and the human threat of unbelonging, becoming unlegible, unnamed, and ungrievable—the analogy possible because of the absence of the human subject's enslavist history. Blackness, in Butler's meditations on Antigone, becomes but a reference horizon for her complex discussion of Antigone's paradigmatic negotiations of "radical kinship" (*Antigone's* 74), which Butler mobilizes to ruminate on the porous but violent borders of human communities. Engaging Agamben and Arendt, she asks, "How are we to understand this realm, what Hannah Arendt described as the 'shadowy realm,' which haunts the public sphere, which is precluded from the public constitution of the human, but which is human in an apparently catachrestic sense of that term?" (81). Seen from an anti-enslavist perspective, however, Black being does not stand in a catachrestic *relation* to the human, being a kind of improper sign for it, as the queer kinship structures Butler observes, but has been evacuated from that relation altogether. It is not (pace Agamben) that Black beings' "ontological status as legal subjects is suspended" (81). The use of "suspended" implies a kind of prior, dysfunctionalized claim. However, thinking ontologically, the status of thingness for the Black post-slave social death was not, as Butler interprets Orlando Patterson, a *deprivation* "of all rights that are supposed to be accorded to any and all living human beings" (73), but a state of sentience a priori outside, categorically split off from the human's trajectory. For the slave, as fungible thing on one side, and for deprived human being on the other side, there is no ontological joint plane; neither in the Greek polis, nor in New

World enslavement and its afterlife, could an easy line be drawn around the "slaves, women and children, all those who were not property-holding males" and were thus "not permitted into the public sphere in which the human was constituted through its linguistic deeds" (82). While of course women and children were not "property-holding," in the case of women, at least in their majority they were part of the *oikos* as legitimate kin, and thus had a claim to it (however patriarchally structured), and, in the case of children, they could be heirs, so that they emerged as born to a legacy of public sociability, freedom, and citizenship. I thus disagree with Butler's argument that Antigone "is not of the human but speaks in its language" (82), catachrestically tied to it, as it were. For me the point is, precisely, that Antigone entered negotiation with the state—even though she lost her life to it—as human kin, antagonizing herself and her claim from slaveness. In this respect, Butler's analogical employment of Carol Stack's investigation of African American extended family networks and Patterson's notion of "social death" repeats Black metaphorical fungibility as a "for instance," its signifying potential to enable thought *about the human*; she wants her reader to "[c]onsider, for instance," the white racism mobilized against the assumed dysfunctionality of African American families, that "of course" dates back to slavery, about which "Orlando Patterson's book *Slavery and Social Death* makes the significant point that one of the institutions that slavery annihilated for African-Americans was kinship" (73). In my view, it is crucial to read the "for instance" literally, as well as to register the shift in Butler's terms of address from a disembodied theoretical first person plural she has been using throughout to a direct interpellation of the reader, a special effect indicating both a plea to register the particular drama of Blackness enacted in this feminist ur-scene and, at the same time, an invitation to disengage from a possible purposeful interest in Black life forms by way of making it an example for something else.

At the point where Butler's text needs the most drastic metaphor available, to characterize the political and social threat of abjection, she takes recourse to Orlando Patterson's concept of social death, without, however, any acknowledgment of the specificity of this term to describe the Black state of unhuman thingness, and not to generalize predicaments of suffering human subjects. Taking on the term for its usefulness to represent the most dramatic horizon of the modern human's fear—not to be a subject—supports anti-Blackness in the present tense. It doubly overwrites Black existence: first, by dis-acknowledging that social death is that very practice that white modern societies and subjects have caused for the slave and its progeny and thus claiming that suffering for the white human; and, second, by implicating Blackness—via quoting Patterson—in this maneuver, without showing any interest at all in Black social death and its cause in white subjectivity's existence at the cost of Black nonbeing. The voiding of enslavism from the subject's purview thus also voids Blackness of potential vulnerability—something to be conceived, logically, only in the purview of human suffering—it pushes Black life forms back into the nothingness inherited from the slave.

Butler, on the contrary, indulges an old white feminist dream, according to which "slaves," "poor people," "women," and "children"—that is, all persons except property-holding white adult males—have been conceptualized as equal in the sense of having been excluded from political, social, and cultural power. This kind of connection by exclusion would then form the materialist base for a vision of alternative alliances, or, in Butler's work, a kind of future kinship across human divisions. This queered kinship, for which she mobilizes Antigone as programmatic icon, makes visible to her "the occasion for a new field of the human" (82). A new field of the human, however, historically speaking, has not opened a space of human life for the (post-)slave. What Butler discusses as Antigone's queer desire is being mobilized against Antigone's powerlessness caused by her gender; it becomes the lever for utopian change, over and against gendered patriarchal interpellation. This displacement of gender, however, works only in the sense that Butler critiques the symbolic fixation of human desire under the law of Oedipus. The question of who is and who is not structurally entitled even to a resistance against patriarchal formations of desire, and the role that Antigone's aggressive abjection of the slave plays in the very constitution of both power and its possible contestation, remains mute.

Subjectivation

Butler's discussion of subjectivation, in my reading, creates a similar problematic. Subjectivation, according to the *Psychic Life of Power*, involves an articulation of the human subject with power that reads it as doubly subjected: as an effect of power and as an agent of its own empowerment—both definitively contoured by and against interpellation from either the state or larger and more amorphous discourses and practices in which the subject is materialized. The concern, that is, is with the subject and its potentiality, or the abortion of that potentiality. Butler writes:

> According to the formulation of subjection as both the subordination and becoming of the subject, power is, as subordination, a

set of conditions that precedes the subject, effecting and subor-
dinating the subject from the outside. This formulation falters,
however, when we consider that there is no subject prior to this
effect. Power not only *acts on* a subject but, in a transitive sense,
enacts the subject into being. As a condition, power precedes the
subject. Power loses its appearance of priority, however, when
it is wielded by the subject, a situation that gives rise to the
reverse perspective that power is the effect of the subject, and
that power is what subjects effect. (*Psychic* 13)

The power of the subject, then, operates within the register of human resistance
and opposition, even though Butler would reject a naive optimism of the
"classical liberal-humanist formulation": "Where conditions of subordination
make possible the assumption of power, the power assumed remains tied
to those conditions, but in an ambivalent way; in fact, the power assumed
may at once retain and resists that subordination" (13). "May" is the crucial
word here, because Butler is most interested in discussing the ambivalence
of subjectivation as the "condition of possibility for a radically conditioned
form of agency" (14–15). She goes on:

The subject might yet be thought of as deriving its agency from
precisely the power it opposes, as awkward and embarrassing
as such a formulation might be. . . . To claim that the subject
exceeds either/or [of pure agency or subordination] is not to claim
that it lives in some free zone of its own making. Exceeding is
not escaping. . . . [T]he subject cannot quell the ambivalence
by which it is constituted. Painful, dynamic, and promising,
this vacillation between the already-there and the yet-to-come
is a crossroads that rejoins every step by which it is traversed, a
reiterated ambivalence at the heart of agency. (18)

Again, note her term of address by which the possibilities of the subject are
supposed to be always already "promising," if painful and conflicted. Butler's
interest in subjectivation is motivated by a compassion for the subject and
its progressive agency:

A critical evaluation of subject formation may well offer a better
comprehension of the double binds to which our emancipatory
efforts occasionally lead. . . . Is there a way to affirm complicity
as the basis of political agency, yet insist that political agency

may do more than reiterate the conditions of subordination. If, as Althusser implies, becoming a subject requires a kind of mastery indistinguishable from submission, are there perhaps political and psychic consequences to be wrought from such founding ambivalence? (30)

The text invites its readers into an empathy with the subject's condition of being interpellated into a rendering of self to power that is at the same time the entry into its potential resistance to power. It goes on to discuss the inevitably "regulatory formations" (18) on the subject's psychic life by reading Hegel and Nietzsche, Althusser, Agamben, and Freud as her philosophical and psychoanalytical interlocutors. Her excessively metaphorical employment of Hegel's master-slave narrative, and her positive discussion of Nietzsche's notion of the trace of "freedom" in the "shackling" of the self, the "productivity of punishment," as the "site for the freedom and the pleasure of the will" (75) refers my readers back to my anti-Hegelian and anti-Nietzschean interrogations, and it also conjures up Benjamin's take on the conflation of masochism and desire. Any citation of "shackling" in the American context cannot but function as a—however symbolically employed and disavowed—reference to enslavement. However, to make the state of being "shackled" into a site of ambivalence, and into a ground for agential subjectivity, for one, misdirects any possible cognition of slavery by connecting it to contingent "punishment" and not to white ownership and abjection. Moreover, its very rhetoric of assigning to the "shackled" being the psychic oscillation between freedom/desire and suffering as a site of subject production appears to me as a cynical maneuver: the thingified Black sentient being had, as a piece of property, precisely, no such means at all to experience, let alone act within such subjectivation. The semantics here, then, betray a human interlocutory position and interest, for which alone "shackling" can figure in its fungibility as a site of affordance of futurity.

Butler's notion of subjectivation, which passes as generalizable, universalist theory, cannot address the Black/slave's thingified state of being. The machinations of power and subjection that Butler so amply dissects, cannot address enslavist operations of white power vis-à-vis the abjected. One needs to consider the way that power in Butler's conception always already awaits, accompanies, and follows the subject, as it were, as a given demanding but negotiable condition prior to, surrounding, and posterior to any subject's particular existence. This fullness and presence of power *for* the subject is precisely what the Black/slave cannot enjoy. In effect, this theory's raison d'être is narcissistic in that it does not have an answer to the question of how power produces a condition of being beyond the realm of its machinations, and which role, precisely, the human, by default white, subject has played in this production.

That a potentiality for the subject has been embedded, historically, in the subject's abjection of Black life forms, is a theoretical and ethical challenge for theory Butler's text evades. From the perspective of the abjected Black/slave, however, theory needs to develop a conception of subjectivation in the transitive sense—that is, of abjection—to begin reading the modern (white) subject as *abjector* and pursue the question, not of why and how has the subject been enmeshed in power to the detriment of its own agency, but of what has been the psychic life of power as enacted over unhumanized, abjected forms of being. Any cognitive theory of the human needs a theory of abjectorship to understand the interpellation of white Western individuals into white modern, as well as postmodern, power, and to abandon post-Enlightenment emphatic melancholy vis-à-vis the continuously reassumed struggles of the human subject against its own disempowerment, erosion, endangerment, and containment.

This issue of the subject's endangerment brings me to Butler's work on what she terms a differential human availability to precariousness, and the ensuing challenge of ungrievable life. On the face of it, and most readers have responded to this appreciatively, Butler's campaign for a more encompassing and more humane distribution of grief propels otherwise precarized forms of living and dying that have been made vulnerable to state and media and other violence, to social visibility and mournability. Emphatically put forward as a political strategy, this becomes a prerequisite and a steppingstone to struggles for more democratic and anti-militaristic forms of conviviality, and to a less brutally differentiated distribution of recognition within and across global space. Of course, this stands as a laudable project against twenty-first-century rampant war-mongering, militant ultraconservatism and fascism, and reactionary state control of nationalist, xenophobic, homophobic, and class-based hysteria. I do want to take issue, though, with the terms of address Butler, as the subject of speech, installs in her argument about and against precariousness. Her appeal for and to a never precisely named collective "we" to turn "our empathy" towards those that "deserve shelter," to live consciously in the "face" of the Other in Levinas's sense, even if it is another that "we" have not chosen for interaction, still argues within a benevolent framework of "bending" one's sympathy towards lives considered "more available to precariousness." Grief here becomes, interestingly, the quintessential and quite theological ersatz signifier for solidarity, which might deserve more discussion because solidarity as a term might much better be able to address relations among the living. It is striking to note how few of Butler's critics have stopped to interrogate that melancholic shift from an erstwhile leftist civil rights vocabulary of solidarity to grief. Grief, of course, remains semantically reserved for human emotional and mental states of post factum response to the wound, the kill, it addresses the victim after devastation. Grief for the other's suffering, that is, presupposes the spectacle of violence to have happened, and to happen in the future. While I do not, of course, want to argue against the urgency of bearing witness, I do wonder if the exclusivity with which grief has been endowed in the discourses of precarious and vulnerable lives, has not in fact worked to preclude and screen another just as urgent debate: that of living struggles to end a world of ongoing violence.

My interest here, thus, is with the gist of bending towards in grief: it seems doubtful to me, whether the ethical impulse of grief will be able to create the transformative politics Butler time and again envisages, with respect to, for example, the prison-industrial complex and its criminal waste of Black men's lives—a trope that reappears throughout all the recent interviews she has given on the matter of precariousness. Again, I see this as Butler's rhetorical partaking of the abjected Black/slave's suffering without, however, assuming or even preparing for a possible politics of Fanonian unreconciliation from the side of the abjected. She writes:

> There is no making of oneself (*poiesis*) outside of a mode of subjectivation (*assujettisement*) and, hence, no self-making outside of the norms that orchestrate the possible forms that a subject may take. The practice of critique then exposes the limits of the historical scheme of things, the epistemological and ontological horizon within which subjects come to be at all. To make oneself in such a way that one exposes those limits is precisely to engage in an aesthetics of the self that maintains a critical relation to existing norms. (Butler, *Giving* 17)

The crucial point to make here is that, again, whereas Butler envisions a "horizon *within which*" human subjects exist as such, Black life as social death has structurally excluded them from that very horizon; from an anti-enslavist point of view, there is no "within" of human horizon that might enable Black subjectivity as human subjectivity.

The Human Frame

Butler argues that only a change in the frame of the subject, at the farthest imaginable borderline of our known epistemologies, contains the ethical chance for becoming human. However, not only does she disregard the hundreds of years of epistemic Black interventions to interrogate the "frame of the human," which positions her argument as belated, and not, as she claims, as a pointer towards a yet to be reached horizon. She also reinstalls the power of change with the "I," with the human subject and its potential to create a more encompassing intelligibility of differential but equally respectable, mournable forms of life (see also "Agencies," about the limits of human intelligibility). By the very frame of this argument, the latent possibility of human life itself being destroyed from its abjected beyond is again denied. That gesture of the (by default) white subject's assumption to be the guarantee for change, does indeed repeat a structural motif in New World history, reaching all the way back to white abolition. Looking at Butler's move towards vulnerability, a critique seems even more pressing *because of* Butler's efforts to go beyond the difference between masculine and feminine, and instead to reformulate the question around the idea of the human.

Attending to *vulnerability* as a concept returns us to the body and its markedness, its demarcation, by the performative categories, which differentialize the subject—at the center of Butler's ruminations on the precariousness of human life. For Butler, "the body before the mark is constituted as signifiable only through the mark," and thus there can be no body as such prior to the phallic assumption of difference (*Bodies* 98). However, this claim is only applicable to those bodies that, by virtue of being human, historically have been made available to the mark. As Brian Carr argues:

> Though it may well be the case that a categorical loss is exacted at the expense of sexed human subject formation, it is also true that, historically, the mechanics of subject formation do not work to elide so easily all livable persons with the category of the bourgeois sexually differentiated human. We must be more nuanced here about the conditions of livability: exclusion from the scene of subjecthood is not always on the order of death proper. (126)

Following Butler's postpsychoanalytical argument, there can be no subject without a body; the subject only may be one in a marked body, so that the mark—of gender, of sexuality, of racial ascription—is at the same time a constraint and an enabler of contestation. By way of introducing her influential concept of vulnerability as a challenge to compassion, witnessing, and compensation, Butler has extended bodily demarcation of the subject to the acutely political markings of bodies, over and beyond her analyses of demarcations, like gender, in the realm of the interpellative symbolic order. Vulnerability, that is, cannot be thought of without a historically, politically situated physicality, and thus woundability of specific bodies. That very woundability of body, though, is always already conditional on some prior untouched shape of a human body, any human body, unviolated by specifically targeted acts to its integrity. The integrity, and a shared human acceptance of its ethical command, is what affords vulnerability. My point, then, is to interrogate the concept of the mark, of demarcation by vulnerability, and bring it in line with modernity's prerequisite for untouchable humanness: (self-)possession. Both desire and the relation to the law, as well as any existing guarantees modern humans have given each other of their principal inviolatability, have been conditioned on that ineluctably prior mark of owning the non-transgressable boundary of a legally and ethically free body (even though the degrees of this freedom from transgression have been certainly differential, and a permanent object of controversy). The human subject, that is, could only acquire its specific materiality, its physicality, and its human right to live an unviolated life in and by being marked as a body in the first place. No subject, in other words, no differentiated human life under the conditions of post-Enlightenment modernity is thinkable without the body's mark as the procurer of inviolatability of one. This entails, crucially that both a human semiotic productivity as well as a violation of the human may be registered as such on the condition of one's embodiedness, even though what post-Enlightenment human societies diachronically and synchronically have registered as either productivity or violation has varied widely. The very fact that there can and has always been ethical and theoretical controversy, however, attests to the persistent and overarching hold of the body's urgency to the human, and to material and social claims to kinship accruing from and to its existence in philosophical ruminations as well as in material life.

This returns us full circle to Hortense Spillers's argument about making a vital distinction between the human body and Black flesh. It seems to me a theoretical incongruity on Butler's part—owed to her posthumanist framework of address—to employ the concept of "social death," on the one hand, and, on the other hand, to evade, or ignore Spillers's crucial theoretical insight. Heeding Spillers's argument would require a shift in Butler's argument in two ways. For one, queer kinship or human grief against vulnerability cannot be envisionable across the divide of "body" from "flesh"; the way it stands, an appeal to queer bodies, as well as an appeal to human vulnerability as such reinstalls the default power of the body to signify humanness—a signification practice in which Black flesh goes missing as semiotic agent, because it, as Spillers argued, adheres to no symbolic integrity. In fact, attending to the theoretical challenge of Black flesh—an epistemic position as philosophically impossible as it is critically urgent—would result in the collapse of kinship, even queer kinship, as a viable concept for political and social struggle. The postanthropological notion of kinship itself, based on productive and reproductive exchange relations of and between human bodies, evacuates the thingified matter of Black flesh from possibly mutual agential interaction in that it, as nonkin matter, does not exist as interlocutor. That this is not an idle speculation becomes visible even in the very textual practice of using Black knowledge as matter, which becomes quotable without commanding embodiedness, either as nameless "Black feminists" or made to signify as fungible metaphor. Moreover, responding to the demands of Black flesh, would thus interrogate gender studies' theoretical operations based on woman's body. At the very least, those needed to be seen as a specific form of repeating rhetorical agnotology of (post)humanist philosophy for which the universal position of the individual human body's sanctity, even when it has come to be understood as an effect of signification and as constituted in the performative practice of gender, as in Butler's work, has served to screen the fungibility of thingified Black flesh.

In fact, Butler's concept of performativity itself, which has mobilized so much critical energy in anti-essentialist readings of gender practices and discourses allowing for gender to emerge as multiple and as reiterated in fluid sets of nonidentical, always already queerable human formations, needs to be bracketed as well. There seems to me to be a violent tension at work between the concept of performativity—after all, a realm of possibilities of human practice, however conflicted, precarious, and vulnerable—and the immobile, time-frozen status of Black thingness. Performativity, if we agree to be talking about the semiotic life of the human subject, always already signifies a mutability in the sense that doing, as Butler herself as called it, implies undoing, redoing, not doing, queer doing. Iteration, then, may result in cracks in the subject's interpellation; it effects futurity and becoming—which has enabled Butler to conceptualize queer kinship as anti-practice to the heteronormative subject of gender. However, the notion of performative iteration by its own logic ignores the deathness of Black social death, in that it ignores the thingness of Black thingified being. Performativity of the thing, as I see it, is by the logic of thingness restricted to performing various services and functions as that thing, which does not make the thing come alive to iteration. The thing can only perform, and perform again, ad infinitum, its changing-same fungibility, various forms of which, depending on context, do not impact on its thingness, however. Gendered human subjectivity, thus, is never outside iteration; whereas Black thingified being is always beyond it, cut off from it. The thing, one could say, in the human subject's purview of things, instead of having the capability of doing, is being remade as such by the very performativity of inherent subjectivity, which refixes the boundary between the human and Blackness. Neither actively nor passively can the thing be a subject of/for interpellation; consequently, Butler's theoretical range delimits it. This is the point at which Butler's retake on the woman-as-slave analogy in the form of her employment of Patterson's social death as analogous metaphor, collapses: if the subject is by definition always already socially existent in the iteration of gender, it cannot be socially dead. In reverse, social death can never be a human social *practice*, fixing, as it does, a state of immutability. The performativity of gender is a signification of human life; which the Black thing has been abjected from.

Five

Post Gender, Post Human

Braidotti's Nietzschean Echoes of Anti-Blackness

The Posthuman concludes by considering the implications of these shifts for the institutional practice of the humanities. Braidotti outlines new forms of cosmopolitan neo-humanism that emerge from the spectrum of post-colonial and race studies, as well as gender analysis and environmentalism. The challenge of the posthuman condition consists in seizing the opportunities for new social bonding and community building, while pursuing sustainability and empowerment.

—"Rosi Braidotti," *Wikipedia*

Reading Braidotti, thinking Deleuze. From where can Black articulation take place, if thinking is structurally, in white philosophy, the name of the human? If philosophy occurs as a scream from within the cage that life can conditionally become, like a particular force of constriction, where then is the Black enslaved thing that is not *in* human life, as a thing, thus, no conatus of it to be made a decipherable practice for, vis-à-vis, in the life of the human. From where does the packaged item on the ship, the dead mass on the ocean floor, the sentient thing on the plantation articulate its being if the basic, to be human life, is not given. The "slave" is not a human in a cage. The "slave" is a shippable, fungible thing outside that orbit where freedom/conatus struggles with conditional en-cagement so that human philosophy can exist. The "slave" is the outside of the cage, that horror which looms beyond the human, that which gives the human the strength to resist the cage, to think. To be human is to be raised to know in oneself that one's conatus will not bear the cage becoming perennial. The "slave" is what

177

makes human philosophy, not the cage. "It" makes human philosophy but only on the condition that its "slaveness" remains a given. This condition of "slaveness" was not changed with abolition, and so-called emancipation. The afterlife of enslavement in modern and postmodern human sociability is the life form of post-enslavement Blackness. So much for me and Deleuze.

—Sabine Broeck, "Towards a Practice of Annotation"

What does Black abjection mean in and for the posthumanist approaches to the contemporary moment? Has Black life now become dispensable in a redoubled way? Because the Black/slave has been structurally abjected from humanity as we know it, it has not been incorporated into humanism's range of concerns. In the critical momentum of the late Anthropocene, then, dedicated, as in Rosi Braidotti's work, to a determined abandon of humanism's tenets—which means, to an abandon of the modern and even the postmodern subject as the embodiment of humanism's meaning and power—has Blackness lost its previous fungibility as a guarantor of that fullness of human subjectivity? If the human subject is no longer the telos of critical thinking, would its demise enable the extension of posthuman, post-Anthropocene conviviality of all modes of speciesness, including life forms hitherto abjected as Black? I argue instead that Rosi Braidotti's work, eminent and vocal in its call for posthumanism, returns readers to anti-Blackness. Her latest book, *The Posthuman*, relegates Black knowledge to a social, political, and cultural immobility and pastness only to be transcended by posthumanist vitalism.

I return to the *Wikipedia* quotation in my epigraph for this chapter. *Wikipedia* is being quoted here, again, because its assemblages of knowledge represent to me the currently sayable—reaching from vernacular to academic epistemic repertoires, much as in a mirror to our present moment. What first struck me about this passage is that a familiar structure of fungibility is written into this anonymous concise summary of Braidotti's work, which actually reiterates the function Black knowledge has always had for Braidotti's texts. In her much celebrated, widely translated and critically productive textual trajectory, Braidotti has indeed argued for "new forms of cosmopolitan neo-humanism that emerge from the spectrum of post-colonial and race studies" (see the recent edited collection by Braidotti and Gilroy). The apparent innocence of this sentence's syntax, though, screens the anti-Black teleological violence on which Braidotti's enthusiastically utopian vision of posthumanism relies. To begin with, the wiki-formulation "Braidotti outlines" assigns white ownership, a human name, to the qualities of oversight, circumspection, erudition, and vision indispensable for the human practice of "outlining." "New forms"—that is, the future of thinking as embedded in her outline—here "emerge from"—that is, they can exist because something else was there before the new which is now no longer valid or necessary in any paradigmatic sense. This something else of Braidotti's before, who with the word "emerge" also owns the flow of thinking in sequential time, is separated from her present. The "from" is left behind, appears as a generically unnamable "spectrum" of "studies" in a vague plural, denoting the absence of particular identifiable owner- or originatorship. The vagueness, then, of "postcolonial and race" enables these two swiftly conjoined terms to function as a useful lump-signifier for fungible Black and indigenous knowledges, however filtered through the white academic industry of "studies." This syntax becomes the grounds for both Braidotti's theoretical emergence and her widely positive academic reception. This syntactic and semantic recapitulation may appear pedestrian to some readers; to me, it serves as a condensed allegorical take-off for my critical view of Braidotti's work.

In the years since the publication of her first book, *Patterns of Dissonance*, Braidotti has emerged—with a consistent series of publications, public appearances, an outstanding web presence, proactive feminist networking, and, not least, her directorship of the widely acclaimed Center for the Humanities at Utrecht University—as one of the most visible, outspoken, and programmatic voices of gender studies, post-Marxist, and post-poststructuralist intellectuals in Europe. There are a great number of appraisals of her work online that have all commented on her sustained success in addressing a broad variety of pressing issues of the post-1989 and also post-9/11 global moment of necropolitical, meta-surveillanced, digitized, and biotechnologized forms of species life. These issues include contemporary feminism's mainstreaming in Europe, the chances and pitfalls of multiculturalism, the challenge not to see gender in simplistic binary terms, the widening of feminist notions of agency to include a politics of location that could address European women's non-homogeneous identities, standpoints, and trajectories. She has earned interdisciplinary reputation beyond gender studies for her critique of humanism, including Marxism, for her arguments with poststructuralist emphasis on language, representation, and performativity, and for her theoretical endeavors to transcend what she considers—post-Deleuze—to be the false negativity of contemporary arrays of critical theory, including Butlerian or Agambian modes of philosophy of vulnerability, precariousness, and the crisis of bare life; all summed up in her suggestions of thinking through a politics of nomadic embodied becoming, with a dedication to the vitalism of matter as her own brand of posthuman zoé.

Braidotti's work figures in the discourses of gender I have been addressing because she belongs to the group of white gender theorists (e.g., Butler;
see also Hemmings; Dietze) responding to the political, social, and cultural
challenges to gender studies caused by the combination of its neutralization
by gender-mainstreaming state politics with accelerating rabid brutaliza-
tion of global capitalism. In a series of conferences at Utrecht University
and in workshops all over Europe, she has schooled a growing number of
younger feminists in a critical epistemology that has not forsaken gender
analysis but has placed it instead into an intricate web of intersectionally
composed philosophical bricolage that, so Braidotti is convinced, will be
the only response to adequately struggle within and against the onslaught
of globally megacapitalized economies and militarized apparatuses that have
recently begun, in her argument, to destruct all planetary forms of life. To
her, there is no single philosophical or theoretical narrative that could deliver
a sustainable framework for addressing the conditions of human life in the
twenty-first century: "Synchronization is the key to consciousness-raising
in so far as consciousness is the ability to self-represent and narrate one's
relationship to the variables that structure one's location in the social space:
woman, adult, white, human, lesbian, healthy, urbanized, English-speaking"
(*Transpositions* 94). Only from those intersectionally determined locations,
she maintains, will life-affirming alliances of resistance against phallogocentric
dominance and control of the planet be possible.

Situated at the crossroads of interlocutions between the New Left,
post-(Enlightenment) continental philosophy, white gender studies, poststructuralism, and, particularly in her latest pronunciations of vitalist nomadism,
Deleuzian thinking, her work has suggested what she has repeatedly called
the politics of life itself (see "Powers"). Inspired by Deleuze's reading of
Spinoza, her predilection for affirmation ascribes far-reaching *potentia* of
post-species conatus to stem the tide of resignation before the contemporary
global neoliberal onslaught of disembodied technologies, surveillance, war
machines, and megacapitalized human subjectivities. In that sense, her work
of bridging and connecting feminist studies, cultural studies, postcolonial
studies, age studies, trauma studies, technology studies, ecology studies,
security studies, and animal studies and species studies is obviously very
much "hip to the times," and an ongoing theoretical challenge to more
myopic, conservative, and staid factions of traditional white middle-class
feminism in Europe. As she argues in "Powers of Affirmation," "[i]n affirmative ethics, the harm you do to others is immediately reflected on the
harm you do to yourself, in terms of loss of *potentia*, positivity, capacity to
relate, and hence, freedom." In an "anti-thesis of the Kantian moral impera-

tive to avoid pain, or to view pain as an obstacle to moral behavior," her project urges to not let "negative passions" (post-Spinoza) negate "the power of Life itself, its *potentia* [*sic*] as the dynamic force, vital flows of connections and becoming." To her "negative passions are black holes," because "they do not merely destroy the self, but also harm the self's capacity to relate to others—both human and non-human others—and thus to grow in and through others," as effects of "arrest, blockage, and rigidification, which comes as a result of a blow, a shock, an act of violence, betrayal, a trauma or just intense boredom." Her version of affirmative ethics "is not about the avoidance of pain, but rather about transcending the resignation and passivity that ensue from being hurt, lost, and dispossessed. One has to become ethical, as opposed to applying moral rules and protocols as a form of self-protection: one has to endure." This capacity of endurance (she claims the word is a "Spinozist code" for the described process) is necessary, based, in her view, on a "vitalist notion of Life as zoé," to realize, in the double sense of the word "that the Life I inhabit is not mine, it does not bear my name—it is a generative force of becoming, of individuation and differentiation: a-personal, indifferent and generative" (all quotes, "Powers" 145). With much rhetorical fire, she suggests to "delink pain from suffering," which would be "not fatalism, and even less resignation, but rather a Nietzschean ethics of overturning the negative. Let us call it *amor fati*: we have to be worthy of what happens to us and rework it within an ethics of relation. Of course repugnant and unbearable events do happen. Ethics consists, however, in reworking these events in the direction of positive relations." Pushing the point even further, she claims that this suggestion does not entail "wilfullness, nor is it carelessness or lack of compassion, but rather a form of lucidity that acknowledges the meaninglessness of pain and the futility of compensation. It also re-asserts that then ethical instance is not that of retaliation and compensation, but it rather rests on active transformation of the negative" (145ff.).

For Braidotti, there is "nothing willful or voluntaristic about this—I think rather the very historical condition of advanced global capitalism make it imperative to raise these questions." She elaborates that "it is not a matter of choosing to stick to the old humanistic and anthropocentric ways of thinking, but rather of being historically propelled into a situation in which we need to think differently about who we are in the process of becoming." Her intervention, she claims, is to "provide detailed and reasoned cartographies of our present historical condition" (141). Time and again, in all of her conversations, lectures, and interviews, for example in "Powers of Affirmation," she has insisted on this point.

The term "cartography" here is crucial, because it announces a quite programmatic turn away from the history, the longue durée, of humanism, away from a thorough analysis, a "protocol," as Spillers phrased it, to read closely the enslavist constitution of the postmodern world of today. Braidotti is resolutely presentist, a lateral thinker, as it were, and massively invested in addressing the global capitalist world, its necropolitical violence, and its overwhelming technological, digitalized, speed as *new*. New, that is, in the sense of a qualitative rupture. Not that she does not know of colonialism, slavery, twentieth-century genocide, and the long histories of exploitation, war-making, and state oppression that have made the global as it is known to global historiography, postcolonial studies, transnational feminism, and other worldly actors today. However, this history of "Man's" white enslavist power, as Sylvia Wynter has analyzed it, does not interest her but as a repertoire of "aspects" that function in her texts in rhetorical nods to other thinkers she has interacted with. Beyond the frame of white European philosophy these are mainly Paul Gilroy and Gayatri Spivak, as well as Edward Said, whose perspectives she engages as indexical markers for her gestures to claim a space for vitalism beyond white Western philosophy. To see the constitution of the Westernized, globalized, supercapitalized planet of today in any way connected to practices and discourses of the longue durée of enslavism does not figure as an urgency in Braidotti's texts. Though she does list racism, sexism, colonial oppression, and the Shoah as sites of engagement for vitalist critique, these "aspects" function, bungled together in an offhanded line with ageism, biotechnology, excessive media power, and other social wrongs but as facile buzzwords in her texts. Thus, claiming a "humble and sincere accountability for historical *aspects* [italics mine] of European culture," she situates "colonialism and fascism . . . in open contradiction with Europe's stated beliefs in humanist ideals and rational principles" (*Transpositions* 29)—a phrasing which in its reliance on the term "contradiction" announces her affinity with the humanism she purports to deconstruct.

How does Braidotti's turn to the posthuman feed off of the human subject's longstanding panic at being rendered the target and not the enslavist executor of abjection, that panic of the subject's horror of various states of its own subjection, which has characterized post-Enlightenment critical thinking through modernity and postmodernity? For Braidotti, all forms of species life, including the human, need to be and may now be—given the state of hyper-technology, ultramobile virtual communication apparatuses, and recent posthumanist scientific research—rendered free of humanism's entropic dictates, which, instead of having realized the subject's full realization, have actually resulted in its eventual subjection to the life-threatening dynamics of late postmodern life, and now threaten the extinction of *all* species.

In this posthumanist configuration, the human subject becomes, precisely by way of its own world destructiveness, a victim of its own practices and discourses of species imperialism. In a stunning *Überbietung* of the Frankfurt School's critique of modern civilization, the subject's humanist rationality, in Braidotti's view, will have caused her own potential apocalyptic annihilation. Reading Braidotti, one hears a kind of post-poststructuralist refrain of Adorno's uptake of *Der Schlaf der Vernunft gebiert Ungeheuer* in *Dialektik der Aufklärung* (see Broeck, "Das Subjekt"). The *Dialektik* oscillated: Was it that because rationality was incapacitated by sleep that monsters were born, or was it that rationality, even in its sleep, unleashed destruction? Similarly, for Braidotti, the humanist logos of man is unredeemable, but she has no qualms to endorse the "enduring legacy" of "the most valuable aspects of the humanistic tradition" (*Posthuman* 29):

> Across the political spectrum, Humanism has supported on the liberal side individualism, autonomy, responsibility and self-determination. . . . On the more radical front, it has promoted solidarity, community-bonding, social justice and principles of equality. Profoundly secular in orientation, Humanism promotes respect for science and culture, against the authority of holy texts and religious dogma. It also contains an adventurous element, a curiosity-driven yearning for discovery and a project-oriented approach that is extremely valuable in its pragmatism. These principles are so deeply entrenched in our habits of thought that it is difficult to leave them behind altogether. And why should we. . . . For me, it is impossible, both intellectually and ethically, to disengage the positive aspects of Humanism from their problematic counterparts: individualism breeds egotism and self-centeredness; self-determination can turn to arrogance and domination; and science is not free from its own dogmatic tendencies. . . . Posthumanism is the historical moment that marks the end of the opposition between Humanism and anti-humanism and traces a different discursive framework, looking more affirmatively for new alternatives. (*Posthuman* 30, 37)

Based on this trajectory, and against the encompassing terror of the late Anthropocene, Braidotti, in a post-Deleuzian and post-Spinozean move, wants to unleash the power of an embrace of capacious species love, of a programmatic departure from humanist telos and logos, in favor of drives, affects, synergies, and cross-species telepathy powered by zoé itself. Humanism needs to be post-ed in order to expand the urgent care of and for life on the planet into the cyborgian state of unison among all species, taking exuberant advantage of hyper-capitalism's technological mobilities and late Anthropocene's forms of life's unfetteredness:

> As far as I am concerned, the challenge of the posthuman condition consists in grabbing the opportunities offered by the decline of the unitary subject position upheld by Humanism, which has mutated in a number of complex directions. For instance: the cultural inter-mixity already available within our post-industrial ethno-scapes and the re-compositions of genders and sexualities sizzling under the apparently sedate image of equal opportunities, far from being indicators of a crisis, are productive events. They are the new starting points that bring into play untapped possibilities for bonding, community building and empowerment. Similarly, the current scientific revolution, led by contemporary bio-genetic, environmental, neural and other sciences, creates powerful alternatives to established practices and definitions of subjectivity. Instead of falling back on the sedimented habits of thought that the humanist past has institutionalized the posthuman predicament encourages us to undertake a leap forward into the complexities and paradoxes of our time. (54)

The proclamation of posthumanist abandon to species-crossing potentia can be successful and seductive as white progressive theory, because it aims to end any preoccupation with or hauntedness by humanism's history. In consequence, this also entails a repeat erasure of enslavism as humanism's constitutive force, an erasure itself complicit with the humanist master narratives Braidotti agonizes against. In fact, she invalidates any possible connections to the "postcolonial and race studies" her work professes to emerge from, to those activists, scholars, and intellectuals that have insistently witnessed to the haunting underside of modernity. That history but functions as a gloss to Braidotti's futuristic concerns, showing up either in references to a rather select number of postcolonial studies scholars, specifically Paul Gilroy, or in her reductive interpellations of colonialism, slavery, and genocide by way of listing those very terms. "Race" and "the colonial" in her perspective, are the remnants of a humanist repertoire of signifiers that deflect attention from envisioning the future of zoé. Consequently, this vision has led her to push for a "fundamental dislocation of anthropocentric premises about agency" ("Powers" 142) which could help realize a new ethical equation in which the "post-human, the inhuman and the non-human" become key players of post-postmodern conviviality on the planet which she sees as not only an urgent but a realizable goal. Thus she also transforms her own critique of gender, and her interim endorsement of the "nomad" as a kind of postgendered subject of postmodernity, into a full-blown vision of supraspecies life as a convivial force whose multifold and fleeting subjectivity is not anchored in fixed human identities (see also Braidotti, *Metamorphoses*).

This raises a theoretical challenge: If modern and postmodern subjectivity are to be displaced and, as it were, enthusiastically shoved on the dung heap of humanist teleology, what then happens to a critique of that subjectivity's history of human abjectorship? Accordingly, Braidotti's recent work, which has ventured beyond both "race" and "gender" as bygone humanist articulations of the modern reign of deadly polarized structural hegemonies, begs the question of how, while the posthuman abandonment of humanist signifiers may overcome limited configurations of human subjectivity, it absents the enslavist character of those configurations from further consideration:

> These dis-identifications [of gender and race struggles, and studies] occur along the axes of becoming-woman (sexualization) and becoming-other (racialization) and hence remain within the confines of anthropomorphism. Yet, a more radical shift is needed to break away from the latter and develop post-anthropocentric forms of identification. The unbearable lightness of being falls upon us as soon as we start running with zoé; non-human life itself. (*Posthuman* 168)

What remains for Braidotti is the mobility of a posthuman "life-force" (104) unhampered by any haunting of its own abjective practices, rid of any dysfunctional responsibility to the past, free to enact, grasp, enjoy the present and presence of cross-speciesness. Braidotti thus suggests what she names and elaborates as a politics of *affirmative vitalism*:

> The key notion in posthuman nomadic ethics is the transcendence of negativity. What this means concretely is that the conditions for renewed political and ethical agency cannot be drawn from the immediate context or the current state of the terrain. They

have to be generated affirmatively and creatively by efforts geared
to creating possible futures. . . . The stated criteria for this new
ethics include: non-profit; emphasis on the collective; acceptance
of relationality and of viral contaminations; concerted efforts at
experimenting with and actualizing potential or virtual options;
and a new link between theory and practice, including a central
role for creativity. (191)

Not wanting to bolster the subject of humanism any longer, even in its
critical poststructuralist incarnations, she calls for "posthuman subjectivity"
located in the "vital, self-organizing and yet non-naturalistic structure of living matter itself": "Life, simply by being life, expresses itself by actualizing
flows of energies, through codes of vital information across complex somatic,
cultural and technologically networked systems. This is why I defend the
idea of *amor fati* as a way of accepting vital processes and the expressive
intensity of a Life we share with multiple others, here and now" (190).

This determined *amor fati* in Braidotti's ("post"-)gender theory only gains
a kind of fragile and ambivalent distance to the acceleration of the current
hyper-capitalist production and reproduction modes of select and exclusive
groups of mobile and empowered global populations, and to the disposability
and extinction of Black life on a global scale, as Braidotti acknowledges in
passing. Braidotti's posthumanist project corresponds to globalized corporate
agendas for the constant mobilization of boundaryless, flexibly operative
transcultural elites: that is, to agendas which structurally exclude majority
populations. Braidotti is of course aware of this problematic, she describes
herself as riding "the wave of simultaneous fascination for the posthuman
condition as a crucial aspect of our historicity, but also of concern for its
aberrations, its abuses of power and the sustainability of some of its basic
premises" (4). However, she proposes posthumanist theory as an overdue
"tool to help us re-think the basic unit of reference for the human in the
bio-genetic age known as 'anthropocene,' the historical moment when the
Human has become a geological force capable of affecting all life on this
planet" (5). Posthumanism to her is an aspiration to affirm a constructive
type of pan-humanity "by working hard to free us from the provincialism
of the mind, the sectarianism of ideologies, the dishonesty of grandiose
posturing and the grip of fear" (11).

Braidotti's notion of affirmation indexes a human collectivity in the
present moment that is always already threatened by disfiguration but capable
of refiguration of life by way of vitalism: "Contemporary bio-political gov-
ernance includes therefore a hefty necropolitical dimension, which fuels a

political economy of negative passions in our social context. We live in a state of constant fear and in expectation of the imminent accident" ("Powers" 142). Affirmation is the charge to be mustered against pending disaster. This universalizing rhetoric of imminence needs to be answered by two points. First, there is, historically speaking, nothing recent about necropolitics, except the extension of those politics to groups of global populations who have hitherto been spared the onslaught of colonial, imperial, and neoliberal violence—in the sense that, as scholars like Ruth Gilmore, Zygmunt Bauman, and Rinaldo Walcott in different modalities have maintained, larger numbers of Western populations have come to live "wasted" and "disposable" lives under the conditions of post-neoliberal triage (see Hall et al.). Second, by speaking of "imminent accident," Braidotti's text obscures the factual history of social and actual death, which for the world's Black populations has not been "imminent" but an everyday reality. Her phrasing couches necropolitics in the present—a move that semantically and politically displaces the historical white abjectorship of Black being and the colonialist destruction of indigenous populations. The genocidal abortion of possibilities (see Césaire, *Discourse*), inappropriately mutates in Braidotti's argumentation into one "aspect" connoting one particular feature of a phenomenon, as opposed to its structure or fundamental character. In the same vein, she reads fascism as a moment of "collapse" of humanist ideals, which signifies ignorance or disconnect vis-à-vis the Black critical perspectives she aligns as points of her emergence.

Bondage and Vulnerability

> Affirmation is about freedom from the burden of negativity, it is about achieving freedom through the understanding of our bondage.
>
> —Rosi Braidotti, "Powers of Affirmation"

With claiming both the subject's bondage and its vulnerability as further key terms for her project, Braidotti, instead of creating a rupture with humanism, prolongs its trajectory of white solipsistic reflections on modernity and postmodernity. My purpose here is not to engage possible political arguments that take up the contingent vulnerability of specific groups of human populations, as in cases of massively exploited child labor, political prisoners, victims of excessive state or individual violence, factual bondage for humans such as sex-trafficked women, or prisoners of war. Instead, I am keen to unpack the epistemic metaphoricity of the term bondage, which, in my view, has fed a very particular white solipsistic mythology.

The human's assumed bondage, the always immanent threat to the human's becoming posed by states of bondage and, accordingly, by the scare of potential psychic, material, individual, and social vulnerability has been an extended topos in Western white philosophy from early Enlightenment onward into postmodernity. Its currency in critical thinking has quite recently and exponentially increased. With the acceleration and intensification of global climate related catastrophes, with the serialization and expansion of technologically militarized war zones, with the accumulation of finance capital scandals, with the proliferation of digital communication media that seem increasingly out of control, and, after 9/11, Madrid, London, and Paris 2015, and ongoing, with the acceleration of terrorist attacks on the public and private safety of Western populations, white Western awareness of the human's latent and constant fragility vis-à-vis human forces or man-made so-called natural disasters has dramatically expanded. That the Red Cross has an extensive agenda concerning human vulnerability on its public site (see under title "What Is Vulnerability?") speaks to a growing awareness on the part of global political actors that leads to acting on behalf of a fast growing number of vulnerable population constituencies under the impact of globally accelerated neoliberal capitalist and military ravages. However, the knowledge of an individual subject's dependency on self-created human sociability has always been the flipside of the secular Enlightenment trope of the human's self-owned *Mündigkeit*; no longer in the hands of God or feudal command, the Western subject discovered a fundamental vulnerability, a status that could be redeemed neither by faith nor by blind trust in given authority (see Wynter, "Unsettling").

This responsibility for one's own life by necessity entails the ability, empowerment, and right to be a legally and nominally free agent of one's destiny; it also entails a panic of unfreedom that might curtail the power and reach of that self-willed, voluntaristic agency. *Bondage*, in this scenario, either refers to those contingent threats to free humans that sum up, phenomenologically speaking, to a sensation of durable state of siege, or to restrictions of human life inflicted by social pressures and vagaries that threaten the subject's sovereignty, pressures which might include the subject's own vices and passions. Even though the Enlightenment's conviction of the human subject's sovereignty has come under erasure in twentieth-century philosophies, what has remained, and what has returned in recent years—for example, most explicitly in Levinas's, Agamben's, and Butler's highly ethically charged philosophical conception of vulnerability—is a shared notion of the universal *human life*, and in Braidotti's case of *all* life, as being potentially violatable and thus, in this potentiality, subject to and within strictures that hamper or even destroy its potential to maintain and reproduce itself without being submitted to injury or lethal force. However, from a point of view of Black abjection, the epistemic validity of the philosophical couple of vulnerability and bondage is thrown into sharp relief. Vulnerability, for Black life under conditions of enslavism, is not bound to specific contingencies (of varying degrees of intensity)—as, for example, to old-age abandonment, to being a soldier, to being forced to become a refugee, to finding oneself in a situation of ecological disaster, to losing one's job, to being sexually harassed, or to being submitted to restrictions or the denial of one's civil rights. The total availability of Black being, as I have already argued in a previous chapter, is a sine qua non for civil society's coherence, as Wilderson has argued most poignantly, which means that for individual and collective Black being to suffer vulnerability is not the effect of any specific cause, but the structural premise of that being's existence. As the more recent media coverage of anti-Black violence—sensationalist and racist as it was, more often than not—could have made obvious to worldwide white audiences, one can be killed with impunity for being Black. One can become a case of collateral or intended damage of all kinds of unprosecuted state policies of extinction, theft, mismanagement, and violence, because one is Black. Enslavism has created a long and ongoing durée of symbolic and factual general killability of Black being. The twin facts of enslavement and killability have constituted modern Black being; they have not been those particular disturbances of civil life for which the term has functioned in reckless white metaphor. Neither bondage nor vulnerability, thus, for Black being, are a rupture, denial, or theft of the subject's sovereignty, but the very condition of its existence. It follows from there that Braidotti's attention to violations of the human does not interpellate Black being because her argument rests on a sense of vulnerability and bondage that assumes its bearers or targets to be free humans and to be, on principle, able and entitled to exert sovereignty over their owned subjectivity and its boundaries. Vulnerability, that is, presupposes a state of civilly granted sanctity and wholeness, a state that *may be* wounded; bondage presupposes a state of unfetteredness that *may be* taken away. Neither of these qualities has marked Black life in the (after)life of enslavement.

A Leap through Pain: Slave Moralities, Recycled

Programmatically, vitalism establishes a counterpoint to the "fear" Braidotti sees as the dominant present sentiment on the New Left—a discourse which she sees as detrimental to any social resistance to necropolitics under neoliberal capitalism:

> In this global context, what used to be the high-energy political activism of the Left has been replaced by collective mourning and melancholia. A great deal, if not most, of contemporary social and political theory stresses vulnerability, precariousness and mortality. As far as I am concerned, our political sensibility has taken a forensic shift: the astounding success of Giorgio Agamben's "bare life" (1998) with its emphasis on destitution and genocidal destruction and the revival of interest in Carl Schmitt's homicidal politics of friends and foes are strong expressions of the contemporary obsession with political violence, wounds, pain and suffering. (Braidotti, "Powers" 142)

Braidotti assures her readers she is not suggesting "that the politics of mourning and the political economy of melancholia are intrinsically reactive or necessarily negative"—retreating somewhat from her claim a paragraph before. In a benevolently generous tone she concedes that she is "also convinced that melancholia expresses a form of loyalty through identification with the wound of others and hence that it promotes ecology of belonging by upholding the collective memory of trauma or pain" (142ff.).

However, she cautions readers not to fall into this conundrum of fear, melancholia, attachment to wounds, memory, trauma, and mourning—a chain of signifiers that her texts sets in motion quite nonchalantly—because it has "become so dominant in our culture that it ends up functioning like a self-fulfilling prophecy, which leaves very small margins for alternative approaches." To counteract this pull of what she perceives as a backwards-bound incapacitating "ecology" of sadness, she argues "for the need to experiment with other ethical relations as a way of producing an ethics of affirmation." For her, a philosophy and a politics of affirmation is the essential lever to work towards a posthuman future, to create a conviviality that accepts, pursues, and builds on continuous "becoming" of a variety of life forms, instead of on the domineering statics, and melancholia—in Braidotti's perception—of the (post-)Enlightenment human subject, as its motoring force:

> Becoming-posthuman consequently is a process of redefining one's sense of attachment and connection to a shared world, a territorial space: urban, social, psychic, ecological, planetary as

it may be. It expresses multiple ecologies of belonging, while it enacts the transformation of one's sensorial and perceptual co-ordinates, in order to acknowledge the collective nature and outward-bound direction of what we still call the self. This is in fact a moveable assemblage within a common life-space that the subject never masters nor possesses but merely inhabits, crosses, always in a community, a pack, a group or a cluster. For posthuman theory, the subject is a transversal entity, fully immersed in and immanent to as network of non-human (animal, vegetable, viral) relations. The *zoé*-centred embodied subject is shot through with relational linkages of the contaminating/viral kind which interconnect it to a variety of others, starting from the environmental or eco-others and include the technological apparatus. (*Posthuman* 193)

I see Braidotti's ruminations partake in the ongoing trajectory of post-Enlightenment conceptualization of self-empowering white voluntarism as liberated (post-)subjectivity. Braidotti mobilizes the legacy of a willed continuity between mid-seventeenth-century white male European (Spinoza) through late nineteenth-century (Nietzsche) to mid-twentieth-century (Deleuze) philosophy for what she sees as her postfeminist, transcultural, posthumanist, anti-racializing, and multiethnic project of affirmation:

> That which is incomprehensible for Lacan—following Hegel—is the virtual for Deleuze, following Spinoza, Bergson and Leibnitz [*sic*]. This produces a number of significant shifts: from negative to affirmative affects; from entropic to generative desire; from incomprehensible to virtual events to be actualized; from constitutive outside to a geometry of affects that require mutual actualization and synchronization; from a melancholy and split to an open-ended web-like subject; from the epistemological to the ontological turn in poststructuralist philosophy. (126)

Under the title "Affirmation versus Vulnerability: On Contemporary Ethical Debates," Braidotti published an article in 2006 that I want to read like a transitory piece. It marks a condensation of her former, more clearly feminist work circling around the metaphors of *dissonance* with the Cartesian canon, of *nomadic embodiment* as a theory of the overcoming of the subject's patriarchal fixation on sexual difference, and of *metamorphoses* to signify her "materialist theory of becoming." These metaphors have become compressed into the aggressive theoretical launch of a *posthuman* ethics of all life forms "beyond the self"—only including, among other forms, the human species. In this concept, some of the older metaphors are being contained, but they are superseded by a valorization of post-anthropocentric affirmation of what she names *zoé* as such, based on her affiliation with Spinoza's notion of conatus.

Her baseline is the assumption that "the charge of moral and cognitive relativism is moved against any project that shows a concerted effort at displacing or decentering the traditional, humanistic view of the moral subject." Accordingly, she argues forcefully against humanist liberal and leftist views of the subject according to which "without identities resting on firm grounds, basic elements of human decency, moral and political agency and ethical probity are threatened"—a "doxic consensus" against which she proposes a posthumanistic vision as an "alternative foundation for ethical and political subjectivity" (Braidotti, "Affirmation" 235). For a statement made in 2006, this seems to me a highly problematic opposition to construct. Arguably, it has just been the predatory success of postmillennium globalized post-neoliberal economies to absorb postmodernist skeptical advances on classical post-Cartesian humanism, the unitary subject, transparent realist notions of self and identity, and rational human agency, and to recapitalize postmodern energies of flow, fragmentation, and diffusion in the shape of a fully mediatized, digitalized, hyper-webbed, technologically overdetermined, seemingly flat and nonhierarchical consumerist culture, in which any identitarian hold on and of the phallic human subject has dramatically lost its power and allure. This observation is of course in no way original, and, in fact, and somewhat self-contradictorily, Braidotti refers at other points in her work to this latest state of postmillennium globalization by way of references to theorists like Donna Haraway.

At this junction, her call for theorizing a conviviality of "the posthuman" moment has become more pronounced and committed. The rise of fundamentalist movements, discourses, and institutional practices must in this context be seen, as Braidotti would agree, as a kind of massive rollback against white postmodernist advances, most manifest in attacks against public education, multiculturalism, sexual rights campaigns, any progress in ethnic integration, and similar Western gains in civility at the end of the twentieth century. In my view, these fundamentalisms are not, however, the manifest symptoms of a resurgence of classical (post-)Enlightenment humanism; quite to the contrary, they must be read as a violent and volatile counterattack against the democratic and civic gains of the civil rights movement generation in the 1960s, and as quite in keeping with a twenty-first-century neoliberal credo that thrives on social dissolution, particularization, the competitive commodification and medialization of whatever scandalizing "identity" can be marketed, and the glorification of anti-social violence. Fundamentalism, that is, is not post-neoliberalism's enemy but its best ally—as witnessed, for example, by the most recent dissolution of the European welfare state–based party spectrum, the resurgence of the radical right in Europe, and Donald Trump's presidency.

In this context, her conjecture of the contemporary moment as one in which the reign of the "traditional" humanist version of the "human" is being reinstated in the "forensic" morality of the left, and in the humanist remnants of postcolonialism and "race" studies becomes highly problematic. I agree that "the human" is still and again being centered in critical thought as the telos of prevailing philosophy and ethics, but not in the mode of an uncontested powerful classic revival. Rather it has come to figure as a thoroughly controversial term, having been embattled by poststructuralism, gender studies, postcolonialism, and Black critique for decades—whereas global neoliberal popular cultures, as well as reactionary fundamentalists, and post–welfare state institutions seem to have happily abandoned it. In face of this mainstream Western abandonment of Enlightenment's modern "human" in favor of prosthetic notions of cyber-agency, of digitally mobilized consumer units, and of sexually and ethnically—though not, importantly, racially—neutralized and mobilized participants in global capital traffic, one needs to ask who benefits from the growing gulf between entitled and empowered posthuman life forms, and what Bauman has called the wasted lives of the planet. It is crucial to keep in mind that this separation between *worthy* and *unworthy* lives (terms that German fascism brought to prominence in the 1930s), which white critical theory has of late discovered with some fanfare, has been constitutive of and characteristic for the modern world system since the conquest of the Americas and the early beginnings of enslavism. In response to Aimé Césaire's notorious intervention in his *Discourse*—where he muses about the "crocodile tears" of European intellectuals' mournful lament over the Shoah, not willing to realize the hundreds of years of aborted possibilities of Black life in the (post)colony—one can observe the rather recent accumulation of critical thought in address to "precarity," "vulnerability," "wastedness" of life, and similar conceptual metaphors at the precise moment when the social wreckage of late imperial and neocolonial capital policies hit white, or whitened, majority populations in the metropolises, who have hitherto been embedded in states of relative empowerment and comfort (see Hall et al.). Western urban spaces have seen and will see major struggles within those metropolitan areas as to whose existence will count for planetary capital flows, whose may be contained, at least contingently, in some kind of parasitical dependency on the mobile class, and whose is entirely unwanted, without function, without use. The US prison-industrial complex and its exportation to Europe by way of the growing accommodation of no-safety camp zones for African and other nonwhite refugees serves as one paradigm, the impact and aftermath of Hurricanes Katrina and Sandy and the so-called water crisis in Detroit (Broeck, "Inequality") are others. What these paradigmatic moments show is that struggle will have—contrary to the postracial mythologies that have dominated the last two decades—an aggressively racist/classist component. Thus, one finds oneself in a historical moment in which Black unhumanized life forms are not even left with the option to appeal and lay claims to the standards of the human; instead, the human being deserted as the defining category for post-neoliberal forms of sociability, without such appeal the dispensability of their very lives has become hyper-absolute, because their very physical lives have been threatened exponentially by a loss of economic fungibility for post-neoliberal capital. In keeping with Wynter, Walcott, and McKittrick, therefore, my point here is not to defend an Enlightenment notion of the human that was constituted in the first instance on the back of the abjected Black/slave, but to question Braidotti's logic of joining in a kind of eulogy to the posthuman at a point when in fact the range of life forms who count as human to begin with has become tightened on a global scale, and within metropolitan North America and Europe, and when Blackness as structurally abandoned life form has become the globally valid certifier for the structural unqualification for future states of worthy posthuman life. As Brian Carr argued almost twenty years ago:

> The obsession with the "post" of the human, while invoking a language of chronology, evacuates any kind of inquiry into the historicity of how the human is categorically accessed, who enters its circuits of symbolization and desire, and who is barred from it. Never able to engage the historicity of the human in its heterogeneity, the rhetoric of the posthuman and its specific rendering of antihumanism opts instead to envision the "post"-ing of the human from the vantage of the human subject, not from the position of the historically dehumanized. (Carr 120)

It is from this perspective that I read Braidotti's decision to privilege "affirmation" over and against "vulnerability." Her programmatic—rather than strengthening radically anti-capitalist thinking in defense of vulnerability, by way of leave-taking from what she considers to be a past-tense bound grief mired in, to her mind, humanism's negativity and antagonisms—supports also a desertion, an abjection of the bearers of grief: those states of Black being that have never even been bound into humanist dichotomies in the first place. Her vision of affirmation is only possible on the basis of her ardent presentism. She stakes life's conatus and her insistence on immanence against history's melancholia, which to me is a theoretical move hard to separate from both the current resolute hollywoodization of enslavist history as fragmented, fungible spectacle and the medial hyper-technologies of presentness.

Claiming an unabashedly "universalist aspiration," even though she envisions it as a politics of transformation embedded in "radical immanence," her project "takes as the point of reference bios-zoé power defined as the non-human, vitalistic, or post-anthropocentric dimension of subjectivity, . . . an affirmative project that stresses positivity and not mourning," and is being posited against a (post-)Kantian defense of morality; against Agamben's identification of the subjection "with its perishability, its propensity and vulnerability to death and extinction" (Braidotti, *Posthuman* 2–3) and against the "Levinas-Derrida tradition of ethics, which is centered on the relationship between the subject and Otherness in the mode of indebtedness, vulnerability and mourning." Her project, again, inspired by Spinoza and Nietzsche through Deleuze, looks at "life itself as a relentlessly generative force," which is characterized by "generation, vital forces and natality," motorized into an ethic momentum "in a set of interrelations with both human and inhuman forces," a project that "moves altogether beyond the postmodern critique of modernity and is especially opposed to the hegemony gained by linguistic mediation within postmodern theory" (237). This turn towards immanent "intensive" embodiment views the subject as "an assemblage of forces or flows, intensities, and passions that solidify in space and consolidate in time," as a "dynamic entity" stable enough "to sustain and undergo constant, though non-destructive, fluxes of transformation" and as one for which "joyful or positive passions and the transcendence of reactive affects are the desirable modes." Anticipating critique, her text alleges that this project does not deny "conflicts, tensions or even violent dis-agreements between different subjects" (238); however, in terms "of the ethics of conatus, in fact, the harm that you do to others is immediately reflected in the harm that you do to yourself, in form of loss of potentia, positivity, self-awareness and inner freedom." A constant circulation of affect enables "subjectivity" to appear as a momentary densification that is nevertheless a fluid construction, on principle, as a "mode of individuation within a common flow of zoé," so that "consequently there is no self-other distinction in the traditional mode, but variations of intensities, assemblages set by affinities and complex synchronizations." Any expectation of "mutual recognition" is replaced by an infinitude of "mutual specification and mutual-codependence," in which "your body will thus tell you if and when you have reached a threshold or limit" (239).

Most of Braidotti's postfeminist critics have responded to her proposals with approval, reading her as a philosopher capable of providing an alternative to the classical humanistic, the left, and the poststructuralist projects, all mired in their respective indifference and contempt vis-à-vis "embodiment, *mater*, and the flesh" (238). However, how can this "monistic ontology" (239) be deciphered from a perspective of Black abjection? How would the terms of Braidotti's project—conatus, the flow of zoé, vulnerability, affirmation, will, positivity instead of mourning—look from within the afterlife of slavery? Braidotti's revamped claim to a nomadic, embodied, vitalist universalism reads like a paradigmatic instance of white voluntarism. That claim is indebted, indeed, to a Nietzschean legacy of the philosophical primacy of *will*; even though she does not locate that will in a Cartesian subject's rational omnipotence and control, but in the relentlessness and desiring power of life's conatus, she nevertheless assumes a universalizing and equalizing existence of zoé as generative force, which has no space for the rememory of the fundamental split between human and unhumanized abjected Black existence, which was cast, thingified as it was, beyond bios *and* zoé.

In Braidotti's work, any insistence on a critique of modernity's history, of the past which is not even past, has become relegated to a lost and detrimental cause of mourning which impedes life's conatus, deters possible resistance, and reanchors itself in futile and reactionary humanism. For her, there is no perspective other than vitalist nomadism that could transcend humanist boundaries; at no point in her texts is there an acknowledgment of the consistent Black, anti-humanist epistemic and ontological critique of modernity and postmodernity, which, in its insistence to first pass through a protocol in Spillers's term of white abjectorship, upsets her voluntarism, which has turned out to be so attractive to large audiences over the last years. In fact, her insistent stress on positivity bespeaks a quite wistful theoretical solipsism, shores up an implicit form of anti-Black contempt, becoming visible in the nonchalance with which she calls upon her readers to consider zoé as an "inhuman force that stretches beyond life, to new, vitalist ways of approaching death as an impersonal event. The process ontology centered on life leads the posthuman subject to confront this position lucidly, without making concessions to either moral panic or melancholia." Negative passions, she exhorts, need to be transformed into positive passions (Braidotti, *Posthuman* 194).

Her dismissal of grief and mourning underwrites the myopic mode of her paradigmatic appeal to "become ethical, as opposed to applying moral rules and protocols as a form of self-protection." The vague exhortation to "become ethical" is negatively and rather flippantly defined in opposition to "morality" caricatured as a "form of life insurance" (*Nomadic* 322). In face of ongoing and escalating Black death and devastation, not only in the United States, but also in Europe and Africa, this instantiates a cynical aggression against earlier and contemporary modes of resistance which necessarily rely on demands for protection and compensation of loss. Closely reading the following, paradigmatic paragraph in full, unravels an articulate disdain for those modes of lament, grief, mourning, negativity, and pained abjection from and refusal of Western humanism's telos of futurity that have necessarily characterized Black life:

> The quantitative leap through pain, across the mournful landscapes of nostalgic yearning, is the gesture of active creation of affirmative ways of belonging. It is a fundamental reconfiguration of our way of being in the world, which acknowledges the pain of loss but moves further. This is the defining moment for the process of becoming ethical: the move across and beyond pain, loss, and negative passions. Taking suffering into account is the starting point; the real aim of the process, however, is the quest for ways of overcoming the stultifying effects of passivity, brought about by pain. The internal disarray, fracture, and pain are the conditions of possibility for ethical transformation. Clearly, this is an antithesis to the Kantian moral imperative to avoid pain or to view pain as the obstacle to moral behavior. Nomadic ethics is not about the avoidance of pain; rather it is about transcending the resignation and passivity that ensue from being hurt, lost or dispossessed. One has to become ethical, as opposed to applying moral rules and protocols as a form of self-protection. Transformations express the affirmative power of Life as the vitalism of bios-zoé, which is the opposite of morality as a form of life insurance. (*Nomadic* 322)

Given Braidotti's allegiance to Nietzsche via Deleuze, it is impossible to ignore a starkly Nietzschean subtext in this paragraph's last sentence. Her very use of the word "morality," which, given her philosophical erudition, must have been chosen proactively, recalls and relies on the intertextual impact of Nietzsche's indictment of "slave morality." Once on this track, the reader begins to perceive a subtle subtextual affinity to Nietzsche's proto-aristocratic contempt. In his diatribe against what he considered the slavishness and democratic decay of meek bourgeois nineteenth-century society, he also advocated for will, a strong affirmation of the power of the elites to rule life, and the immanence of *amor fati*—a phrase that Braidotti also uses approvingly. An attachment to past social woundedness and the political struggle to gain recognition and recompensation, in Braidotti's post-Nietzschean register appear as a nostalgic, counterproductive interference with the voluntaristic exhortation to "jump through pain." In the lingering pain, which, in her casting, "race studies" still and again see themselves bound and indebted to, she sees but a "political economy of melancholia" that deters from affirmation. The mode of "will" she projects is incarnated in the term "desire": "The idea of desire as plenitude and not as lack produces a more transformative and less negative approach to the nomadic relational subject than previously allowed, for instance by the split subject of psychoanalysis" (*Posthuman* 189). Her juxtaposition, then, of mourning, as a melancholic posture to overcome, and vitalism's "desire," as a sign of the future, fixes Black being, still and again, on the side of death, precisely because it remains attached to loss, fear, and want for compensation—all those terms echoing Nietzsche's "slave morality" of social blackmailing by way of meek suffering, superior morality, and weakness of character. In view of this juxtaposition, Black being cannot embody zoé's force. In a wild twist of primitivism, it is now no longer Black being, that stands, in its "animal energy" as the antipode to white rationality's entropy, but it is posthuman "life itself" and its conatus which will be the agent of an affirmative transformation of the planet's sustainable reproduction. *The Posthuman* thus ends on an almost aggressive note of affirmation, based on the hubris of a reuniversalizing "we":

> Are we going to be able to catch up with our posthuman selves, or shall we continue to linger in a theoretical and imaginative state of jet-lag in relation to our lived environment? This is not Huxley's *Brave New World*, that is to say a dystopian rendition of the worst modernist nightmares. Nor is it a trans-humanist delirium of transcendence from the corporeal frame of the contemporary human. This is a new situation we find ourselves in: the immanent here and now of a posthuman planet. It is one of the possible worlds we have made for ourselves, and in so far as

it is the result of our joint efforts and collective imaginings, it is quite simply the best of all possible posthuman worlds. (197)

Cross-species zoé has become the guarantee for a future beyond man's civilization—as in Braidotti's exuberant vision of the human-becoming-animal, -becoming-machine, -becoming-posthuman—whereas Black being remains abandoned to its grief.

Ever since Wollstonecraft, white feminists have been trying to get as far away from "matter" and its implied thingness, as possible. They were not supposed to be enslaved things. Separating white feminism from anti-enslavism, they managed to fight successfully for white women's entry into the human, into poiesis, into forms of legitimized being as possessors, shapers, and controllers of matter. On the backs of Blacks, as Morrison would say, they taught the world to accept the distinction between themselves as women and (post-)enslaved states of being. Now matter matters? Matter now—with the fancy post-cyber technology planetary post- and anti-humanism being haloed—appears as the site of "a self-organizing principle," the site of conatus. Matter lives. It is becoming-machine. It is a globally impacting principle—in short, it resembles a post-technologically reassembled white subjectivity. Thus, now that posthuman matter as a "living force" has been both neatly disentangled from the human (who used to want to be in control of it) and thereby also demarcated against the human's underside, the ongoing inert stillness of abjected Blackness, it has become the much needed substitute for the subject.

Six

On Dispossession as a False Analogy

In his dissertation, *On Jubilee: The Performance of Black Leadership in the Afterlife of Slavery*, Omar Ricks discusses various instances of unacknowledged belatedness of white philosophy or critical theory in modern and postmodern instances of conflict. Insights into the diachronic and synchronic working of global capitalism and its political ideologies, social formations, and cultural hegemonies circulate as surprising, unexpected, and groundbreaking, although, when seen from the perspective of Black existence, they are nothing if not (too) late vis-à-vis the challenge of Black radical critique. My project obviously shares in this belatedness, very consciously so. In order to unthink philosophies of human liberation which over and again return to enslavist premises by way of the slave's or its incarnation's (abjected Black life's) fungibility to think human freedom (Walcott 109), it has been necessary to acknowledge white abjectorship, instead of clinging to (post-)Hegelian mutually reversible subject-object constellations or (post-)Nietzschean paradigms of both structural and semiotic contempt for Blackness. The established realm of the political, as well as that of the epistemic, if one takes Afro-pessimism seriously, is an impossible space for Black articulation, because it has been reserved for the human. Theorizing the end of the world—as unimaginable as it might be at this point—will be brought about by what Fred Moten calls Black noise, what Frank Wilderson calls the arriving coffle, and what Christina Sharpe calls the raging grief of the wake.

As my exit acknowledgment of the Black feminist critique of gender, I want to foreground an antagonism in political ontology, bearing on the scene of gender theory, by way of reading the following interventions from two oppositional locations. The first is represented by a pertinent conversation between Judith Butler and Athena Athanasiou (Butler and Athanasiou).

The second is grounded in both Christina Sharpe's *Black Scholar* essay "Black Studies: In the Wake," a precursor to *In the Wake* of 2016, and Saidiya Hartman's most recent "The Belly of the World: A Note on Black Women's Labors." The selected texts approach the necessity for a critical reflection on the late neoliberal onslaught from radically juxtaposed angles. Even though the respective sides have not engaged in direct a controversy, I am reading Sharpe's and Hartman's arguments as a critique of Butler and Athanasiou's approach.

All these interventions revisit gender, albeit indirectly, speaking back to gender studies respectively from a position of post-Marxist, postfeminist meditation on the possibilities and exigencies of struggle against late neoliberalism's global production of permanent crisis for human life, in Butler and Athanasious's case, and from a Black feminist, anti-enslavist critical meditation on the very impossibility of human life for Black being, in Sharpe's and Hartman's case.

Butler and Athanasiou have taken up the condition of human life's vulnerability and precariousness—of "politics, theory, embodiment" under the late liberal "economies of abandonment" (Elisabeth Povinelli qtd. in Butler and Athanasiou vii) by way of a joint intersectional, queer, anti-racist, and radical leftist address. The issue most pertinent for my discussion is taken up in the chapter "The Logic of Dispossession." The exchange opens with a broad statement that assembles a well-known list of analogously paradigmatic ethical and political wrongs besetting human life:

> In general, dispossession speaks to how human bodies become materialized and de-materialized through histories of slavery, colonization, apartheid, capitalist alienation, immigration and asylum politics, postcolonial liberal multiculturalism, gender and sexual normativity, sectarian governmentality, and humanitarian reason. (Butler and Athanasiou 10)

Their conversation then goes on to acknowledge that, in postcolonial usage of the term, dispossession refers to colonial theft of land from indigenous people:

> [D]ispossession works as an authoritative and often paternalistic apparatus of controlling and appropriating the spatiality, mobility, affectivity, potentiality, and relationality of (neo-)colonized subjects. In such contexts, "dispossession" offers a language to express experiences of uprootedness, occupation, destruction of

homes and social bonds, incitation to "authentic" self-identities, humanitarian victimization, unlivability and struggles for self-determination. (11)

However, both then extend the term's meaning to address "today's global market economy of neo-liberal capitalism," which signifies as economic precarity, "debtocracy" (11) and austerity, and the overall contemporary precarization of life on the planet in general.

Even though they mention in an aside that "certain bodies—paradig-matically so the bodies of slaves—are excluded" from the biopolitical ontology of "being" as "having" property (13), they explicitly abject this point, and the history of Black enslavement, in their focus on the "newness" of global neoliberal practices which turn "human life into capital." In a telling way, this insistence reproduces the enslavist distinction between the slave—who has sine qua non been human property and thus has always already herself been capital, structurally barred from a human *oikos*—and "human life":

> But new life forms and forms of subjectivity are also being pro-duced (that is, human life turned into capital), as "debt" becomes a fundamental technology of biopolitical governmentality—a political and moral economy of life itself. This is, in fact, the original meaning of "economy": the allotment and management of the *oikos* (the house, the household) as the site par excellence of human capital. This etymology is very suggestive of the cur-rent shift taking place in the domain of power, from the rule of law and the production of the ordinary to measures of crisis-management and therapeutic decrees of emergency (which, in turn, inculcate another order of ordinariness). (12)

In disidentification with the argument's gist, I read this passage with a focus on a subtextual logic that hinges on the structural split between the biopolitically produced human and the slave. Seeing through the prism of the slave's abjection from the human, one can perceive the particular urgency of their insistence on the "newness" of precariousness: the attention is geared towards what happens to human life, from which, in Butler and Athanasiou's own demarcation, the slave is evacuated—an insight which they consequently abandon by directing readerly identification to *human* life. However, by acquiring this specific demarcation, the slave as a term figures for them paradigmatically for the precarious horizon of contemporary human life, without any further consideration bestowed on enslavement as

204 | Chapter Six

a condition antagonistic to but necessary for the (neo)liberal biopolitics of contemporary human life. This rhetorical gesture gives value to the slave only as a metaphor, again, without interpellating the authors or their readers into a critique of enslavism, so that it, still and again, disarticulates Black being from the human, and as such from possible dispossession. Being property cancels out dispossession; thus, if one speaks of dispossession as a general condition, one cannot speak of the (post-)slave.

Where there has been no possession of self, let alone of property, of land, or other things, structurally speaking, but instead propertied thingness of being, there can be no dispossession; thus, the term does not address Black life.

Biopolitics has not articulated the slave, as the authors argue, but their critique refuses to address the (post-)slave, either. It leaves unattended the question of how Black life in the afterlife of slavery could be "present" (18) to the world if it has been structurally abjected from human subjectivity and if the human needed the slave only as paradigmatic figuration for an excessive and threatening beyond of biopolitical precariousness, as in Butler and Athanasiou's conversation. "Social death" (with reference to Patterson, who—along with Mbembe's "Necropolitics" and Gilmore's work on the prison—is one of three references to Black thought in the entire conversation) consequently only appears as the extreme marker for newly excessive human vulnerability, which they see as a "politically induced" and "socially assigned disposability" calculated on a differential scale of "modalities of valuelessness" (19) of people marked by "injury, violence, poverty, indebtedness, and death" whose " 'precarity' " describes exactly the lives of those " 'whose proper place is non-being.' " Apart from the intellectual recklessness of placing "death" on a differential scale with "poverty," their employment of "social death" as an analogy for the human's precarity, and dispossession evades any Black address of the structural rupture between the human (even in all her precarity) and Black nonbeing. Again, Black existence, by way of those references to Patterson, Mbembe, and Gilmore, becomes but an example of how the "violent logic of dispossession seeks to reassert the propriety of both spatiality and subjectivity as it bodies forth displaced and displaceable subjectivities" (20).

The very term "subjectivities," as well as the employment of "(de)subjectivation" (31), tellingly loops readers back to an exclusive concern with the human, because the slave and Black life (in the split from humanness, as they themselves pointed out), signify only the absence of even the possibility of subjectivity altogether, as opposed to a suffering from something that gets done, as in displacement, to a subjectivity. In the same mode, Rosa

Parks makes an appearance only to be mustered as an instance of a desirable politics, for human subjects, of not staying in one's proper temporality and spatiality (21). The logic repeats. Since the slave and its offspring, Black life, in a (post)humanist, biopolitical framework, have not had either time or space (proper or improper), the reference to Parks becomes part of a fungible repertoire of radical Black existence that can only aspire to a status of metaphorical excess vis-à-vis the human. In Park's case, it stands as a promise and a strange desire. Why would the human desire articulation with Black practice, if the condition of Black radical agency is Black nonlife as human, except as a desire for becoming—by association—politically and socially improper without paying the Black price for it? In the case of "social death" Blackness figures a haunt and fear of necropolitics, but structurally remains in the same function. Butler and Athanasious's focus is, again, on the human who, precipitated by the "economies of abandonment" (31), has arrived in a state of "differential allocation" of humanness, even though certain humans are still privileged with "performative bio-productivity in capacitating modes of living subjectivity as well as in inculcating normative fantasies and truth-effects of the 'good life' in self-owned subjects (a life defined, for instance, by property ownership, commodity fetishism, consumer excitement, securitarian regimes, national belonging, bourgeois self-fashioning and biopolitical normalcy)"(30–31). Neoliberal subjectivation, then, in the present moment, in its "politico-affective dynamic" renders certain lives "disposable and perishable"—a statement that again evades the issue of enslavism's longue durée as the genealogy of neoliberalism.

At this moment in the conversation, we are offered a hint, a nod towards an argument based on antagonism between the human and the slave. Athanasiou talks about the conception of the "inhuman as necessary for the human," referencing Adorno: "[T]he violation of a life that has been discursively figured as inhuman, or that has been omitted from human discursivity, or that has been conditionally included as an uncannily authentic human, is not perceived as violation. Address and redress of this violence cannot find a place in the world as it is" (33). This sentence gestures towards a post-Fanonian argument, but Athanasiou immediately abandons this trace. Even though she demands a subversion of the proper human norm, to "open the human to radical rearticulations of humanness" (34), she does not include gender as a marker of the human in her critique. For her, gender does not function as an apparatus of intrahuman differentiation staked against Black being as flesh. She sees gender exclusively as a function of patriarchal power: "the proper of the human, that is, its presumed self-evidence" is "a man with property and propriety," the paradigm of the discourse of the human, which "has historically become a default mechanism for upholding the intersecting matrices of colonial expansion, phallocentrism, heteronormativity and possessive individualism" (32). The human, to Athanasiou, suffers from overdetermination by those patriarchal, neoliberal transgressive "matrices": "To whom does the human belong, or who owns the human?" (32). The crucial question not asked here is, who did the human own? Butler follows the proposition, asking, "Who and what is excluded from 'the human,' and how has the category of the 'human' come to be formed against the background of the abject or disavowed? In other words, how has the 'human' been formed and maintained on the condition of a set of dispossessions?" (35–36).

My comment here sums up the point of this book. I disagree with speaking about the formation of the human in the passive form, as in *is excluded from the "human," come to be formed, has been formed and maintained.* This sentence, in its very grammar, lacking a subject of the practice in question, evades the issue of human abjectorship of Black life. And I maintain that the heuristics of gender in/as theory—even if large parts of the world's female population are still and again subjected to intrahuman violation and, indeed, dispossession, and even if freedom from gendered oppression and injustice justice remains a dream for the majority of women—has served to promote woman to the definitional legal, political center of the realms of the human. While the political, social, cultural, and epistemic push to undo gendered suppression thus has, into the twenty-first century, impacted on Euro-American societies as a powerful anti-patriarchal epistemic lever, gender theory and its ("post"-gender) interlocution has been evading the issue of its implication in enslavist abjectorship. The proper human, at this point, is not a masculine, patriarchal domain.

In sharp contradiction to the concern with human dispossession, Christina Sharpe, to whose thinking my objection has been massively indebted, writes with reference to the property laws of Black enslavement about

an order of knowledge that produces and enforces links, discursive and material, between the womb and the tomb in order to represent black maternity and therefore black childhood or youth as condemning one to a life of violence; condemning one to black life in/as proximity to knowledge of death. . . . A "condemnation of blackness" (to borrow Khalil Gibran Muhammed's apt phrase) taken, now, as so much "common sense" and traceable back to slavery's law of *partus sequitur ventrem* that established that the children of a slavewoman inherited the mother's condition. The mother's condition (her non/status) reappears in the present in ways that all black people, regardless of sex/gender, but especially the young and poor and working class have become in the United States (and not only in the United States) the symbols of the less-than-Human being condemned to death. (Sharpe, "Black" 62)

That word, condemnation, as the overall tenor of Sharpe's work, based as it is in Spillers's, Hartman's, and Wynter's previous insights, makes it very clear that the "less-than-human"-ness of Black being does not signify a recent development of dispossession, a neoliberal crisis, or an extreme of human suffering, but an inherited and inheritable, intergenerationally repeated, permanent positionality of structural evacuation from the essential grammar underpinning Human relationality (Wilderson, *Red* 73). As I have shown in this book, this exclusion from the human's grammar entails an exclusion from the human significations of gender as well. As Sharpe elaborates:

Reading together the middle passage, the coffle, and, I argue, the birth canal, we see how each has functioned separately and collectively over time to disfigure black maternity, to turn the womb into a factory (producing blackness as abjection much like the slave ship's hold and the prison), and turning the birth canal into another domestic middle passage with black mothers, after the end of legal hypodescent, still ushering their children into her condition; her non-status, her non-beingness. . . . Womb to tomb all over again. ("Black" 63)

Even though Sharpe does not say this explicitly, I read this as an injunction against the concept of gender: the insistence that Black abjection, through the unhumanization of the maternal line, reproduces Black abjection, overrides the teleology of gender as both a function of critique and of human liberation. Black (re)generation's trajectory of the inheritability of nonbeingness does not articulate with such dialectic teleology. From womb to tomb, or the womb as predictable tomb: the metaphorical equation excludes analogy with human dispossession, in that the prefix tellingly assumes, at the very least, a metaphysical disposition to see the human—*including woman*—in possession, of his life, of herself, of a cartography of humanness, however embattled, if not altogether in possession of other property. Human life, philosophically speaking, attains to sacrality or equivalent secular notions. It acquires contingent vulnerability after the fact of being born into this ontological shelter; Black life as/in possession—through *partus sequitur ventrem*—is condemnation by way of birth.

Hartman poignantly expands Sharpe's point. On the face of it, she also does not take explicit issue with gender studies. Explicitly, her argument wrestles Black women's suffering and struggles from neglect by other discursive strands of Black knowledge, like Black nationalism or Black leftism. Implicitly, it effects a powerful negation of gender theory, which has claimed the possession of genderedness and gendered interpellation as a pre-structuring, preemptive characteristic of normative sociability. For Hartman, like for Sharpe, the argument is about Black life's structural exclusion from this human interpellation and from gender's teleology. In direct reference to Sharpe's allusion to *partus sequitur ventrem*, she maintains: "The sexual violence and reproduction characteristic of enslaved women's experience fails to produce a radical politics of liberation or a philosophy of freedom." And, taking recourse to Spillers, she goes on to argue: "Flesh provides the primary narrative rather than gendered subject positions. . . . [T]he wanton uses of the black body for producing value or pleasure, and the shared vulnerabilities of the commodity, whether male or female, trouble dominant accounts of gender" ("Belly" 167–68). This however, does not contradict the primacy of "sexual differentiation in the making of the slave" (168), because, as Hartman notes with recourse also to Jennifer Morgan's work on reproduction and its importance for the legal codification of slavery, "[t]he reproduction of human property and the social relations of racial slavery were predicated upon the belly. Plainly put, subjection was anchored in Black women's reproductive capacities" (168). Accordingly, "[n]o uniform or shared category of gender included the mistress and the enslaved" (170).

By polemical extension, this chasm between "mistress" and "slave" holds for gender studies and Black female narratives of struggle. It has been feminism's and gender studies' achievement to have made effective, in political, social, and cultural terms, woman's predicative function as structurally discoupled from reproduction and from availability to segregation, abuse, and violence. If women as humans are dispossessed, poor, or vulnerable in specific ways, as most of the world's women still and again are, their demand, their by now philosophically widely recognized a priori birthright to self-possession gives them the lever to lay claim to a full realization of human rights. Also, this chasm needs to be connected to Butler's and Athanasiou's insistence that the "proper of the human is a man with property and propriety" (32). As the Euro-American history (the social life and the culture) of enslavism has shown, gender struggle has in fact mobilized the self-possessed woman to become her own stakeholder in property (of all kinds) and propriety, or at least it has disseminated a vision of such stakeholding in human recognition and kinship as proper liberation. In contradistinction to this trajectory, Black being's, including Black women's, predicative impact on the human world as we know it, has been made an impossibility by enslavism: the afterlife of being slave property is the freedom of fungibility to provide matter to the human's world-making: Black life is still, to signify on Spillers, awaiting (its) verb (see Spillers, "Interstices" 75).

The goal of this book has been to make visible the *white practice* of anti-Blackness within and as part of Western Eurocentric modernity while avoiding voyeuristic repetition of Black abjection, which, as Hortense Spillers already warned readers decades ago, is a very fine and slippery line to walk in the face of rampant pornotroping of Black suffering. My text's main terms of address have been white-on-white critical reflections of epistemic practices that have supported, mobilized, energized, disseminated, or at least tolerated our practices of anti-Blackness, even though those practices have been part of Western white discourses of liberation. The book's counter-hermeneutics (that is, reading feminist emancipatory texts not in identification with but against the white grain of their arguments) suggested a modality of epistemic allegiance to Black knowledges in order to lay bare crucial lines of (post) humanist anti-Black inquiry. Such critical acts of witnessing, because of their limitations as textual practices that are inescapably contained with the institutional apparatuses of higher education and racist-capitalist knowledge dissemination, are of course a rather mediated and restricted form of solidarity with Black struggles. The deadly social, cultural, and political grammars of anti-Black abjection, enacted by white life under the sign of the human, challenges us white people, following Wynter, McKittrick, Walcott, and Sharpe, to "lose" our "kin" (Sharpe, "Lose"). "Lose" here is meant not as a passive form, but as an active mode on our part to combat anti-Black abjection on a daily basis, which will require, indeed, a loss and a giving up of white loyalty—not as one-time acts of declarative and proclamative hubris, but as ongoing labor. Modes of day-to-day militancy need to be practiced that do not rely on Black people's fungibility both as victims of lethal and other forms of violence and as the sole agents of resistance against it; modes which deassign the ethical obligation to struggle against anti-Blackness and the challenge of "ending the world as we know it" from their exclusionary command over Black people's lives, and reassign both of these ethical prerogatives to white anti-white complicity. In other words, the mode this book calls me and its readers to, as its ethical consequence, is not one of benevolent, but essentially passive and narcissistic empathy, but an interventionist anti-racist struggle alongside Black resistances. Nevertheless, this book has been written in the conviction that the struggle against white humanist epistemology and its particular anti-Black violence remains one of the crucial terrains of this necessary anti-enslavist political intervention.

Bibliography

Abel, Elizabeth, et al., editors. *Female Subjects in Black and White: Race, Psychoanalysis, Feminism*. U of California P, 1997.

Adorno, Theodor W., and Max Horkheimer. *Dialektik der Aufklärung: Philosophische Fragmente*. Querido Verlag, 1944.

Ahjum, Sharifa. "The Law of the (White) Father: Psychoanalysis, 'Paternalism,' and the Historiography of Cape Slave Women." *Women and Slavery: Africa, the Indian Ocean World, and the Medieval North Atlantic*, edited by Gwyn Campbell et al., vol. 1, Ohio UP, 2007, pp. 83–110.

Ahluwalia, Pal. *Out of Africa: Post-Structuralism's Colonial Roots*. Routledge, 2010.

Ahmed, Sara. "White Men." *feministkilljoys*, 4 Nov. 2014, feministkilljoys. com/2014/11/04/white-men/.

Ansell-Pearson, Keith. *Nietzsche contra Rousseau: A Study of Nietzsche's Moral and Political Thought*. Cambridge UP, 1996.

Arp, Kristana. *The Bonds of Freedom: Simone de Beauvoir's Existentialist Ethics*. Open Court, 2001.

Bambara, Toni Cade, editor. *The Black Woman: An Anthology*. U of Michigan P, 1970.

Bannerji, Himani. "Mary Wollstonecraft, Feminism and Humanism: A Spectrum of Reading." *Mary Wollstonecraft and 200 Years of Feminisms*, edited by Eileen Janes Yeo, Rivers Oram Press, 1997, pp. 222–42.

Barnes, Sherri L. *Black American Feminisms: A Multidisciplinary Bibliography*. UCSB Libraries, blackfeminism.library.ucsb.edu/.

Baucom, Ian. *Specters of the Atlantic: Finance Capital, Slavery, and the Philosophy of History*. Duke UP, 2005.

Beal, Frances M. "Black Women's Manifesto; Double Jeopardy: To Be Black and Female." *World History Archives*, www.hartford-hwp.com/archives/45a/196.html.

Beauvoir, Simone de. *The Ethics of Ambiguity*. Translated by Bernard Frechtman, Kensington, 2000.

———. *The Second Sex*. Translated by H. M. Parshley, Vintage Books, 1989.

Beckles, Hilary. *A History of Barbados: From Amerindian Settlement to Nation-State*. Cambridge UP, 1989.

Bell, Vikki. "On Speech, Race and Melancholia: An Interview with Judith Butler." *Theory, Culture and Society*, vol. 16, no. 2, 1999, pp. 163–74.

Benjamin, Jessica. *The Bonds of Love: Psychoanalysis, Feminism, and the Problem of Domination*. Pantheon Books, 1988.

———. "Letter to Lester Olson." *Philosophy and Rhetoric*, vol. 33, no. 3, 2000, pp. 286–90.

———. *Like Subjects, Love Objects: Essays on Recognition and Sexual Difference*. Yale UP, 1995.

———. "Master and Slave: The Fantasy of Erotic Domination." *Powers of Desire: The Politics of Sexuality*, edited by Ann Snitow et al., Monthly Review Press, 1983, pp. 280–99. New Feminist Library.

———. *Shadow of the Other: Intersubjectivity and Gender in Psychoanalysis*. Routledge, 1997.

Bernasconi, Robert, with Sybol Cook, editors. *Race and Racism in Continental Philosophy*. Indiana UP, 2003.

Best, Stephen, and Saidiya Hartman. "Fugitive Justice." *Representations*, vol. 92, no.1, 2005, 1–15.

Bhabha, Homi K. *Nation and Narration*. Routledge, 1990.

Bhandar, Brenna, and Denise Ferreira Da Silva. "White Feminist Fatigue Syndrome." *Critical Legal Thinking*, 21 October 2013, criticallegalthinking. com/2013/10/21/white-feminist-fatigue-syndrome.

Birulés, Fina. "Interview with Judith Butler: 'Gender is Extramoral.' " *MRZine*, 16 May 2009.

Blackburn, Robin. *The Making of New World Slavery: From the Baroque to the Modern, 1492–1800*. Verso, 1997.

Bogues, Anthony. *After Man, towards the Human: Critical Essays on Sylvia Wynter*. Ian Randle, 2005. Caribbean Reasonings.

Braidotti, Rosi. "Affirmation versus Vulnerability: On Contemporary Ethical Debates." *Symposium*, vol. 10, no. 1, 2006, pp. 235–54.

———. *Metamorphoses: Towards a Materialist Theory of Becoming*. Polity Press, 2002.

———. *Nomadic Theory: The Portable Rosi Braidotti*. Columbia UP, 2012.

———. *Patterns of Dissonance: A Study of Women in Contemporary Philosophy*. Polity Press, 1989.

———. "Posthuman, All Too Human: Towards a New Process Ontology." *Theory, Culture and Society*, vol. 23, nos. 7–8, 2006, pp. 197–208.

———. *The Posthuman*. John Wiley and Sons, 2013.

———. "Powers of Affirmation: Response to Lisa Baraitser, Patrick Hanafin and Clare Hemmings." *Subjectivity*, vol. 3, no. 2, 2010, pp. 140–48.

———. *Transpositions: On Nomadic Ethics*. Polity Press, 2006.

Braidotti, Rosi, and Paul Gilroy, editors. *Conflicting Humanities*. Bloomsbury Academic, 2016.

Breines, Winifred. *The Trouble between Us: An Uneasy History of White and Black Women in the Feminist Movement*. Oxford UP, 2006.

Broeck, Sabine. "Comments on Gines." *Symposia on Gender, Race and Philosophy*, vol. 12, no. 1, Spring 2016, web.mit.edu/sgrp/2016/no1/Broeck0516.pdf.

———. "Enslavement as Regime of Western Modernity: Re-reading Gender Studies Epistemology through Black Feminist Critique." *Gender Forum*, no. 22, 2008, pp. 3–18, genderforum.org/wp-content/uploads/2017/04/0822_BlackWomensWritingRevisited.pdf.

———. "Gender Trouble in the Deep South: Women, Race and Slavery." *Objet identité: Epistemologie et transversalité*, special issue of *Cahiers Charles V*, vol. 40, 2006, pp. 115–34.

———. "In the Presence of Racism: Response to Heike Paul." *American Studies Today: Recent Developments and New Perspectives*, edited by Hubert Zapf et al., Universitätsverlag Winter, 2014, pp. 289–95.

———. "Inequality or (Social) Death." *Rhizomes*, no. 29, 2016, doi.org/10.20415/rhiz/029.e11.

———. "Legacies of Enslavism and White Abjectorship." *Postcoloniality—Decolonality—Black Critique: Joints and Fissures*, edited by Sabine Broeck and Carsten Junker, Campus Verlag, 2014, pp. 109–28.

———. "Lessons for A-disciplinarity: Some Notes on What Happens to an Americanist When She Takes Slavery Seriously." *Postcolonial Studies across the Disciplines?*, edited by Jana Gohrisch and Ellen Grünkemeier, Rodopi, 2014, pp. 349–57.

———. "Never Shall We *Be* Slaves: Locke's Treatises, Slavery, and Early European Modernity." *Blackening Europe: The African American Presence*, edited by Heike Raphael-Hernandez, Routledge, 2004, pp. 235–49.

———. "Property: White Gender and Slavery." *Gender Forum*, no. 14, 2006, pp. 3–20, genderforum.org/wp-content/uploads/2017/04/200614_Raceing QuestionsIII.pdf.

———. "Re-reading de Beauvoir after Race: Woman-as-Slave Revisited." *International Journal of Francophone Studies*, vol. 14, nos. 1–2, 2011, 167–84.

———. "Das Subjekt der Aufklärung—Sklaverei—Gender Studies: Zu einer notwendigen Relektüre der Moderne." *Gender Kontrovers: Genealogien und Grenzen einer Kategorie*, edited by Gabriele Dietze et al., Helmer Verlag, 2006, pp. 152–80.

———. "White Mythologies." *Thinking Away*, moderated by Sabine Broeck, weserhag.tumblr.com/.

———. *White Amnesia—Black Memory? American Women's Writing and History*. Peter Lang, 1999.

Broeck, Sabine, and Carsten Junker, editors. *Postcoloniality—Decoloniality—Black Critique: Joints and Fissures*. Campus Verlag, 2014.

Buck-Morss, Susan. *Hegel, Haiti and Universal History*. U of Pittsburgh P, 2009.

Burnard, Trevor. *Mastery, Tyranny, and Desire: Thomas Thistlewood and His Slaves in the Anglo-Jamaican World*. U of North Carolina P, 2004.

Butler, Judith. "Agencies of Style for a Liminal Subject." *Without Guarantees: In Honour of Stuart Hall*, edited by Paul Gilroy et al., Verso, 2000, pp. 30–37.

———. *Antigone's Claim: Kinship between Life and Death*. Columbia UP, 2002.

———. *Bodies that Matter: On the Discursive Limits of "Sex."* Routledge, 1993.

———. *Frames of War: When Is Life Grievable?* Verso, 2009.

———. *Giving an Account of Oneself.* Fordham UP, 2005.

———. "Longing for Recognition: Commentary on the Work of Jessica Benjamin." *Studies in Gender and Sexuality*, vol. 1, no. 3, 2000, pp. 271–90.

———. *Precarious Life: The Powers of Mourning and Violence.* Verso, 2004.

———. *The Psychic Life of Power: Theories in Subjection.* Stanford UP, 1997.

———. "Rethinking Vulnerability and Resistance." June 2014, bibacc.org/wp-content/uploads/2016/07/Rethinking-Vulnerability-and-Resistance-Judith-Butler.pdf.

———. *Undoing Gender.* Routledge, 2004.

———. "What Is Critique? An Essay on Foucault's Virtue." *Transversal*, June 2001, eipcp.net/transversal/0806/butler/en.

Butler, Judith, and Athena Athanasiou. *Dispossession: The Performative in the Political.* Polity Press, 2013.

Carr, Brian. "At the Thresholds of the 'Human': Race, Psychoanalysis, and the Replication of Imperial Memory." *Cultural Critique*, no. 39, 1998, pp. 119–50.

Carruth, Mary C., editor. *Feminist Interventions in Early American Studies.* U of Alabama P, 2006.

"The Celia Project." Institute for Research on Women and Gender, University of Michigan, irwg.umich.edu/news/celia-project.

Césaire, Aimé. *Discourse on Colonialism.* Translated by Joan Pinkham. Monthly Review Press, 2000.

———. *Discours sur le colonialisme.* Présence africaine, 1950.

———. "Notebook of a Return to the Native Land." *The Collected Poetry*, translated, with introduction and notes by Clayton Eshleman and Annette Smith. U of California P, 1983, p. 55.

Chanter, Tina. *The Picture of Abjection: Film, Fetish, and the Nature of Difference.* Indiana UP, 2008.

———. *Whose Antigone? The Tragic Marginalization of Slavery.* State U of New York P, 2011.

Chodorow, Nancy J. *The Reproduction of Mothering: Psychoanalysis and the Sociology of Gender.* U of California P, 1999.

Combahee River Collective. *The Combahee River Collective Statement: Black Feminist Organizing in the Seventies and Eighties.* Kitchen Table / Women of Color Press, 1986.

Commentaries on Kathryn T. Gines. Special issue of *Symposia on Gender, Race and Philosophy*, vol. 12, no. 1, Spring 2016, http://web.mit.edu/sgrp/2016/no1/SGRPv12no1(2016).pdf.

Cooper, Anna Julia. *A Voice from the South.* Aldine Printing House, 1892.

Cornell, Drucilla. *Moral Images of Freedom: A Future for Critical Theory.* Rowman & Littlefield, 2008.

Davies, Carole Boyce, and Elaine Savory Fido. *Out of the Kumbla: Caribbean Women and Literature.* Africa World Press, 1990.

Davis, Adrienne. " 'Don't Let Nobody Bother Yo' Principle': The Sexual Economy of American Slavery." *Sister Circle: Black Women and Work*, edited by Sharon Harley and the Black Women and Work Collective, Rutgers UP, 2002, pp. 103–27. Available on author's webpage, law.wustl.edu/faculty_profiles/documents/davis/ The%20Sexual%20Economy%20of%20American%20Slavery.pdf.

———. "The Private Law of Race and Sex: An Antebellum Perspective." *Stanford Law Review*, vol. 51, no. 2, 1999, 221–88.

Davis, Angela. "Reflections on the Black Woman's Role in the Community of Slaves." *The Black Scholar*, vol. 3, no. 4, 1971, pp. 2–15.

———. *Women, Race and Class*. Vintage Books, 1983.

Deutscher, Penelope. *The Philosophy of Simone de Beauvoir: Ambiguity, Conversion, Resistance*. Cambridge UP, 2009.

Dietze, Gabriele. *Weiße Frauen in Bewegung: Genealogien und Konkurrenzen von Race- und Genderpolitiken*. Transcript Verlag, 2006.

Donnan, Elizabeth. *Documents Illustrative of the History of the Slave Trade to America*. Carnegie Institution, 1930–35. 4 vols.

DuBois, Ellen Carol. *Feminism and Suffrage: The Emergence of an Independent Women's Movement in America, 1848–1869*. Cornell UP, 1978.

Fabre, Michel. *The Unfinished Quest of Richard Wright*. Morrow, 1973.

Farley, Anthony Paul. "The Black Body as Fetish Object." *Oregon Law Review*, vol. 76, no. 3, 1997, pp. 457–535.

Federici, Silvia Beatriz. *Caliban and the Witch: Women, the Body and Primitive Accumulation*. Autonomedia, 2004.

Felman, Shoshana, and Dori Laub. *Testimony: Crises of Witnessing in Literature, Psychoanalysis, and History*. Routledge, 1991.

Fox-Genovese, Elizabeth. *Within the Plantation Household: Black and White Women of the Old South*. U of North Carolina P, 2006.

Fraser, Nancy. "How Feminism Became Capitalism's Handmaiden—and How to Reclaim It." *Guardian*, 14 Oct. 2013, www.theguardian.com/commentis free/2013/oct/14/feminism-capitalist-handmaiden-neoliberal.

Freud, Sigmund. *The Ego and the Id*. Translated by Joan Riviere, Hogarth Press / Institute of Psycho-Analysis, 1949.

Garrison, William Lloyd. *Liberator*, 21 Apr. 1854.

Gewertz, Ken. "Four Decades Later, Scholars Re-examine 'Moynihan Report.'" *Harvard Gazette*, 4 Oct. 2007, news.harvard.edu/gazette/story/2007/10/ four-decades-later-scholars-re-examine-moynihan-report/.

Gilmore, Ruth Wilson. *Golden Gulag: Prisons, Surplus, Crisis, and Opposition in Globalizing California*. U of California P, 2007.

Gilroy, Paul. *The Black Atlantic: Modernity and Double Consciousness*. Harvard UP, 1993.

———. *Postcolonial Melancholia*. Columbia UP, 2004.

Gilroy, Paul, et al. *Without Guarantees: In Honour of Stuart Hall*. Verso, 2000.

Gines, Kathryn T. "Comparative and Competing Frameworks of Oppression in Simone de Beauvoir's *The Second Sex*." *Graduate Faculty Philosophy Journal*, vol. 35, nos. 1–2, 2014, 251–73.

Gordon, Lewis R., editor. *Existence in Black: An Anthology of Black Existential Philosophy*. Routledge, 1996.

Gore, Dayo F. *Radicalism at the Crossroads: African American Women Activists in the Cold War*. New York UP, 2011.

Gouges, Olympe de. *Déclaration des droits de la femme et de la citoyenne; suivi de, Préface pour les dames ou le portrait des femmes*. Edited by Emanuèle Gaulier, Mille et une nuits, 2003.

Gumbs, Alexis Pauline, et al. *Revolutionary Mothering: Love on the Front Lines*. PM Press, 2016.

Hall, Stuart, et al. *After Neoliberalism? The Kilburn Manifesto*. Lawrence and Wishart, 2015.

Harris, Cheryl I. "Whiteness as Property." *Harvard Law Review*, vol. 106, no. 8, 1993, pp. 1707–91.

Hartman, Saidiya. "The Belly of the World: A Note on Black Women's Labors." *Souls*, vol. 18, no. 1, 2016, pp. 166–73.

———. *Lose Your Mother: A Journey along the Atlantic Slave Route*. Farrar, Straus, and Giroux, 2007.

———. *Scenes of Subjection: Terror, Slavery, and Self-Making in Nineteenth-Century America*. Oxford UP, 1997.

———. "Seduction and the Ruses of Power." *Callaloo*, vol. 19, no. 2, 1996, pp. 537–60.

———. "Venus in Two Acts." *Small Axe*, vol. 12, no. 2, 2008, pp. 1–14.

Hegel, Georg Wilhelm Friedrich. "Independence and Dependence of Self-Consciousness: Lordship and Bondage." *Phenomenology of Spirit*, translated by A. V. Miller. Oxford UP, 1977, pp. 111–18.

———. *Phenomenology of Spirit*. Translated by A. V. Miller. Oxford UP, 1977.

Hemmings, Clare. *Why Stories Matter: The Political Grammar of Feminist Theory*. Duke UP, 2011.

Hesse, Barnor. "Afterword: Black Europe's Undecidability." *Black Europe and the African Diaspora*, edited by Darlene Clark Hine et al. U of Illinois P, 2009, pp. 291–304.

Hill Collins, Patricia. *Black Feminist Thought: Knowledge, Consciousness, and the Politics of Empowerment*. Unwin Hyman, 1990.

Horstmann, Rolf Peter. Introduction. *Beyond Good and Evil: Prelude to a Philosophy of the Future*, by Friedrich Nietzsche, edited by Rolf Peter Horstmann, translated by Judith Norman. Cambridge UP, 2013, pp. vii–xxviii.

Hull, Akasha (Gloria T.), et al., editors. *All the Women Are White, All the Blacks Are Men, but Some of Us Are Brave: Black Women's Studies*. Feminist Press, 1982.

"Introducing: Omar Ricks." *The Feminist Wire*, 10 Feb. 2012, www.thefeministwire.com/2012/02/introducing-omar-ricks/.

John, Mary E. *Discrepant Dislocations: Feminism, Theory, and Postcolonial Histories*. U of California P, 1996.

Jones-Rogers, Stephanie. *Mistresses of the Market: White Women and the Economy of American Slavery*. Yale UP, forthcoming.

Judaken, Jonathan, editor. *Race after Sartre: Antiracism, Africana Existentialism, Postcolonialism*. State U of New York P, 2008.

Judy, R. A. T. "On the Question of Nigga Authenticity." *boundary 2*, vol. 21, no. 3, 1994, pp. 211–30.

Kaplan, Caren, et al., editors. *Between Woman and Nation: Nationalisms, Transnational Feminisms, and the State*. Duke UP, 1999.

Katz, Phyllis A., editor. *Towards the Elimination of Racism*. Pergamon Press, 1976.

Khanna, Ranjana. *Dark Continents: Psychoanalysis and Colonialism*. Duke UP, 2003.

Knott, Sarah, and Barbara Taylor, editors. *Women, Gender and Enlightenment*. Palgrave Macmillan, 2004.

Kojève, Alexandre. *Introduction to the Reading of Hegel: Lectures on the Phenomenology of Spirit*. Assembled by Raymond Queneau, edited by Allan David Bloom, translated by James H. Nichols. Cornell UP, 1980.

Kristeva, Julia. *Powers of Horror: An Essay on Abjection*. Translated by Leon S. Roudiez, Columbia UP, 1984.

Laclau, Ernesto. *New Reflections on the Revolution of Our Time*. Verso, 1990.

Larsen, Nella. *Passing*. Penguin, 2003.

Leong, Diana. "The Mattering of Black Lives: Octavia Butler's Hyperempathy and the Promise of the New Materialism." *Catalyst*, vol. 2, no. 2, 2016, pp. 1–35.

Linebaugh, Peter, and Marcus Rediker. *The Many-Headed Hydra: Sailors, Slaves, Commoners, and the Hidden History of the Revolutionary Atlantic*. Beacon, 2000.

Loeb, Elizabeth. "Making It Work: Audre Lorde's 'The Master's Tools' and the Unbearable Difference of GSOC." *Workplace*, no. 14, 2007, pp. 40–58, http://ices.library.ubc.ca/index.php/workplace/article/view/182201.

Lorde, Audre. "The Master's Tools Will Never Dismantle the Master's House." *Sister Outsider: Essays and Speeches*, revised ed., Crossing Press, 2007, pp. 110–14.

———. *Uses of the Erotic: The Erotic as Power*. Out and Out Books, 1978.

Lowe, Lisa. *The Intimacies of Four Continents*. Duke UP, 2015.

Maart, Rozena. "Decolonizing Gender in the Academy: From Black Power and Black Consciousness to Black Rebellion." *Postcoloniality—Decoloniality—Black Critique: Joints and Fissures*, edited by Sabine Broeck and Carsten Junker. Campus Verlag, 2014, pp. 331–52.

———. "Race and Pedagogical Practices: When Race Takes Center Stage in Philosophy." *Hypatia*, vol. 29, no. 1, 2014, pp. 205–20.

Macdonald, D. L., and Kathleen Scherf, editors. *The Vindications: The Rights of Men and The Rights of Woman*. By Mary Wollstonecraft, Broadview Press, 1997.

Marriott, David. "Inventions of Existence: Sylvia Wynter, Frantz Fanon, Sociogeny, and 'the Damned.' " *CR: The New Centennial Review*, vol. 11, no. 3, 2012, pp. 45–89.

———. *On Black Men*. Columbia UP, 2000.

Martin, Valerie. *Property*. Abacus, 2008.

May, Vivian M. *Anna Julia Cooper, Visionary Black Feminist: A Critical Introduction*. Routledge, 2007.

———. " 'It Is Never a Question of the Slaves': Anna Julia Cooper's Challenge to History's Silences in Her 1925 Sorbonne Thesis." *Callaloo*, vol. 31, no. 3, 2008, pp. 903–18.

Mbembe, Achille. "Necropolitics." Translated by Libby Meintjes. *Public Culture*, vol. 15, no. 1, 2003, pp. 11–40.

McKittrick, Katherine. *Demonic Grounds: Black Women and the Cartographies of Struggle*. U of Minnesota P, 2006.

———. "Mathematics Black Life." *The Black Scholar*, vol. 44, no. 2, 2014, pp. 16–28.

———, editor. *Sylvia Wynter: On Being Human as Praxis*. Duke UP, 2015.

McLaurin, Melton A. *Celia: A Slave*. U of Georgia P, 1991.

Mignolo, Walter D. *Local Histories / Global Designs: Coloniality, Subaltern Knowledges, and Border Thinking*. Princeton UP, 1999.

Mills, Charles W. *The Racial Contract*. Cornell UP, 1997.

———. "White Ignorance." *Race and Epistemologies of Ignorance*, edited by Shannon Sullivan and Nancy Tuana. State U of New York P, 2007, 11–38.

Mohanty, Chandra Talpade. *Feminism without Borders: Decolonizing Theory, Practicing Solidarity*. Duke UP, 2003.

Moi, Toril. *Simone de Beauvoir: The Making of an Intellectual Woman*. Blackwell, 1993.

Moraga, Cherríe L., et al. *This Bridge Called My Back: Writings by Radical Women of Color*. Persephone Press, 1981.

Morgan, Jennifer L. *Laboring Women: Reproduction and Gender in New World Slavery*. U of Pennsylvania P, 2004.

Morrison, Toni. *Beloved*. Alfred A. Knopf, 1987.

———. *Playing in the Dark: Whiteness and the Literary Imagination*. Harvard UP, 1992.

———. "Unspeakable Things Unspoken: The Afro-American Presence in American Literature." *Michigan Quarterly Review*, vol. 28, no. 1, 1989, pp. 1–34.

Moten, Fred. *In the Break: The Aesthetics of the Black Radical Tradition*. U of Minnesota P, 2003.

Moynihan Report (1965). BlackPast.org, www.blackpast.org/primary/moynihan-report-1965.

Myrdal, Gunnar. *An American Dilemma: The Negro Problem and Modern Democracy*. Transaction, 1996.

Nietzsche, Friedrich. *Beyond Good and Evil*. Translated by Helen Zimmern. Prometheus Books, 1989.

———. *On the Genealogy of Morality*. Edited by Keith Ansell-Pearson, translated by Carol Diethe. Cambridge UP, 2007.

No Subject: An Encyclopedia of Lacanian Psychoanalysis. nosubject.com/Main_Page.

Nussbaum, Felicity A. *Torrid Zones: Maternity, Sexuality, and Empire in Eighteenth-Century English Narratives*. Johns Hopkins UP, 1995.

Oates, Joyce Carol. *Uncensored: Views and (Re)Views*. Harper Collins, 2005.

Olson, Lester C. "A Reply to Jessica Benjamin." *Philosophy and Rhetoric*, vol. 33, no. 3, 2000, pp. 291–93.

On the Future of Black Feminism. Special issue of *The Black Scholar*, vol. 45, no. 4, 2016.

On the Future of Black Feminism, Part 2. Special issue of *The Black Scholar*, vol. 46, no. 2, 2016.

Painter, Nell Irvin. *Soul Murder and Slavery*. Markham Press Fund / Baylor UP, 1995. Charles Edmondson Historical Lectures, 15.

———. *Southern History across the Color Line*. U of North Carolina P, 2002.

Patterson, Orlando. *Slavery and Social Death: A Comparative Study*. Harvard UP, 1982.

Proctor, Robert N., and Londa Schiebinger, editors. *Agnotology: The Making and Unmaking of Ignorance*. Stanford UP, 2008.

Quanquin, Hélène. " 'There Are Two Great Oceans': The Slave Metaphor in the Antebellum Woman's Rights Discourse as Redescription of Race and Gender." *Interconnections: Gender and Race in American History*, edited by Carol Faulkner and Alison M. Parker. U of Rochester P, 2012, pp. 75–104.

Quijano, Anibal. "Coloniality of Power, Eurocentrism, and Latin America." *Nepentla: Views from the South*, vol. 1, no. 3, 2000.

Réage, Pauline. *Story of O*. Preface by Jean Paulhan, translated by Sabine d' Estrée. Grove Press, 1965.

Rehmann, Jan. Review of *Nietzsche, il ribelle aristocratico: Biografia intellettuale e bilancio critico*. *Historical Materialism*, vol. 15, no. 2, 2007, pp. 173–93.

Ricks, Omar Benton. *On Jubilee: The Performance of Black Leadership in the Afterlife of Slavery*. 2014. U of California, Berkeley, PhD dissertation. *eScholarship*, escholarship.org/uc/item/5rj160xp.

Rosenbaum, Alan S., editor. *Is the Holocaust Unique? Perspectives on Comparative Genocide*. 2nd ed., Westview Press, 2001.

"Rosi Braidotti." *Wikipedia*, en.wikipedia.org/wiki/Rosi_Braidotti. Accessed 25 May 2016.

Roth, Benita. *Separate Roads to Feminism: Black, Chicana, and White Feminist Movements in America's Second Wave*. Cambridge UP, 2004.

Rothberg, Michael. *The Implicated Subject: Beyond Victims and Perpetrators*. Stanford UP, forthcoming. www.academia.edu/7734709/The_Implicated_Subject_Beyond_Victims_and_Perpetrators.

———. *Multidirectional Memory: Remembering the Holocaust in the Age of Decolonization*. Stanford UP, 2006.

Ruhe, Doris. "Simone de Beauvoir, Sartre und Fanon: Le deuxieme sexe 'en situation.' " *Geschlechterdifferenz im interdisziplinären Gespräch: Kolloquium des Interdisziplinären Zentrums für Frauen- und Geschlechterstudien an der Ernst-Moritz-Arndt Universität Greifswald*, edited by Doris Ruhe. Königshausen und Neuman, 1998, 171–95.

Said, Edward W. *Orientalism*. Routledge and Kegan Paul, 1978.

Salih, Sarah. *Judith Butler*. Routledge, 2002.

Sánchez-Eppler, Karen. *Touching Liberty: Abolition, Feminism, and the Politics of the Body*. U of California P, 1993.

Sandoval, Chela. *Methodology of the Oppressed*. U of Minnesota P, 2000.

Senghor, Léopold Sédar. *Anthologie de la nouvelle poésie nègre et malgache de langue française*. Preceded by "Orphée noir," by Jean-Paul Sartre, Presses universitaires de France, 1948.

Sexton, Jared. "Ante-Anti-Blackness: Afterthoughts." *Lateral*, no. 1, 2012.

———. "The Social Life of Social Death: On Afro-Pessimism and Black Optimism." *InTensions*, no. 5, 2011, www.yorku.ca/intent/issue5/articles/pdfs/jaredsextonarticle.pdf.

Shange, Ntozake. *For Colored Girls Who Have Considered Suicide When the Rainbow Is Enuf.* MacMillan, 1977.

Sharpe, Christina. "Black Studies: In the Wake." *The Black Scholar*, vol. 44, no. 2, 2014, pp. 59–69.

———. *In the Wake: On Blackness and Being.* Duke UP, 2016.

———. "The Lie at the Center of Everything." *Black Studies Papers*, vol. 1, no. 1, 2014.

———. "Lose Your Kin." *The New Inquiry*, 16 Nov. 2016, thenewinquiry.com/lose-your-kin/.

Sharpley-Whiting, T. Denean. *Negritude Women.* U of Minnesota P, 2002.

Simson, Rennie. "The Afro-American Female: The Historical Context of the Construction of Sexual Identity." *Powers of Desire: The Politics of Sexuality*, edited by Ann Snitow et al. Monthly Review Press, 1983, pp. 229–35.

Simons, Margaret A. *Beauvoir and* The Second Sex: *Feminism, Race, and the Origins of Existentialism.* Rowman & Littlefield, 2000.

Spelman, Elizabeth V. *Inessential Woman: Problems of Exclusion in Feminist Thought.* Beacon Press, 1988.

Spillers, Hortense J. " 'All the Things You Could Be by Now If Sigmund Freud's Wife Was Your Mother': Psychoanalysis and Race." *Critical Inquiry*, vol. 22, no. 4, 1996, pp. 710–34.

———. *Black, White, and in Color: Essays on American Literature and Culture.* U of Chicago P, 2003.

———. "Interstices: A Small Drama of Words." *Pleasure and Danger: Exploring Female Sexuality*, edited by Carole S. Vance. Pandora, 1992, pp. 73–100.

———. "Mama's Baby, Papa's Maybe: An American Grammar Book." *Black, White, and in Color: Essays on American Literature and Culture*, U of Chicago P, 2003, 203–29.

———. "Mama's Baby, Papa's Maybe: An American Grammar Book." *Diacritics*, vol. 17, no. 2, 1987, pp. 65–81.

Spillers, Hortense, et al. " 'Whatcha Gonna Do?'—Revisiting 'Mama's Baby, Papa's Maybe: An American Grammar Book': A Conversation with Hortense Spillers, Saidiya Hartman, Farah Jasmine Griffin, Shelly Eversley, and Jennifer L. Morgan." *Women's Studies Quarterly*, vol. 35, nos. 1–2, 2007, pp. 299–309.

Spivak, Gayatri Chakravorty. *A Critique of Postcolonial Reason: Toward a History of the Vanishing Present.* Harvard UP, 1999.

Suleiman, Susan Rubin, editor. *The Female Body in Western Culture: Contemporary Perspectives.* Harvard UP, 1985.

"Third-Wave Feminism." *Wikipedia*, en.wikipedia.org/wiki/Third-wave_feminism.

Thomas, Greg. "Proud Flesh Inter/Views: Sylvia Wynter." *ProudFlesh*, no. 4, 2006.

Traylor, Eleanor W. Introduction. *The Black Woman: An Anthology*, edited by Toni Cade Bambara, reprint ed. Washington Square Press, 2005.

Vance, Carole S., editor. *Pleasure and Danger: Exploring Female Sexuality.* Pandora, 1992.

Vergès, Françoise. *L'homme prédateur: Ce que nous enseigne l'esclavage sur notre temps.* Editions Albin Michel, 2011. Bibliothèque idées.

Walcott, Rinaldo. "The Problem of the Human: Black Ontologies and 'the Coloniality of Our Being.' " *Postcoloniality—Decoloniality—Black Critique: Joints and Fissures*, edited by Sabine Broeck and Carsten Junker. Campus Verlag, 2014, pp. 93–108.

Walker, Alice. "In Search of Our Mothers' Gardens: The Creativity of Black Women in the South (1974)." *Ms. Magazine*, Spring 2002, www.msmagazine.com/spring2002/walker.asp.

———. *In Search of Our Mothers' Gardens: Womanist Prose.* Harcourt Brace Jovanovich, 1983.

———. *Meridian.* Harcourt Brace Jovanovich, 1976.

Wallace, Michele. *Black Macho and the Myth of the Superwoman.* Verso, 1979.

Wallerstein, Immanuel. *The Modern World-System I: Capitalist Agriculture and the Origins of the European World-Economy in the Sixteenth Century.* Academic Press, 1974.

———. *The Modern World-System II: Mercantilism and the Consolidation of the European World-Economy, 1600–1750.* Academic Press, 1980.

———. *The Modern World-System III: The Second Era of Great Expansion of the Capitalist World-Economy, 1730s–1840s.* Academic Press, 1989.

Walton, Jean. *Fair Sex, Savage Dreams: Race, Psychoanalysis, Sexual Difference.* Duke UP, 2001.

Weier, Sebastian, et al. "Consider Afro-Pessimism / Responses by Christopher M. Tinson, Rinaldo Walcott and Elizabeth J. West." *Amerikastudien / American Studies*, vol. 59, no. 3, 2015, pp. 419–45.

"What Is Vulnerability?" International Federation of Red Cross and Red Crescent Societies, www.ifrc.org/en/what-we-do/disaster-management/about-disasters/what-is-a-disaster/what-is-vulnerability/.

Wiegman, Robyn. *American Anatomies: Theorizing Race and Gender.* Duke UP, 1995.

Wilderson, Frank B. *Red, White and Black: Cinema and the Structure of US Antagonisms.* Duke UP, 2010.

———. "The Vengeance of Vertigo: Aphasia and Abjection in the Political Trials of Black Insurgents." *InTensions*, no. 5, 2011, http://www.yorku.ca/intent/issue5/articles/pdfs/frankbwildersoniiiarticle.pdf.

Williams, Eric. *Capitalism and Slavery.* 1944. U of North Carolina P, 1994.

Williams, Patricia J. *The Alchemy of Race and Rights.* Harvard UP, 1991.

Winks, Christopher. "Comments on Sylvia Wynter." *The Caribbean Commons*, 26 Mar. 2012, caribbean.commons.gc.cuny.edu/2012/03/26/comments-on-sylvia-wynter/.

Wollstonecraft, Mary. *A Vindication of the Rights of Woman.* Dover, 1996.

Wood, Marcus. *Slavery, Empathy, and Pornography.* Oxford UP, 2002.

Wynter, Sylvia. "Beyond Miranda's Meanings: Un/silencing the 'Demonic Ground' of Caliban's 'Woman.' " *Out of the Kumbla: Caribbean Women and Literature*, edited by Carole Boyce Davies and Elaine Savory Fido. Africa World Press, 1990, pp. 355–72.

———. "The Ceremony Must Be Found: After Humanism." *boundary 2*, vol. 12, no. 3–vol. 13, no. 1, 1984, pp. 19–70.

———. "Unsettling the Coloniality of Being/Power/Truth/Freedom: Towards the Human, After Man, Its Overrepresentation—An Argument." *The New Centennial Review*, vol. 3, no. 3, 2003, pp. 257–337.

Yeatman, Anna. "A Two-Person Conception of Freedom: The Significance of Jessica Benjamin's Idea of Intersubjectivity." *Journal of Classical Sociology*, vol. 15, no. 1, 2015, pp. 3–23.

Yeo, Eileen Janes, editor. *Mary Wollstonecraft and 200 Years of Feminisms*. Rivers Oram Press, 1997.

Young, Robert. *White Mythologies: Writing History and the West*. Routledge, 1990.

Index

www.ingramcontent.com/pod-product-compliance
Lightning Source LLC
Chambersburg PA
CBHW070405270326
41926CB00014B/2714